Common
Sense
Business

Common Sense Business

Starting, Operating, and
Growing Your Small Business—
in Any Economy!

Steve Gottry

Foreword by Ken Blanchard

COMMON SENSE BUSINESS. Copyright © 2005 by Priority Multimedia Group, Inc. All rights reserved. Printed in the United States of America. No part of this book may be used or reproduced in any manner whatsoever without written permission except in the case of brief quotations embodied in critical articles and reviews. For information address HarperCollins Publishers, 10 East 53rd Street, New York, NY 10022.

HarperCollins books may be purchased for educational, business, or sales promotional use. For information please write: Special Markets Department, HarperCollins Publishers, 10 East 53rd Street, New York, NY 10022.

FIRST EDITION

Designed by Nancy Singer Olaguera

Library of Congress Cataloging-in-Publication Data

Gottry, Steven R.
    Common sense business : starting, operating, and growing your small business—in any economy / Steve Gottry.—1st ed.
        p.   cm.
    Includes index.
    ISBN 0-06-077838-5
    1. Small business—Management. 2. New business enterprises—Management. I. Title.

HD62.7.G698   2005
658.02′2—dc22   2005040215

05 06 07 08 09 ❖/RRD 10 9 8 7 6 5 4 3 2

Dedication

The lessons in this book come not only as the result of starting and operating businesses of my own, but also as one of the many benefits of my marriage.

A marriage is, in part, a small business. Every married couple must create a legal partnership, locate a "facility" in which to "set up shop," and manage cash flow, payables, and investments to maximize return.

As children "join the firm," there are personnel issues to resolve and facilities-expansion matters to evaluate.

Ultimately, the disposition of the company's assets enters into consideration.

I am fortunate to have a first-rate marriage partner, Karla Styer Gottry, to whom I dedicate this book. Knowing that writing this was important to me, she packed me up and sent me alone on trips to quiet destinations where I could work long hours with few interruptions. She even let me spend time in beautiful, inspiring Sedona, Arizona, without her. That's sacrifice! And, hopefully, it was a sound business decision, too.

Without my wife's support, patience, and understanding, this book would never have been anything more than an idea churning around somewhere in the back of my mind. Thank you, Karla!

Contents

Acknowledgments   ix
Foreword by Ken Blanchard, Ph.D.   xiii
Preface   xvii
Introduction   xxi

PART ONE

The Small Business Life Cycle   1

1. The Dreaming Stage   5
2. The Planning Stage   17
3. The Implementation Stage   49
4. The Growth Stage   65
5. The Preservation and Evolution Stages   111
6. The Selling/Divesting Stage   117

The Alternate Route   125

7. Downsizing—Voluntary and Involuntary   127
8. Bankruptcy   139
9. The Second Start-Up   145

PART TWO

Building on Your Assets   153

10. Yourself   155
11. Your Employees   175
12. Your Customers   211
13. Your Vendors   219
14. Your Capital   225
15. Your Relationship with Your Community   245

PART THREE

Conquering Your
Natural Enemies   251

16. Busy-ness   253
17. Busybodies   267
18. Sloppiness   271
19. Debt   281
20. The Government   287
21. Addiction   293
22. Fear   301
23. There's Always Tomorrow!   307

      Appendix   313
      Index   319

Acknowledgments

I have benefited from the friendship of, and advice and mentoring from, a number of people over the years. It would be impossible to thank them all, but several deserve a special mention.

My parents, **Roger and Helen Gottry,** taught me the value of independent thinking and provided sound moral teaching. And from my wonderful children, **Jonathan, Michelle,** and **Kalla Paige,** I have discovered the rewards of instilling those values in the next generation.

Many of my high school teachers—especially **Ole Loing**—believed that encouragement and personal involvement were an integral part of education, and thereby helped me capture a vision of what my future could look like.

College professors who had an immeasurable influence on my career path include **Jack Mark** and the late—and forever admired—**Drs. Harold Wilson** and **Leonard Bart,** all of the University of Minnesota.

During some difficult periods in my business ventures, I received invaluable support and advice from **Richard Young, Dudley Ryan, Jim Gilbert, Steve**

Kalin, John Hanson, and **Chuck Wanous.** Special thanks are offered to my brother, **Dan "Leggo" Gottry,** who has been a supporter of my business pursuits since day one. (Dan's nickname came about because he is a leg amputee with remarkable faith and perseverance—always bolstered by a great sense of humor and his loving wife, **Sandy**.)

Clients and friends who deserve my gratitude are **Michael** and **Lindsey Clifford; Chuck Wenger; Pam** ("Always-There-for-Me") **Benoit** and her husband, **Gary; Ric** and **Joy Jacobsen; Linda Jensvold Bauer; Bill** and **Joan Brown;** and especially **Richard Baltzell,** my publishing mentor, who has lent his encouragement and invaluable assistance to every book project.

It would be impossible to overlook **Duane Pederson,** who gave me some tremendous opportunities to express my creativity while I was yet in high school (and who today devotes his life to aiding runaway teens, the homeless, the poor, and the imprisoned); **Tom Cousins,** former promotion director of WCCO-TV; and **George Johnson** and **Reid Johnson** (no relation), who never stopped believing in me. Thanks to **Ken Blanchard** and **Doug Ross** for giving me a huge measure of hope and to **Kathy Styer** for "lending me her ear."

During life's toughest moments, my personal faith has been a source of immeasurable strength. My fellow Rotarian **Father Dick Smith** has helped me better understand that, through faith, I don't have to fight my battles alone.

Thanks, **Elaine Ralls,** for the use of your wonderful cabin in the cool high pine country of Arizona. What a great place to write!

Chuck Riekena, I know I can be a pest sometimes. But I had lots of legal questions throughout the writing of this book, and you are by far the best guy I know to answer them. A lawyer I actually trust! **Ann,** sorry about the dinner interruptions.

Kevin Klimas, your advice on employee background checks could be invaluable to a lot of small businesses.

Dave Gjerness and **Eric Walljasper**—thanks for being the two former employees who still talk to me . . . and help me on so many projects today.

The people at HarperBusiness are a pleasure! I could not have asked for a more caring and involved editor than **Herb Schaffner.** He is the definition of "professional," and is supported by some wonderful people, including **Jessica Chin** and **Knox Huston.**

Perhaps my most unusual acknowledgment is to **Steve Jobs,** the creative genius at Apple Computer who "powered up" my Macintosh PowerBook laptop and provided a compact way for me to transport 10,000 songs (on my iPod) so that my writing retreats had musical accompaniment. (I don't leave home without them!) I value innovation, aesthetics, and functional design, so even though Apple has but a tiny share of the PC market, I will always be a loyal addict and evangelist.

One more. Sorry. But the great people at the **Dobson/Isabella Starbucks** and at the **Chandler Fashion Mall Starbucks** (near my favorite Apple store) provided great "getaway space" for writing and kept me going with my "Iced-Quad-Grande-Half-Soy-No-Water-Ice-to-the-Top-No-Room-Americanos!"

Aren't friends wonderful?

Foreword

By Ken Blanchard, Ph.D.,

coauthor of *The One Minute Manager, Raving Fans,*

Gung Ho!, and *The On-Time, On-Target Manager*

How many times have you heard the phrase "That's what it's all about"? Those five words are as overused as any in the English language—and can refer to anything from sinking a thirty-foot putt to seeing a newborn baby for the first time.

You are about to come face-to-face with the essence of those words once again. Because if you own a small business or plan to begin a new venture in the future, *this book is what small business is all about!*

Common Sense Business is an energizing, inspiring, provocative personal "letter" to you from my friend and coauthor of *The On-Time, On-Target Manager,* Steve Gottry. In fact, until now, I had never seen so much solid business advice dispensed in a single book.

Steve will carefully guide you through the six stages of the small business "life cycle"—from the Dreaming

Stage, through the Growth Stage, all the way to the Selling/Divesting Stage.

Next, he will teach you how to build a successful, ongoing organization by taking advantage of your strengths—beginning with your own personal skills and goals, then capitalizing on your employees as well as on your customers and vendors. You will be able to construct solid, lasting "people-oriented" relationships by discovering how to avoid the pitfalls that have led to disaster for countless entrepreneurs.

Finally, Steve will reveal the secrets that will help you conquer the "natural enemies" of any business venture. As I read this section of the book, I realized that my company has faced many of these challenges, and we have had to overpower them in order to survive the many ups and downs of our economy.

The bottom line is, this stuff goes far beyond mere theory. There are no "maybes" in this book. Follow Steve's sound advice, and your business *will* be successful. Ignore it, and your hopes and dreams could become rubble at your feet.

"But," as they say, "there's more!" There is another dimension of this book that caught me completely off guard—and that's the intensely personal, candid nature of Steve's story.

Steve lost a very successful small business—one that he built from scratch with nothing more than a dream, a strong desire, and a handful of cash. He lost it because, somewhere along the line, he lost sight of his primary focus. He got taken up with the *evidence of success,* rather than the *elements of success.* He freely admits to that in this book, so I'm not betraying his trust in any way.

The result of his decisions—as well as the impact of some other unfortunate factors that he will share with you—led to the failure of his business.

Please notice that I used the word "failure" instead of "bankruptcy."

Despite the advice of many of his business advisers, Steve made the decision to pay off all of his debts through a combination of cash payments and the bartering of his creative work. It took him eight years to settle all of his debts—1993 to 2001—but he did it!

How does he feel about that accomplishment? "It's the only decision that I could have made," he told me. "I've been stuck for tens of thousands of dollars by a number of my clients in the past, so I knew how it felt. I didn't want to do that to anyone else."

How do Steve's past creditors feel about what he accomplished? Here's an excerpt from a letter he received from one vendor after Steve sent in his final payment on his old debt: "I consider myself fortunate to have known a man of your integrity. I have dealt with thousands of people since 1965 and I can honestly say, I don't think any one of them would have paid a bill six years after leaving the state. You have restored my faith in humanity and you stand head and shoulders above anyone I have ever done business with. If you ever come back to the Twin Cities area, please give me a call and I would be honored to take you to lunch."

Throughout this book, Steve will share both his greatest failures and his most significant achievements in a sincere desire to help you become as successful as you can be.

As I read about his many triumphs and setbacks,

something remarkable occurred to me. Steve Gottry's biggest failure is also his greatest success. This may seem to be a paradox, but it's absolutely true. It became clear that Steve indeed possesses two enviable qualities that would empower any businessperson who aspired to succeed. They are *tenacity* and *integrity*.

This book is about both. Clearly, confidently, and completely.

Helen Keller, who overcame the handicap of being born both blind and deaf, once said, "Character cannot be developed in ease and quiet. Only through experience of trial and suffering can the soul be strengthened, ambition inspired, and success achieved."

That quotation is framed and has a permanent home on Steve's desk—not only because he truly knows what it means, but also because he believes it applies in his own life in a highly personal way.

My challenge to you is, *read this book!* Read every page. Contemplate every word. Learn from every sentence. Find a nugget of truth and success in every chapter. *Common Sense Business* is Steve's heartfelt gift to you. Accept it with gratitude!

—Ken Blanchard
Escondido, California
June 2005

Preface

In the business sense, I believe there are just four basic types of people:

1. Those who have started their own businesses. These are people who have acted on their dreams. They have an entrepreneurial spirit and the desire to be their own bosses. They want to exercise a measure of control over their own destinies.

2. Those who *want* to own a business and become their own bosses. Their ambitions, however, are limited by something that seems to them to be insurmountable. Perhaps they believe they don't have access to the necessary financial resources. Perhaps they are secure and comfortable in their jobs and feel they can't afford to take the risk. Maybe their dreams aren't backed by sufficient drive. Maybe they're stalled by fear.

3. Those who have started companies sometime in the past but have watched them fail. The death of a business is, in my opinion, one of the most painful things an owner can ever witness. I know. I've been there.

4. Those who don't have a clue of what I'm even talking about. They want the perceived security and stability (at least in good economic times) of working for someone else. They can't imagine the joys and joyous tribulations that accompany business ownership. They are limited because their dreams are limited.

You've probably already realized that this book is written for the first group of people. But it's also written for the second group, to help them explore the possibilities of business ownership as seen from the perspective of someone who has been there.

In addition, it's written for the third group, because, if they still possess the entrepreneurial spirit, they may be considering a "second start-up" or a new business—and this book will help them take more of the necessary basics into account.

The fourth group probably won't see this book—or even hear about it. They don't hang out in the business sections of bookstores, nor do they care about the subject matter. But if they *were* to read it, they would gain a new insight into the struggles their employers face. They would realize that their bosses aren't necessarily in the enviable positions they thought they were.

Sadly, there's another group who may never see this book. They are the current MBA students as well as the recent recipients of MBA degrees—the brilliant people who may not yet fully understand the blood-drenched battleground of small business. They will likely seek careers in corporate America and never glimpse the world of the entrepreneur. But I hope they give *Common*

Sense Business the opportunity to heighten their under-standing of what we "noncorporate types" go through.

This book is clearly written from the perspective of a "typical" small business owner. I have made enough mis-takes to see one business—an ad agency that was successful for twenty-two years—fail. I've also learned enough about small business to regroup, reapply my knowledge and skills, and redesign my future.

What's in it for you? If you're planning a business start-up, Part One, "The Small Business Life Cycle," will guide you through all of the stages of starting, operat-ing, growing, and even closing down a business. Already own a business? Begin reading at the point that best describes where your business is at right now. But give some thought to reviewing the earlier stages, just to make sure that you're not missing out on some vital concept—the FANAFI Principle or the pro forma, for example.

Part Two, "Building on Your Assets," will help you understand your own role as well as the roles of your employees, customers, and vendors, and how all of this comes together to form a successful business. You will find valuable ideas that will help you gain more from your employees and cement your relationships with your customers and vendors. There are solid, proven techniques for managing your capital, and I'll even offer some reasons why your community is one of your assets—and why you will want to do your part to make it a better place. (If it sounds as though I've climbed onto a soapbox, I'm sorry.)

Part Three, "Conquering Your Natural Enemies,"

will help you ward off those threats that could eat away at your resources and peace of mind. You will discover the keys to gain control of "busy-ness," busybodies, sloppiness, debt, addiction, and other likely challenges.

If there is but one nugget of wisdom in this book that helps your business—or your future business—prosper, I will feel that I have accomplished something of purpose.

Introduction

If I had the power to turn back time, I guarantee you that I wouldn't. I most certainly wouldn't want to relive 1993, even if I could change virtually everything about it.

It was pure purgatory. My personal Dante's *Inferno*. Murphy's Law was fully in force in every area of my life. If there was even the slightest chance things could go wrong, they did. Not just a "little wrong," either. A *lot* wrong.

The year 1993 was so awful that in early December, my wife walked by a Hallmark store and spotted a holiday ornament that immediately captured her attention. It was a small skunk holding the number '93. *That fits,* she thought, *because '93 sure stunk!* She bought the ornament and brought it home. (Today we can laugh about it, but it was bitterly ironic at the time.)

As I unfold my story for you, parts of it may sound boastful. That's not my intention at all . . . and as the story progresses, you will come to understand that a "new, improved Steve Gottry" is writing these words.

You see, I had invested twenty-two years building a successful advertising agency and video production subsidiary in Bloomington, Minnesota, a suburb of Minneapolis. I had ten employees who generated an amazing amount of quality creative work for such clients as Warner Bros. Distribution, HarperSanFrancisco, Prudential Realty Group, NewTek, Inc., United Properties, and Standard Publishing.

My team and I created "special markets" campaigns for more than twenty-two motion pictures, including *Chariots of Fire, Pale Rider, The Hiding Place, The Prodigal,* and *Joni.* We helped create national best sellers for authors such as Zig Ziglar, Dr. Denis Waitley, Madeleine L'Engle, and Dr. Robert Schuller.

We won numerous prestigious local and national advertising competitions, including two awards from the International Advertising Festival of New York. The Bloomington Chamber of Commerce named us "Small Company of the Year" in 1991. This honor was bestowed upon us at a luncheon attended by hundreds of business leaders and was accompanied by a proclamation signed by the governor of Minnesota.

Yep, readers, we were successful by every commonly accepted measure. And, trust me, I was enjoying our success in every way possible.

Naturally, I decided to "invest" a significant portion of our profits in the luxuries I had always wanted.

Cars always seem to surface to the top of the list of status goodies, so I eagerly got into that game. In 1993, I owned five automobiles—an Italian convertible sports car, a minivan for video production gigs, a front-wheel-drive German car for use on snowy winter days, and, of course, the obligatory S-Class Mercedes sedan with heated leather seats, alloy wheels, a great audio system, power everything, and even a special gold-plated Mercedes three-pointed star on the hood.

That's four. So what about the fifth car? Well, to entertain clients properly, I would phone the livery service that managed my Cadillac Sedan DeVille stretch limousine, and I'd book it—along with a chauffeur dressed in a tuxedo. As we headed toward one of the better restaurants or clubs in town, we'd watch a video on the color TV, listen to the stereo, or make phone calls to those fine restaurants and clubs to confirm our reservations. Or maybe we'd just buzz the chauffeur on the intercom to chat. (I hope you know that I'm poking fun at myself here, but, well, yes, at that time my head was major swelled.)

If you're guessing that it didn't stop there, you're right. Sadly, you're 100 percent correct.

A boat would be fun, I thought. So I bought one. Actually, I bought four. No "lowly" aluminum fishing boats, either. I started out with a 15-footer with a 75-horsepower outboard motor. I quickly moved up to a 22-foot inboard/outboard. Then a 26-foot cruiser with a complete galley (kitchen, for you nonboaters), two cabins, and a bathroom (head, for you boaters) with a shower. Next came the 30-footer with dual steering stations, twin engines, and a flybridge that offered panoramic views of my domain—beautiful Lake Minnetonka. Every few years, I traded for bigger and better.

I entertained existing clients at any one of several wonderful waterfront restaurants and took them on leisurely starlit cruises. The positive side of this activity was that, by entertaining prospective clients on the boat, I was able to generate several million dollars in cumulative new business.

Can you guess what came next on this list? You got it! Airplanes! For a number of years, I'd been interested in flying. Finally, I had enough money to take flying lessons. I learned how to fly in my own airplane. I earned my instrument rating in my second airplane—a high-performance little hummer with retractable gear that had all the bells and whistles I'd always wanted, from (forgive me, nonpilots) digital VOR and VHF communications radios, to Loran-C navigation (the predecessor to GPS), autopilot, and thunderstorm-detection and distance measuring equipment—the stuff of an aviator's dreams. As I traveled to my business destinations, I listened to music on CD, played through my special Bose noise-canceling headset connected to my stereo intercom system.

What a great life, I thought, never realizing how temporary it could all be.

On and on it went.

If I wanted a new television, I'd choose one with a 50-inch screen. Or a video projector that displayed a 100-inch picture on a movie screen that could be lowered from the ceiling with the touch of a button. A new stereo had to be an exotic Danish model—a Bang & Olufsen. When I went shopping for a new sofa—for office or home—it was covered in Italian top-grain leather. All of my computer cases and travel bags were made by Hartmann, Zero Halliburton, or Tumi. My pens were Montblanc or Waterman. Every new camera I purchased was a Hasselblad, a top-of-the-line Nikon, or the best, most-current camcorder Sony or Canon had on the market.

I spent my vacations with my wife and children in

Hawaii, Mexico, Aruba, and the Bahamas and at Disneyland. Karla and I cruised the Caribbean on five different cruise ships. I golfed with high-powered executives at exclusive country clubs and dined with senators, members of congress, and mayors.

Great life, right?

Not really.

I had become so downright materialistic in my approach to business, success, and living in general that nothing else mattered. The things I've told you only serve to underscore one simple fact: I had lost sight of all the real priorities in life.

Then, beginning in 1992 and culminating in 1993, it all crashed down around me. The noise of unexpected failure was deafening.

A chain of seemingly irreversible events began to take place . . . and I watched my business—and my life—unravel right in front of me.

Our nation was in the midst of a recession, so most of our clients had slashed their advertising budgets drastically.

Several clients decided to take advantage of the revolution in graphic design offered by the newest Macintosh computers and the software developed by Quark, Adobe, and (at that time) Aldus. They decided to do their ads and literature in-house, thereby cutting us out of the picture.

One of our clients in the medical field was suddenly notified by the FDA that their primary product was to be immediately banned from the marketplace. With no product, there would be no need for advertising.

Two of my employees surreptitiously concocted a

plan to start their own competing ad agency. Armed with my complete contact lists, proprietary information about my pricing structure, and fresh new letterheads designed on my computers after business hours, they easily managed to walk off with several key accounts with whom they had been working to establish relationships. All this in blatant violation of the noncompete nondisclosure contracts that they (and every other employee of the company) had willingly signed.

Because my overhead was quite high—thanks to a fairly luxurious office, my many fancy cars, a sizable boat, a fast airplane, and the best business equipment a company of our size could desire—and because the loss of business was quite significant, it wasn't long before I was losing in excess of $50,000 a month. The losses began in April 1992 and continued at that level or higher through July 1993. Ouch!

I wish I could tell you that all of the disasters in my life at that time were confined to my business life.

But wait! There's more.

Things weren't going much better in my personal life.

Our house was struck by lightning. No, I'm not kidding. A small fire started in some electrical wiring, but, thankfully, it went out on its own. Still, the wall had to be ripped out and the wiring replaced. Cost? A few hundred bucks.

Next, our house was attacked by giant carpenter ants. Not kidding again. The damage? Over $7,000.

Our very young daughter, Kalla, paid a visit to my office, tripped and fell into a sharp corner, and broke her tailbone. Cost? Lots of pain, lots of tears, lots of medical bills, plus $30 for a blow-up plastic doughnut that she had to sit on for weeks.

July 1993. The accident. Karla and Kalla were caught driving in a violent thunderstorm accompanied by torrential rains, when another driver swerved into their car, forcing them off the freeway and into a ditch filled with three feet of rainwater. Cost? Well, the car was totaled and my wife and daughter could easily have been killed. Fortunately, they both survived. The emergency room attendants were able to remove the chunks of shattered glass from their bodies with a special "vacuum cleaner," and our daughter sustained no major injuries.

But I'm sure you can imagine how bad I felt when, two weeks after the accident, Karla was riding around my office in a wheelchair—her broken leg in a splint—attaching price tags to all of the furniture and equipment we were forced to sell (most of it for less than what we owed on it) in order to help pay off our massive debt.

The worst news of all surfaced shortly thereafter. My dad, who had always done his utmost to avoid doctors, was diagnosed with colon cancer in its late stages. I closed down what was left of my ad agency and took a job as a marketing director for a former client of mine, so that I could work just two miles away from the hospital where my dad underwent four major surgeries. That way, I could visit him every day. And be there for him and my mom when he died.

Funny how unimportant toys, cars, gadgets, money, power, and prestige become when one's spouse and child are threatened by a near fatal accident and one's parent is facing a life-ending illness. No, not funny. More of a reality check. An awakening.

What's the point of all of this? Very simply, the point is this book. My goal is to help you start the business of your dreams, nurture it to success, avoid poor choices, maximize your assets, minimize your risks, and assure your long-term success. And have your priorities straight throughout the entire process.

I want to pass along the commonsense things I've learned the hard way . . . so that you don't have to learn them on your own.

I've learned the hard way that serving customers is more important than serving myself.

I've learned the hard way that it is easier to lose customers than it is to retain them . . . or to find new ones, and that I'd better focus on their needs rather than on boats, planes, and automobiles.

I've learned that by empowering the members of my team, I empower my business.

I've learned that there are certain irrefutable laws observed by successful businesspeople—and that I'd better know and understand them.

I've learned that it's important to put together a solid support group well before I need it.

I've learned that meaningful, loving relationships with family and friends offer more satisfaction than the smell of the leather interior of a new car, the high-definition picture on a 64-inch TV, or the luxurious stateroom on a 78-foot yacht. "Things" *ain't* where it's at.

I've learned that "faith," by whatever name you call it—"self-esteem," "a belief system," "hope," "drive," "aspirations," "the dream"—is absolutely essential if you expect to have any chance of confronting challenging times and surviving.

I am pleased that you are giving me the opportunity to share what I've learned, so that you can add it to all of your personal experiences and knowledge in order to achieve your dreams.

I'm also pleased to report that—as bad as '93 "stunk"—life is better, Karla and I have healed, and we have a positive outlook for the future! In fact, we're living that brighter future right now!

PART ONE

The Small Business Life Cycle

New Realities

We live in an economic era unlike any our nation—or our world—has ever seen. The term that describes it is "global economy." Manufacturing jobs once solidly ensconced in the United States have been steadily moving overseas. Long-standing, holdout "American brands," such as Levi Strauss jeans, have even caved in and joined the migration. Clothing, electronics, toys, and printed books bear foreign labels in increasing numbers. American companies still design and engineer their share of innovative products, but those products are built elsewhere. The resulting job losses have become a daunting challenge for so many of our workers—even for the very best of them.

Many of us who long ago realized and accepted the fact that offshore manufacturing had simply become a way of life never thought we'd see the day when customer support, technical service, and inbound/outbound telemarketing activities for American companies would be handled in such places as India, the Philippines, and Thailand. More jobs lost to cheap labor.

Monetary systems are in flux, too. The core nations of Europe have standardized their own joint currency, the Euro, to compete more effectively with the American dollar. More changes in currency are likely in the future. The ebb and flow of foreign stock and commodities exchanges creates waves that are felt with increasing impact in the United States.

Governments try to control the economy by controlling the flow of their natural resources—oil, steel, and coffee among them—or by assessing tariffs to reduce competition and limit imports. At the same time, they engage in unbridled deficit spending, adding more risk to the future of their citizens.

While major companies are off-shoring their manufacturing and customer support to such countries as India in order to gain an economic advantage, there are countless small businesses in the United States who can't afford even a round-trip ticket to India to begin to explore the possibilities.

As I'm sure you realize, this is just a brief glimpse of the economic environment in which you currently operate your small business—or hope to do so one day.

The good news is, there's a place in this world for your business venture, and you *can* succeed!

My objective, throughout the pages of this book, is to give you reasons to dream, to hope, to apply basic commonsense "smarts" to every aspect of your business, and to overcome the threats and challenges that you will most certainly face.

I've heard small business described as a "roller coaster." If it is, it must operate in "amusement park hell." Sometimes it's outrageous fun, but other times it's undeniably terrifying.

I invite you to follow me through the various stages of the business life cycle. Learn from the good decisions I've made, as well as from my many mistakes. Become stronger, more focused, more successful. Discover how to achieve victory no matter what changes the global economy forces upon you.

Begin with me where we all begin in business—at square one.

1

The Dreaming Stage

Everyone has dreams—perhaps without knowing it, we are even born with them.

They begin at age five . . . perhaps earlier . . . sometimes later.

When I was a child, most boys my age wanted to become a "Roy Rogers" cowboy, a fireman, or a policeman. Most girls dreamed of becoming nurses, schoolteachers, secretaries, beauticians, or housewives. (C'mon, give me a break here . . . this was the 1950s . . . we had no clue that girls could become astronauts, bioengineers, news anchors, or senators. It was nurse, teacher, secretary, beautician, or housewife. Period.)

At age eleven, my dream was Annette Funicello—the effervescent brunette with the killer smile on *The Mickey Mouse Club* who stirred the hearts of nearly every prepubescent boy in America.

At fourteen, my dreams turned to radio broadcasting. So my friend Jack and I started our very own illegal AM radio station in our small Minnesota hometown. Things were going quite well until the federal government—specifically the FCC—caught word of our operation and traveled the 135 miles from St. Paul to Mountain Lake to pull our plug. Literally. Physically. Completely. Forever.

Undaunted, I decided to study hard and take the test to earn a real FCC radio operator's license and get a job at a real, legitimate radio station. So I did, and I got a DJ job at the local radio station at age sixteen.

As part of my job, I had to write commercials for a variety of sponsors, which sparked a new interest and a new dream. At age eighteen, I decided to attend the University of Minnesota and take a double major in advertising and radio-television production.

While attending college, I devised a personal goal—a new dream. I decided I wanted to be rich.

There was just one catch. Because I had grown up in a modest home in a small farming town in southwestern Minnesota, I had never *seen* wealth, let alone experienced it. Still, I thought it might be worth a try.

As a caring, giving person—thanks to my upbringing—I knew that I didn't want money just for myself and my own selfish goals. No, not I! I wanted it for the other people for whom I could create a better life. My family. Worthy charities. The starving people in Third World countries that my mother brought up every time I didn't want to clean my plate. The nearest Mercedes dealer. Fortunately, I had learned something crucial from watching my father, my grandfathers, and the employed fathers and mothers of my high school friends. Most people do not get rich as the result of working for others.

After considerable thought about the matter, I concluded that there were only eight ways to gain great wealth:

1. Win some form of contest or lottery—one of those multistate Powerball-type lotteries would be perfect!
2. Develop an idea that can be widely franchised. Another McDonald's would be the ticket!
3. Invent something that everyone needs, preferably on a regular basis. (I've heard that the person who invented those little plastic "whatevers" on the ends of shoelaces retired in utter opulence.)
4. Become a movie, television, recording, or professional sports star.
5. Invest in stocks, bonds, buildings, and land—but only when such investments are absolutely guaranteed to increase in value.
6. Inherit big bucks.
7. Create and own intellectual property (books, music, stage plays, film, television programming) and earn royalties and residuals in perpetuity. (Neil Simon makes money every time actors in any theater in the world step onstage to perform *The Odd Couple* or any of his other plays.)
8. Start a business, devote a tremendous amount of energy to it, and make it prosper and grow.

Great ideas, one and all. But upon further thought, I ruled out the first six of the eight methods.

The statistical odds against winning some form of contest or lottery are astronomical, in spite of the widely held belief that "Someone has to win it; might as well be me."

As to the others?

I'm no Ray Kroc of McDonald's, and besides, the world probably doesn't need another fast-food chain. (Although if there were a drive-through sushi bar in my neighborhood, I'd be a regular!)

I don't have a mechanical mind, so inventing something new would be a pointless pursuit on my part.

I can't act, sing, or dance, and I was always chosen last for every sport or game. (I remember the fights between the team captains. "You take Gottry." "No, *you* take him; I had him last time." It doesn't do much for a seventh grader's self-esteem.)

I thought stocks could be the answer, but those investments have not worked out as well as others—real estate, for example. Some of the companies in which I have invested are out of business. (Ever hear of Fingermatrix or New World Computer? I didn't think so!)

Inheritance sounds like a plan, but I don't have any wealthy relatives or friends. (I know a fellow about my age who, for years, has actually befriended wealthy elderly people in the hope that they will put him in their wills. That's unbelievably tacky, but I'm pleased to report that it hasn't worked for him—yet.)

As to intellectual property, well, I've written two stage plays, and neither one has been produced. If you buy a copy of this book, and everyone you know buys a copy, and everyone they know buys a copy (and so on . . .), maybe the royalty thing could work.

It then seems that the best option for most of us hardworking, highly motivated people is to start a business and nurture it to growth and profitability.

For many years, when my wife, Karla, and I would talk at the end of a long day at the office or on the road, she would ask jokingly, "Are we rich yet?"

Today's answer, of course, would be "No." Not in terms of material goodies, at least. But Karla and I are a long way from where we started more than thirty years ago. I'm a long way from the small house with linoleum floors and asbestos siding in the small farming town where I grew up. I'm a long way from the late-night hours of pumping gas and doing oil changes and grease jobs to earn money for college. I still pump gas, but I only pump it into my car—at several times the price it was back then. Indeed, I have many blessings to count!

These days—very honestly—the accumulation of money is not my primary goal. Any money I do make is simply the result of providing a viable service at a fair price—or writing a helpful book that gets into the hands of readers who will benefit—and being in demand as a result.

The good news is that there will always be a place—in virtually any economy—for well-run businesses that provide meaningful and necessary products or services at competitive prices. And they will always provide jobs for others.

Your business—existing now or in your future plans—could be among them. But only if you play the game smart. You must know what to do in both good times and bad. You must be prepared to make tough but logical decisions. You must understand where you are in the business life cycle and use that knowledge to your advantage.

YOUR BUSINESS BEGINS WITH A DREAM

You may dream about starting a business, but perhaps you seek some guidance on how to transform that dream into reality. You may be concerned that you need more money than you have, or that you have less experience than you need. That's why I'm scattering my personal story throughout this book. The thoughts and processes that worked for me—even through the failure of my business and the start-up of a new one—may well work for you.

My company began as a dream in high school, when my senior-year social studies teacher assigned a term-paper project on the subject of personal career choices. I knew exactly what I was going to write. I wanted to start my own advertising/public relations business. That was my dream. And now, years later, that term paper is still filed in the lower-right-hand drawer of my desk. (Yes, I *did* receive an A on the paper.)

From my first day at the University of Minnesota, I knew what my majors were going to be. I worked my way through college—with as much help as my parents could give me (only about $40 a month for food)—as a hospital orderly, as a freelance designer and wedding photographer, and as a gofer in the promotion department of the local CBS Television Network affiliate. I graduated without honors and without debt.

A few weeks before commencement exercises, my graphic design professor confirmed what I already knew would be my career decision. He said, "Of all the students I've had over the years, you're the only one I have ever advised to hang out his own shingle." That's all I needed to hear!

Despite the need to pay for most of the costs of my education, I had managed to save about $125 through my freelance design and photography work. That seemed like plenty of money with which to start an advertising agency, but my lawyer at the time—a wonderful elderly gentleman who offered to handle the incorporation process for me if I simply paid his out-of-pocket expenses—didn't seem to agree. He pointed out that in the state of Minnesota, $1,000 was the minimum capital investment required for incorporation. "Well, I have other assets besides cash," I told him. "I have a well-worn IBM electric typewriter that my father bought for me. I have a four-drawer file cabinet, a drafting board and a T square, and a nearly antique manual adding machine. Why, the typewriter alone has appreciated dramatically over the past several years, to the point where I'm sure it's worth at least a thousand dollars!" With a sly little wink, he agreed, and I became an "Inc." My dream was marching toward reality.

All dreams, though, need a foundation of reality. I believe you have to possess a deep personal interest in the business you are contemplating, as well as training in, and knowledge of, the field. Your dreams must be based on a measure of research. You need to know whether or not you have a reasonable chance for success.

If your dream is to open a sushi bar in a small Missouri town of 400 residents, you're probably doomed to fail. If you plan to set up a bait-and-tackle store in the dustiest part of Nevada, 150 miles from the nearest good-fishing lake or stream, good luck! If your dream is to open a DVD rental store in a strip mall that already has two or three DVD rental outlets, you may find that the pickings get pretty slim.

THE FANAFI PRINCIPLE

The secret to small business success is something I refer to as FANAFI. It's the acronym for the old saying "Find a need and fill it."

If you want to start a business for the purpose of filling a need that no longer exists (horse-drawn carriage repair, for example), or for the purpose of filling a need that is declining too much to assure your profitability (VCR/DVD player repair is a less viable option than it was a few years ago, because it's cheaper to buy a new one than to repair a broken unit), or for the purpose of filling a need that only the strongest of economies will support (selling only $1,500-and-up vacuum cleaners), you're not taking the FANAFI principle into consideration.

Take a moment to reflect on the needs that have recently come to the forefront and the businesses that have been formed to fill those needs.

The desire to shop at home combined with the growth of the Internet and the ease and security of ordering online has spawned countless new retail ventures. (Is there some product line you could sell online?)

The time crunch that most of us face, coupled with our impatience and unwillingness to wait in lines, has resulted in thirty-minute photo processing and twenty-minute-or-less automobile oil change facilities. We are all in a hurry.

Digital photography has cut into the sales of film but has also led to those freestanding "make your own photos" kiosks. And you know who got into the digital business, right? Kodak, the people whose film sales are in decline.

Pizza-delivery services were a great idea. They saved time and gave busy people a night off from kitchen duties. But we all get tired of pizza sometimes. That's why there are services that offer to deliver meals from a wide range of restaurants. You simply order from a "catalog" of restaurant menus.

New needs, new technologies, and new generations of consumers will lead to a multitude of new business opportunities. The businesses that succeed will be those that fulfill a genuine need for a large enough market—and are well managed.

It doesn't matter whether your plan is to manufacture a new product, compete in an existing product category, distribute goods manufactured by others, or start a service-based business; you'll find that the same principles will apply no matter what business you enter.

You will, on an ongoing basis, have to confront certain realities.

- If you have a good idea, you will be copied. Even if you are able to patent or trademark your innovation, others will attempt to compete. "But I have a patent/trademark," you argue. That may be true, but the reality is that it costs an enormous amount of money to defend your patent or trademark. These days, some companies don't even bother to file for patents, because by not doing so, proprietary information is kept out of the hands of competitors for a longer period of time—enough time to make enough money to move on to the next big idea.
- Technology changes so rapidly that your earthshaking idea of today may be worthless tomorrow.

- If the "barrier to entry" in your field is high, you will buy yourself some time to establish your brand and build a loyal share of the market. But if the barrier to entry is just a few thousand dollars, competitors will crop up quickly.

What does this mean to you? As you dream, make certain those dreams mesh with reality, and you will have a good shot at success!

THINKING IT THROUGH

My greatest dream is to: _____

_____

_____

A need that someone has mentioned to me is: _____

_____

_____

A need I can fill is: _____

_____

_____

The business I would *most* like to start is: _____

_____

_____

My perception of the barrier to entry that potential cus-

tomers would face is: _____

_____

_____

The business start-up I admire most is: _____

_____

_____

The reason is: _____

_____

_____

2

The Planning Stage

One of the most amazing individuals I've ever known was my late friend Jack Liemandt. He was in his eighties—nearly twice my age—when I met him at my Rotary Club.

Jack started a small men's-clothing business nearly seventy years ago. He grew the business into a chain of men's clothing stores that was so successful that it eventually attracted the attention of Hart Schaffner & Marx, which offered Jack a tidy sum in order to become the new owners. (Most of us dream of a similar scenario!)

Jack once told me that his business career had been guided by a simple, straightforward principle found in the ancient but timeless Proverbs of King Solomon:

> Any enterprise is built by wise planning, becomes strong through common sense, and profits wonderfully by keeping abreast of the facts.

This little nugget of truth is incredibly obvious to everyone in business. Or at least it should be. A multitude of costly mistakes and disastrous business failures could be avoided if entrepreneurs paid attention to its three components—wise planning, common sense, and up-to-date information.

I started making critical mistakes from the day I opened my doors. The first one was that I had not developed a business plan. No five-year plan. No three-year plan. No one-year plan. Not even a one-month plan. In fact, I had no plan for the next day.

All I knew for sure was that my brand new ad agency had one client from day one, and that that client had promised two months of work in the form of one project. Although I was fortunate in that one order was all I needed to get started, that's usually not enough to get a business up and running and keep it going.

After you've dreamed your dreams, you have to plan your plan. A good initial plan takes several things into account. Just as a news reporter asks the basic **who, what, when, where,** and **how** questions to establish the facts behind a fast-breaking story, you have to ask—and answer—some essential questions to establish the direction of your business.

- **When** are you going to start your business?
- **Where** are you going to start it?
- **What** are you going to name it?
- **How** are you going to position it?
- **How** are you going to determine your investment needs and finance them?
- **What kind** of business structure are you going to establish? Sole proprietorship, partnership, limited liability company (LLC), corporation, or S corporation?

- **How many** employees will you need, and what will they have to accomplish?
- **What policies** will apply to those employees?

These questions are so simple—so fundamental. Yet it's surprising how many small business owners overlook one or more of them.

ANSWER THE ESSENTIAL QUESTIONS OF BUSINESS

All of these questions demand answers. They must be explored in depth. Every facet of that exploration must be written down, evaluated, and discussed with trusted advisers.

Let me be one of your advisers, and share some thoughts on each of these questions.

1. WHEN are you going to start your business?

The obvious answer is, "When the time is right. When the cosmic forces of concept and financing come together." That's almost correct.

The answer is, "When there is a *valid need* that *someone* can *fulfill* at a *profit*, and *you* are in the *best position*—by virtue of interest, expertise, and financial capability—to *meet it*." Hopefully, you'll be in the best position to meet that need **ahead** of everyone else. The late entrant usually has a tougher go of it, unless he or she can come up with a new slant or better pricing or can outmarket the competition.

This statement presupposes a number of things. Enough residents of Desert Wasteland, Nevada, have to *need* and *want* a local bait shop, even if there's no fishing within miles. Each and every one of the people in that Missouri town of 400 souls had better *crave* sushi three or four times a week. I can't overemphasize that your planning must begin with the FANAFI Principle: Find a need and fill it.

If you are considering leaving your current job, no matter what it is or how much you are paid, you must be in a position to accept a major reduction in pay for the first several weeks, months, and possibly even years, when you start your own business. If you can't do that, you can't answer the question "When?" and you should probably pass this book along to a more courageous friend.

The fact is, you *will* face hard times. You more than likely will take at least a temporary cut in pay. Maybe not from day one, if you have a few "ducks in a row" before you start your business—but soon thereafter.

Back in 1970, I was offered a full-time, likely secure job with our metropolitan area's only (highly regulated) phone company. They wanted to start me in the advertising department at $9,800 per year. Today, those would be virtually poverty-level wages. But back then, it was a fairly enticing offer, especially for a college student who had been making $1.90 an hour at a part-time job.

I said, "Sorry, no thanks," and struck out on my own. The first few months, while I was fulfilling the terms of my initial contract with my first client, and had taken on some additional assignments, I was actually making what amounted to the monthly equivalent of the $9,800 annual income I had been offered by Ma Bell.

Then I hit my first dry spell. I experienced my first bad receivable, along with a reduction in work orders. Just five months before my first child was due, my gross income was $60—for the *entire* month. Four months before his birth, it increased to the whopping sum of $75. In fact, in order to keep the roof of our apartment over our heads, we had to become caretakers for the apartment building in which we lived. The young ad agency president had to clean toilets, mow lawns, and shovel sidewalks to provide a home for his growing family.

I had traded a sure thing (the phone company) for an unsure thing (my own business). And for some strange, indefinable, entrepreneurial reason . . . I loved it!

It was difficult. It still is. The tough times have been mixed in with the good times. But the good times always seem to win out. Even when I'm locked in a battle with our nonsense economy.

2. WHERE are you going to start it?

Every real estate broker can quote the oldest axiom on the books: "The three most important things about real estate are *location, location, location.*"

When it comes to most new businesses, location is only one of several important considerations. But it's still vital.

As you investigate a prospective location, take a look at the neighborhood. Is the population sufficient to support your business? Are the demographics—age, income, gender—a good match for your business? You won't sell much baby furniture in a retirement community.

Is the neighborhood clean, safe, and inviting, or is it deteriorating? Are other businesses in the area successful?

Then, consider traffic counts. If most of the traffic sticks to a main artery three blocks north of where you want to locate your business, better think again. When your business is one that relies on high traffic to be successful, you must be situated on a well-traveled street.

Make sure you have good access, especially if you're planning to locate along a freeway or major highway. All roads may lead to you, but do all exits?

Next, carefully consider the prospects for growth in the area. Are people building new homes? Are apartment buildings going up? Is vacant land being developed into malls and office parks? If there are a lot of "For Lease" or "For Sale" signs in the windows, find out why. Chances are, the businesses there have failed because of the location.

If you're setting up a manufacturing or distribution operation, naturally you'll have to look at all aspects of area services, zoning, rail spur access, roads that can handle trucking loads, availability of a good labor pool, and so on—issues too varied and complex to fully explore here.

Avoid the temptation to take the second-best location based on lower lease rates. Where you open your business has a tremendous impact on whether or not you will succeed.

3. WHAT are you going to name it?

Think carefully about the name you plan to give your business.

When I first began my company, our name was Visual Communications Services, Inc. We were an ad agency, but we didn't sound like it. We got calls from people looking for duplicates of slides, for audiovisual equipment, and for multimedia shows for use at conventions.

Stubbornly, I stuck to the name for seventeen years. But when we moved our office in 1987, and had to reprint all of our letterheads, envelopes, business cards, and forms, I gave in to the urging of my account executive, who said that it was too difficult to explain to prospects that we're really an ad agency and marketing communications firm. The consensus among the staff was that we change our name to Gottry Advertising & Marketing, Inc.

A few years later, the word "advertising" seemed to have fallen into almost the same category as "lawyer." We "got no respect." So we became The Gottry Communications Group, Inc. We sold ourselves as the company that could handle any communications assignment—advertising, public relations, video, corporate events, newsletters—you name it.

The best approach is to give your business the "perfect" name right from the start—and then stick with it. It's expensive to change a name (signs, forms, business cards, letterheads, yellow pages ads, all have to change). But the biggest disadvantage of a name change is that you lose the cumulative marketing benefits of name recognition, and you have to start over. It wasn't a huge problem for us either time we changed our name, because an ad agency has very few clients and a limited number of prospects, and they can all grasp the change quickly.

On the other hand, if you've developed an insurmountable negative image problem (hopefully through no fault of your own), a name change could be your salvation.

Regardless of the name you ultimately choose, you'll have an easier time promoting your company if your name accurately describes the products or services you offer. If it's short and memorable, all the better!

> **TIPS:**
> * The thoughts and opinions of others can be helpful throughout this process.
> * Make sure the company name you choose is available, whether you are filing a trade name for a sole proprietorship or you're forming an LLC or a corporation. Generally, you find this out by contacting your secretary of state or corporation commission.

4. HOW are you going to position it?

Every company and every product need what ad people call a "Unique Selling Proposition," or USP. The essence of the term is this: What makes your company, product, or service different from every other competing company, product, or service? Why are you unique?

Your distinguishing benefit could be price, quality, variety, convenience, service, or a strong guarantee. Or maybe you just outpromote, outadvertise, and outspend your competition.

Whatever it is, you must focus on your competitive edge—and use it to build your business and your market share.

For example, what competitive edges do you automatically think of when these brands come to mind: Mercedes-Benz, Maytag, Charmin, Apple Computer, Chick-fil-A, and Fox News?

For Mercedes-Benz, the competitive edge is safety and quality German engineering.

For Maytag, it's dependability.

For Charmin bathroom tissue, it's "squeezable softness."

For Apple Computer, it's user-friendliness.

For Chick-fil-A, you might think of the cows urging you to "Eat Mor Chikin."

For Fox News, it's "Fair and Balanced" reporting.

I'm sure you can recall the slogans and/or Unique Selling Propositions for scores, if not hundreds, of companies and brands. These companies have spent major amounts of money to make sure that you can.

There are other companies that seem to have never-ending difficulty positioning themselves in the consumer's mind. They struggle with one ill-conceived idea after another. Certain fast-food chains and hotels come to mind. People simply don't know why these companies are different or better—or even *if* they are. The companies in question haven't determined who they are and, as a result, are unable to establish a strong selling proposition.

Your Mission Statement

One of the most effective ways to begin to focus on your Unique Selling Proposition is to draft a concise mission statement. This statement should be relatively brief (it should fit on less than one page), and it should be widely circulated among your employees, your customers, your vendors, and your prospects. Your mission statement is, in effect, your reason for being in business, and thus it helps you position your company.

There's nothing profound about the mission statement we drafted. It has three components: our mission, how that helps our clients, and how fulfilling that mission benefits us. "The Benefits to Us . . ." section is important because we wanted our employees to "buy into" the mission of the company, since most of them weren't around when it was drafted.

Our Mission

The mission of this company is to become **"partners in spirit and purpose"** with our clients, to enable them to more effectively sell their products or services to a larger market at a greater profit, while at the same time satisfying our need to be creative, fresh, and innovative, and, in the process, grow in our careers.

The Benefits to Us . . .

As we succeed in meeting this goal, we will—as a natural by-product—make a reasonable profit as a company. The result of this profit will be greater personal income for each of us, better short-term and long-range benefit programs, an enhanced working environment, and the acquisition of new tools to make us more productive in our jobs.

By performing our jobs to the best of our abilities, we will be able to demonstrate through our portfolios or résumés that we are highly skilled and knowledgeable members of our profession.

Your mission statement may focus on your desire to be known as the company that provides fast and dependable service, or does contract manufacturing to the strictest tolerances with the fewest rejected parts, or offers the widest selection of a particular category of durable goods.

As we will discuss in subsequent chapters, your mission statement—and the way you choose to position your business—is only the starting point. It may work only for today. Times change, products change, and needs change. To remain a viable business in the years ahead, you will have to accept and adapt to change.

KEN BLANCHARD AND JESSE STONER ON VISION AND MISSION

Your organization's vision has to be a compelling one in order to have the desired impact on leaders, team members and customers. The tests of a compelling vision are straightforward:

- Does our vision help us understand what business we are really in?
- Does it provide guidelines that help us make daily decisions?
- Does it provide a picture of our desired future that we can actually see?
- Is it enduring?
- Is it about being "great"—not solely about beating the competition?
- Is it inspiring—and not expressed solely in numbers?
- Does it touch the hearts and spirits of everyone?
- Does it help each person see how he or she can contribute?

Fall short on even one of these tests and your vision will not be as compelling as it could be.

—From *Full Steam Ahead!* by Ken Blanchard and Jesse Stoner

5. *HOW are you going to determine your investment needs and finance them?*

No matter how carefully a financial plan for a start-up business is drafted, no matter how detailed and thorough the planning, some costly things are going to be overlooked. I've never come in contact with any businessperson who didn't ultimately need much more money for the start-up than originally anticipated.

Conservatively, I would estimate that new businesses need 30 to 50 percent more capital than what they, in their wildest dreams, imagined they would need. And, in virtually every case, an insufficiently capitalized new business opens its doors with one side of the coffin lid nailed down.

One of the older "business" books around—the Bible—advises builders to count the cost before they start construction, so that they don't run out of money before they finish—and, as a result, look like fools to their neighbors.

Hidden Costs

I've personally come across a few fascinating accounts of companies that underestimated their capital needs, or failed to "expect the unexpected."

A printing company decided to build a new plant to accommodate their rapid growth. (This isn't a start-up story, but it's the kind of thing that happens to start-ups.) They completed their beautiful new building and ordered a huge multicolor printing press. Only when it arrived in crates did they discover that, when assembled, it would be too heavy for their brand-new concrete floor. At substantial cost, they had to break up the floor, haul it out in pieces, and pour a new reinforced floor that offered three times the strength.

Another company, a start-up manufacturer of energy-efficient furnaces, ordered some new robotic welding equipment and had to rewire their leased space to handle the extra demand for electricity.

Yet another company purchased new state-of-the-art computers that promised to make every employee more productive and efficient. They discovered that the machines themselves were only a small part of the investment. Every one of them needed additional memory, higher-capacity hard drives, extensive backup systems, a variety of accelerator boards and video cards, and other goodies too numerous to mention. Of course, all the old software was outdated, so another major investment had to be made. And the lines of employees waiting for the output from the new laser printer could be shortened only through the purchase of additional laser printers. I know the details of this story firsthand. This happened at my company ... way back in 1987.

It's vital that you explore, investigate, and understand all the hidden costs associated with an investment, to maintain control over that investment.

Inventory Control

Another common trap is that of inventory imbalance. As an example, the new business owner has reason to believe that he or she will sell a certain number of each of hundreds or thousands of items over a certain period of time.

But then something unexpected happens. Half of the products move off the shelves more quickly than projected, and the other half just sits there. Realizing that he or she must now stock twice as many of the items that do sell in order to meet demand, the owner increases the purchase of those items. Suddenly there's a problem with display space, with warehousing, and with the fact that the business operator has money tied up in that portion of the inventory that simply isn't moving.

An inventory-based business must have product to sell and must be able to meet demand in a timely manner. Customers today are impatient; they want immediate gratification and will go where their needs can be met. By gathering as much information as possible on the sales trends in your industry—from trade journals, visits to the competition, and the study of competing advertising, you will be able to do more accurate forecasting.

Outside Costs

You must also determine what outside resources and services your business will require, what they will cost, and whether or not they are readily available. The list could be endless—legal and accounting services, hazardous and nonhazardous waste disposal, recycling services, shipping and mail handling, advertising and direct mail, sign painting, phone system purchase and installation, architectural design services and construction, and so on. Onetime costs will be included in your start-up budget; recurring costs will be a part of your operating budget. Thus, your initial capital must be sufficient to handle all of your start-up expenses, and your operating capital, sales, and cash flow must be able to meet or exceed your operating expenses.

Sources of Financing

Very few businesses get established without some source of outside financing. And very few keep going without additional financing. As long as you remain in business, you will probably always be paying interest to someone for something you have financed.

Traditionally, business start-ups are financed through venture capitalists, family investors, second-mortgage loans, or equity financing through banks. I believe one of your primary goals should be to find those sources of capital that do not require you to transfer control of your concepts, patents, or ownership to others. An investor can own your building without owning your business.

Throughout the ups and downs in my business, I did everything within my power to avoid selling off pieces of my business under duress. I did not want to wake up some morning, go into my office, and discover that the new owner was sitting in my chair. I wanted a new owner to take over when *I* was ready for it, and when it was to my advantage. Of course, that is no longer an issue. My creditors ended up sitting in my chair—for the eight long years it took me to pay off all of my debt.

Generally, when I needed cash, I did considerable financing through personal lines of credit at banks and through loans against the cash value of my life insurance policies. I had many of my insurance policies for so long that I had accumulated considerable cash values.

I also used receivables financing extensively. Those who choose this route must be aware of the fact that banks have limitations on how old those receivables can be. For lending purposes, my bank disallowed *all* of the money due from a particular client if *any part* of that money was ninety days past due. Don't count on money the bank won't let you have.

Sales and Cash Flow

An essential part of the business forecasting process is to know what you will need in monthly sales and cash flow to operate the business, and to determine whether it is feasible to attain that level of sales and cash flow. Some businesses simply can't be operated at a profit—or even at break-even levels—based on the way they are structured. Example: a restaurant that doesn't have enough tables to serve the number of customers at a certain average meal cost that would be required to break even won't be able to do so. Wishing it so won't make it happen. Neither will projecting the customer count based on beginning lunch service at 9:00 A.M. or continuing dinner service until 2:00 A.M. Traffic counts won't materialize during off-hours. Most people eat lunch at lunchtime and dinner at dinnertime.

Your Pro Forma

Your business needs a pro forma. Simply stated, *how much must you sell at what price to how many customers over what time frame at what fixed cost in order to break even?* If you do not meet the pro forma, you will lose money. If you meet it exactly, you will break even; if you exceed it, you will make a profit.

If you are losing money, you must change at least one of the variables of the pro forma. You must increase your prices, increase your number of customers, change your hours of operation, or reduce your fixed costs.

If you invoice your customers, expecting payment later, part of your pro forma must take into consideration what share of your customers will pay within terms (say, thirty days), what share of your customers will be late with payment (and how late), and how you will fund the interim? How much will the money you need to continue to operate cost you in terms of interest?

Any business—even one with a solid backlog of orders, good employees, and efficient production—can get in severe trouble or go under if cash flow is insufficient to sustain day-to-day operations.

6. WHAT KIND of business structure are you going to establish?

Every business is viewed by the law as a "person" or "body." In other words, as a legal entity with a legal name. What kind of person or legal entity the business is determines how it, and its owners, are treated under the tax laws and other statutes.

In establishing your business, you will have to determine how you want to be treated by those laws, and you will have to become the compatible legal entity.

The most common options are sole proprietorship, partnership, limited liability company (LLC), corporation, and S corporation.

Sole Proprietorship

In a sole proprietorship, you, the individual, are the company. Your equity in your business assets belongs to you, and your personal assets belong to the business. There is no separating them. You are taxed as one entity, and the personal income tax rates apply to all of your income. Your personal tax return will include all the special forms that relate to the operation of your business, and you can usually charge all operating expenses and losses against your gross income.

This option, in my mind, has two major drawbacks. First, you have little or no legal insulation, such as you would have if your business were an LLC or a corporation. If the business goes away, your house, car, and boat may go away, too, depending on how much debt you have accumulated. Secondly, if you plan to actively seek outside lenders, those potential lenders may not perceive you as "distanced" enough from your business and may be less likely to loan money for purposes they may not see as being of a purely business nature. They certainly won't want to loan you money to enhance your lifestyle. They want their loans secured and protected.

If your dream is to build a profitable, growing business, I believe a sole proprietorship has too many limitations, and I would recommend looking at other options.

Partnership

A business partnership reminds me of a marriage—two people, usually of widely diverse backgrounds, who think they will always understand each other and get along, come together under one roof. And then the trouble begins.

But unlike married couples, who can experience the bonds of sex and children and the benefits of marriage counseling, partnerships, by comparison, are held together by cellophane tape and baling twine.

Of all the partnerships I have personally observed, not one has remained successful and intact over the long term. One partnership of two brothers failed miserably within two years, despite the fact that the business was growing and prospering. Being brothers, they let some minor details, such as written contracts, slip by them. The relationship was further complicated because one was the operating partner and the other was the not-so-silent silent partner.

If you think divorces can be ugly, you should be on hand when business partners split up. (I must add that I'm not including those partnerships that are, in essence, professional associations—medical practices, accounting firms, and the like. Their larger size and purpose for being, coupled with the individual accountability of the partners, give them a much greater success rate.)

When a partnership splits up, there are assets to divide. This usually precipitates war. I've read many reports in the *Wall Street Journal* and other newspapers about the demise of well-known partnerships. One story about a leading architectural firm described the problem as an "irresolvable conflict between Mr. So-and-so and his longtime partner . . ." and observed that "the profession is rife with stories of partners stiffing partners as firms shrink, restructure and dissolve."

My observation has been that there are three basic reasons partnerships don't often succeed.

The first is that the partner who believes he or she is working the hardest has the perception that the other partner isn't pulling his or her share of the load.

The second is that if the partners have an equal voice in the operation of the business, a stalemate often develops with regard to critical decisions, and the business becomes immobilized.

But the greatest cause of failure, from what I've witnessed, is that each partner can individually act on behalf of the partnership. Each partner can sign contracts, bring suits, and incur debt. Yet, in each case, both partners are individually and jointly liable for the debt, responsible for the decisions, and legally bound by the actions of one of them. One ill-advised move can doom what both individuals initially believed would be a lasting and mutually beneficial relationship.

Basing a business on the hope that your partnership can beat the odds is like building a house on a sandy beach.

Limited Liability Company (LLC)

This is a major step above a sole proprietorship but just a small step below a corporation.

Most states make it easy to apply for LLC status. The forms are simple and the fees are usually very low.

Karla and I have an LLC in place for a piece of rental property we own. We initially owned it under our names, but thanks to the advice of Robert Kiyosaki (of *Rich Dad, Poor Dad* fame), we realized that if some disaster occurred for which we could be held liable, we could potentially lose not only that property, but our house and every other asset as well. An LLC protects your personal assets, but the structure is less complicated than a corporation, because the income and expenses of the LLC are included on your personal 1040 tax forms.

Generally, the members of an LLC are required to conduct annual meetings and keep records of the decisions made. In short, an LLC must be run like a business, and not like a "hobby" designed to avoid taxes.

Corporation

A corporation is a distinct and separate legal entity. It, in effect, has a life of its own. A corporation can go down without dragging its owners or shareholders along with it. In the event of business failure, you are no more legally responsible for the debts of your corporation than you are for the debts of your next-door neighbor. (Unless, of course, you and your board of directors have engaged in some illegal activity, in which case you may face some lawsuits, jail time, and other unpleasant outcomes.)

I use the term "legally responsible," because I believe that insofar as we are able, we are all *morally* responsible for the debt we incur, whether we incur it under the auspices of a corporation or not.

There are certain circumstances under which the courts may not uphold that protection. In these cases, the so-called "corporate veil" is pierced. The attorneys for your creditors can argue that you did not adhere to corporate formalities—such as electing a board of directors and keeping minutes of shareholder and board meetings. The court could determine that your corporation was set up primarily for the purpose of isolating you from your obligations and responsibilities and could hold you personally liable.

If you form a new corporation, have limited assets, have little experience in your field, and have not yet established a solid credit rating, your vendors or suppliers may seek an extraordinary measure of financial protection.

If their confidence in your ability to succeed in business is limited, they may insist that you personally guarantee the financial obligations of your corporation.

They may require that you—as a tenant in their office building, warehouse, or mall, as a borrower from their bank, or as a buyer of their raw materials, products, or services—pledge to pay them personally the money you owe them in the event of corporate insolvency. For a very small business, personal guarantees have some meaning. For a larger business, these guarantees mean next to nothing, because it's virtually impossible for an individual to guarantee all of the debts and obligations of a multimillion-dollar business.

The real beauty of incorporation is that it provides the best legal and business context for future growth. As a corporation, you can attract outside investors, sell shares of the company, and, ultimately, go public with a stock offering—subject to all of the rules and regulations our government has devised to protect the innocent investor.

S Corporation

An S corporation—or closely held corporation—is a twist on the regular corporation. Essentially, it involves a provision of federal tax law that permits the principle stockholder to pay the company's taxes and claim the company's losses on a separate tax return that is filed in conjunction with that individual's personal tax forms.

The advantages of the S corporation are that you don't pay taxes twice on the same income, and that you are not double-taxed when the time comes to sell assets or liquidate the company. This can be a very real benefit.

In determining the legal structure of your company, choose the option that puts you in the best position to obtain needed financing or investors, while at the same time providing the greatest measure of protection for your personal assets. Since, in general, lack of capital kills businesses, and availability of capital helps them grow and prosper, incorporation often becomes the most attractive option.

7. HOW MANY employees will you need, and what will they have to accomplish?

When it comes to personnel, the two great mistakes made by businesspeople are *understaffing* and *overstaffing*.

The problems of each are obvious.

If you are understaffed, you are unable to meet the demands, in terms of service, delivery, and deadlines, that your customers or clients make. And if someone calls in sick or goes on vacation, your problems are compounded.

If you are overstaffed, you will often be paying people to sit around and do nothing. Customer service will be outstanding, because you may have two or three employees to handle the needs of every customer.

The problem for the small businessperson is that it is difficult to maintain the proper balance between the supply of employees and the demand of customers. The solution can be cross-training and the restructuring of specific jobs within your company.

During the peak years of my business (in terms of employment levels), I had eight people in the creative department, who generated sufficient revenues to pay for themselves, plus three people in the support areas. If I had needed to add a ninth person, the overhead associated with that person would have been apportioned among the eight income-producing staff members. The added burden would have been easy to bear.

But, as the result of a recession (combined with some really crummy business decisions), we were forced to cut back to three income-producing people in the creative department, and three support persons. As the result of our reduced workload, we had fewer than half as many income-producing creative people carrying the load for the same number of support persons as we had before.

Not only was the pro forma not working, but we would have had to take on a higher percentage of new business (33 percent) to pay for one new person, rather than the 12.5 percent we would have needed when we had eight people generating income.

We dealt with this problem as best we could by computerizing some of the functions that were previously performed manually, by restructuring and eliminating some of the support positions, and by hiring an extremely efficient part-time person to take on the income-producing responsibilities that had been handled by an underworked full-time employee. This was the first of many steps we took to make our company more productive and better able to meet the challenges we faced over the next several months.

8. WHAT POLICIES will apply to those employees?

There was a young pup (at least I think of twenty-five as young) who operated a small business of his own in the same office building where I leased space. This likable, upbeat young entrepreneur had been in business for three or four years and oversaw a team of commissioned salespeople along with one salaried office assistant.

For a variety of reasons, we became friends, and he occasionally approached me with questions about business. One day, he stopped into my office and asked if I had a minute. I said I did. This was his question: "My assistant will have been with me a year next week, and I was wondering, should I do something special? Should she get a vacation or a raise or something?" (I *said* he was a young pup!)

My question to him was, "What is your company policy? What does it say in your employee handbook?"

He looked at me with a totally blank expression on his face. "Handbook? What handbook? Do *you* have a handbook?"

I showed him a copy of our employee handbook. He was awestruck. I said, "Young Pup (not his real name), if you would like, I'll give you a copy of our handbook on computer disk. You can print it out, change the name of the company wherever it appears, make any other changes you want, and—presto—you'll have an employee handbook." He was grateful for my help, although, to this day, he still owes me a lunch.

Most major corporations would never dream of operating today without setting forth all of their employment practices and policies in writing. Yet, many small business owners feel that they are too small to be concerned about such matters. Nothing could be further from the truth. Even if you have only one employee—even if your handbook has its beginning as a two- or three-page memo—begin today to put one together.

Without an employee handbook, you have no framework on which to base such matters as hiring and firing procedures, vacation and sick pay, raises and promotions, and a myriad of other matters.

There are some words of caution that apply to the compilation and distribution of employee handbooks.

First, you must make certain that the policies apply fairly to all employees in a specific class. You can have some policies that apply to part-time employees, some that apply to full-time employees, and some that apply to commissioned employees, but the policies for a specific group must apply to all persons in that group.

Second, remove any ambiguity from your policy statements. Clearly define your policies, and make certain they are easy to understand and apply.

Third, study the laws and labor practices that apply to your business. Make sure your handbook does not contain policies that contradict local, state, or federal law. Consult with an attorney for accuracy and compliance with applicable laws.

Fourth, most states interpret the contents of your employee handbook to be a part of an "employment contract." In other words, be careful what you promise in your handbook, and examine the various possible interpretations of each statement, so that you don't get caught in a legal trap later. Again, have a competent attorney (they're out there; I actually know some!) review the contents. You may discover that your attorney will advise against publishing an employee handbook, simply because of the fact that they are often interpreted as binding contracts in the courts. Many law firms do not have employee handbooks of their own for this very reason. Though not privy to the nature of and facts related to the cases that have made their way through the judicial system, I still believe it is better for both the company and its employees to set forth your policies and procedures in a handbook.

Finally, make sure that you follow through on the policies you've set forth. Prevent your day in court at the hands of a disgruntled employee who feels that you enforced your policies with some employees and not with others. The most critical case in which this could come up is in a suit alleging "wrongful discharge," wherein the former employee charges that you fired him or her without cause, or for violations of policies or procedures that were not applied or enforced equally and consistently among all employees. The laws are different in "right to work" states, so make sure you know the statutes that apply to you.

YOUR FIRST PLAN

When you have developed your answers to these eight basic business questions . . .

- **When** am I going to start my business?
- **Where** will it be?
- **What** should I name it?
- **How** am I going to position it?
- **How** am I going to find the money?
- **What kind** of business structure should I establish?
- **How many** employees will I need, and what will I want them to accomplish?
- **What policies** will apply to these employees?

. . . and you have written them down in logical sequence, you will have your first business plan in front of you. I say "first" plan deliberately, because no plan will ever be your final plan. As we will discuss later, your new business is likely to evolve and change over the years, and you will need to draft new plans, secure new financing, and perhaps change the very structure of your business.

But with your first plan in place, it's time to move ahead!

YOUR JOB!
THE ROLE OF THE BOSS:

As the owner of the company, you have certain duties, responsibilities, and obligations. They begin in the Dreaming Stage, are refined in the Planning Stage, and continue throughout all of the subsequent stages.

Here they are . . .

1. **Conceptualize:** What business will you be in? What product or service will you offer? Where will you offer it? What will you charge for it? Who will your target customers be?
2. **Organize:** This is a key management responsibility. You need to decide who does what. When does it need to happen?
3. **Implement:** You need to put everything into place. Buy or rent your facility. Hire key people. Connect with your key support group. Accountants, lawyers (yes, you will need them!), marketing people, Web designers . . .
4. **Motivate:** The support team you have brought into your company won't do much of anything unless they are clear on what they need to do . . . and you motivate them to do it. Pep talks? Incentives? Prizes? Contests? This is all up to you.
5. **Serve:** Great leaders serve. One of the keys to motivating people is to be a "servant leader." There is no place for unbridled ego in a true leader's portfolio of skills. Two thousand years ago, a humble, uneducated Jewish carpenter with profound leadership skills demonstrated servant leadership by washing the

dusty, dirty feet of his followers. He said, "The great-est among you must become the least." Those words apply in business today.

6. **Analyze:** You need to look at what's going on in your business and analyze it. No "head in the clouds" stuff here. Face reality. Know what's happening. Run the numbers! What are you doing right or wrong? What is the competition doing right or wrong? What do you need to change? This is all about measuring. Reviewing. Cross-checking. Comparing.

7. **Adapt:** If your competitors are blowing you away, you better change *at least* one thing! If you've analyzed correctly, you will know what you need to change.

But guess what? If you go through all of these steps and your business is not working, be prepared to go back to *step one:* Conceptualize.

Business is all about constant, continuous change. Refinement. Reinvention. Ford Motor Company would not be in business today if it were still building Model T's.

As the founder, owner, and employer in your business—these seven responsibilities belong to you!

KEN BLANCHARD AND MARK MILLER ON SERVANT LEADERSHIP

"What's-in-it-for-me" leaders are rarely successful. Throughout history, the leaders who have had the greatest impact have taken the position that they are "servants."

There are five steps to servant leadership—easy to remember because of the SERVE acronym.

S—See and Shape the Future. A servant leadership has a clear vision and does what is necessary to move the organization toward the future.

E—Engage and Develop Others. Get people to "buy into" the vision and give them the motivation, the education and the tools to develop.

R—Reinvent Continuously. Your organization cannot be a stagnant pool. It must be a river through which new ideas are constantly flowing.

V—Value Results and Relationships. Some organizations are numbers driven, at the expense of people. Others are the opposite. It is possible to value both results and relationships.

E—Embody the Values. Leaders gain credibility by "walking the talk"—by modeling the actions and attitudes they want others to pursue.

—From *The Secret* by Ken Blanchard and Mark Miller
Copyright © 2004 by the Blanchard Family Partnership and T. Mark Miller
"SERVE" is copyrighted © 2000 by Chick-fil-A

THINKING IT THROUGH

When am I going to start my business? (Target date)

_____

Where will it be? (Location) _____

What should I name it?_____

How am I going to position it? (Unique Selling Proposition)

_____

How am I going to find the money?_____

_____

What kind of business structure should I establish?

_____

How many employees will I need? _____

- What will they need to do? _____

  _____

- Who should I consider? _____

  _____

What policies will apply to these employees?

_____

3

The Implementation Stage

There comes a day when the Dreaming and Planning Stages have been completed, and it's time to actually start the business. As the result of the Planning Stage, you will have named your business, determined what products and services you will offer, chosen your location, established your pro forma, and obtained your initial financing or investment capital.

Your next steps are all inextricably intertwined. Because each business has its own specific requirements, I won't go into detail. What may apply to a manufacturing operation will have little or no bearing on a retail or service business. But there are certain tasks that every new businessperson must complete.

In the preopening, or setup, phase, you'll have to prepare your facility for business. The steps involved may include the build-out of office space; remodeling of an existing facility; interior decorating; installation of phones, fixtures, computers, or manufacturing equipment; and purchasing of forms and supplies.

You will have to order raw materials or inventory, and arrange for shipping, delivery, and warehousing, as well as for payment to your vendors.

And you'll need to hire and train competent employees to get your business off to a positive start.

The primary goal is to make sure that all the right pieces of the puzzle come together at the same time, and fit perfectly—or at least close enough to create the desired picture . . . a successful, well-run new venture.

FILL IN THE MISSING PIECES

How many people do you know who are experts in every field? Someone who knows all there is to know about every subject? The answer, of course, is obvious. Yet, for some reason, when we start a business, we are expected to know everything about every aspect of that business. That's simply not possible.

I have a friend who began an advertising agency about the same time I began mine. This man is a brilliant salesman. He knows how to network, prospect, gain an audience, and close the sale. His agency, as a result, grew much more quickly than mine.

In some ways, I was envious. His accounts were major food companies, government agencies, and international conglomerates, while mine, at the time, were small local companies. His staff was outgrowing his office space. I added people only when my staff was being stretched beyond reasonable expectations.

Yet, today, his agency—the one I envied—is long gone. He freely admits to me now that while he knew how to network, prospect, "schmooze," and sell, he didn't pay attention to the numbers. He didn't understand receivables, payables, cash flow, and long-term debt, and he didn't hire a competent manager who did.

The point of this illustration is: **Fill in the missing pieces.**

If you don't know finances, learn—or hire someone who already knows.

If you don't excel in sales, find someone who does.

If customer service isn't your area of strength, look for someone who is strong in that area.

The fewer missing pieces you fill in, the bigger your problems will become. And these problems seem to grow and multiply exponentially.

But what do you do when you're just starting out in business, and you don't have the capital resources to hire all the right people for all the needed positions?

The answer is in two parts: **Learn where to look for answers,** and **learn.**

INTERNAL RESOURCES

When we employed a new person at The Gottry Communications Group, we made it very clear that we were not limiting them by locking them into a specific job that would never change. The reason for this is that people have talents and skills, interests and possibilities, that cannot be ascertained fully at the time of hiring. We wanted to enable people to grow in their careers, while at the same time making sure that all of the tasks we'd hired them to perform were being completed in a timely and efficient (read that: profitable) manner.

One of the methods we implemented to bring the best ideas forward was a variation on the old suggestion box. We called it "the Idea of the Month Club," or **"Innovations for Success."**

The problem with suggestion boxes is that they often provide little more than an opportunity to crab and complain with anonymity. There is no incentive to contribute meaningful ideas.

Our Innovations for Success Program provided two of the most time-honored incentives there are—money and recognition.

The original criterion for judging was that the idea had to save the company a minimum of $50 per month or add a minimum of $50 to monthly income. (I realize that for many companies, this is small potatoes, so you can make it $5,000 or $50,000, or whatever you want. The principle is the same. And remember, this idea was implemented back when $50 could buy lunch for two.)

What we discovered through this program is that people have ideas—good ones. And if they were a part of the team, they'd help us implement them.

There *are* drawbacks. Despite the fact that you want to hire people who are eager to grow, these same people are always eager to redefine their jobs so that they can do exactly what they want to do—and do very little of what *you want* them to do, or *need* them to do, in order to operate a profitable business.

I had an employee who was hired to be an art director. It was his job to manipulate type and pictures or graphics into a pleasing, compelling, and often colorful design—an ad, a brochure, a mailer, poster, or whatever. To fulfill his tasks, he used a Macintosh computer loaded with various graphic design and illustration programs.

In the process of using these programs, he became both proficient in the use of computers and addicted to all of the newer, better, faster peripherals and software programs that could be added to them—for a price. He convinced me that he was the right guy, in the right place, at the right time, to computerize all of our job lists, purchase orders, time cards, and other records. Because I was eager to see all of this happen, I gave him the green light to proceed.

The result? While he was busy satisfying his "computer addiction," his productivity, as well as that of those under his direction, slipped dramatically. He was no longer being paid for what I had hired him to do; I was paying him for what *he* wanted to do. The moral? **Gain the ideas you want** from your employees, but make sure you also **gain the output you need** from them.

OUTSIDE SOURCES OF HELP AND INFORMATION

When it's not possible to employ the right person for every job—or when you can't obtain the information and ideas you need for success from your current pool of employees—you need to turn to outside sources for help.

Often, as I have discovered, these resources are readily accessible and are not necessarily costly. Here are the ones I have felt are most helpful, along with what I feel they most effectively provide.

1. Books and Magazines—
Your Source of Information

You are reading *this* book because you believe it will provide you with at least one idea of enough value to compensate you for the purchase price.

This book isn't the only . . . isn't the best . . . isn't the most recent one on business that could benefit you. Read others. Many others.

Buy them; check them out of the public library; borrow them from friends. It doesn't necessarily cost money to learn. It costs time. True, time is money, but not *all* time is money. *Some* time is an investment. Time spent in sleep refreshes you for the next day. Time spent reading and learning gives you a foundation on which to build your business, your family, and your life.

If you find it difficult to set aside large or consecutive blocks of time for reading, magazines provide an excellent alternative. In fact, magazines, because of their frequency of publication, often provide a more up-to-date source of information than books. The latest in-depth news, information, and ideas are found in magazines.

My wife would tell you that I subscribe to more magazines than any living human being. I'm sure that's not true, but I do receive about sixty-five magazines each month. (Not counting numerous publications I receive on a complementary basis simply because I still do video production.) Some relate to my hobbies—boating, flying, and travel. A few provide information on computers and software. But the most useful ones cover general business topics. They tell me what's happening locally, regionally, nationally, and globally. They provide clues to the changes, developments, and innovations that could help or hinder my ongoing and future business ventures.

I rely on two specific publications, *Wired* and *Fast Company,* to tell me what's happening in the future. That may seem like an odd statement, but both of these publications have their eyes on emerging technologies, business trends, and "happening" people—and they are both fun to read.

The minimum number of nonhobby, non-news publications to which you subscribe should be **eight.** In addition to *Wired, Fast Company, Inc., Fortune, Forbes, BusinessWeek,* and your local business magazines, they should include one or two leading publications in your industry. If you have major clients in industries with which you are unfamiliar, add those related periodicals as well. (Do you see how easy it is to come up with sixty-five publications?)

2. The Internet

There's a lot of garbage on the Internet and a ton of it is passed on via e-mail. I'm still waiting for Bill Gates to send me $45 for every e-mail I forwarded to my friends. Ex-friends, I should say. "C'mon, Bill, share your wealth with all of us gullible people!" And, of course, there's that $26 billion waiting for me in some bank in Africa, thanks to the untimely demise of some guy who has no next of kin. The fact is, I've received at least thirty of those e-mails, so I actually have $780 billion waiting for me. How exciting!

Yes, scams abound. You can't believe everything you read.

But I do tend to trust the information on the Web that's furnished by reputable, long-established organizations and institutions. I love the fact that I can research anything from Hank Aaron's achievements in baseball to the history of NASA's manned space flights.

The ability to immediately retrieve information is what makes the Internet so useful.

As to e-mail . . . I have both positive and negative feelings about it. On the positive side, I can communicate with busy people and we can respond to one another on our own schedules. I also like the fact that I can document the exchanges on my hard drive, so I don't have to print more pages to be filed. Hard drive space is far less expensive than file cabinets.

On the negative side, junk e-mails are naturally at the top of the list. I have received as many as 320 spam-mails in one day. My servers have occasionally been filled, and I have to go through the time-intensive process of clearing them out. Fortunately, spam filters are continually being improved. I was amazed by how many unwanted e-mails went away when I entered "Britney Spears," "free" and "Viagra" in my filtering program.

My other issue with e-mail is that its use is turning us into lazy communicators, and the English language is suffering serious setbacks as a result. I have a good friend and client who uses a BlackBerry PDA cell phone to communicate by e-mail. Because he has a lot going on (and probably because the BlackBerry's keyboard is so small), he sometimes responds to my questions with a single letter. He used to type "Yes." He cut that back to

"Si," and now it's just "C," which also means "Cool." It took me a while to figure that one out!

3. Videos/DVDs—A Resource for Training

Videos/DVDs are great training tools because they have the ability to demonstrate in real time. That's something that books and magazines simply can't do, although the Internet comes in a close second.

I have always believed in using video to train new employees on computer programs—such as Microsoft Word, QuarkXPress, Adobe Photoshop, and Final Cut Pro. Video/DVD training offers a multitude of advantages:

- You reduce the amount of time your staff has to spend in training new people.
- They can be used during off times—even after hours— when a trainer may not be available.
- They are rewindable and repeatable. Your employees can go over steps and procedures they don't understand again and again, without feeling stupid or fearing that they are wasting the trainer's time. Often, this fear blocks learning, and the trainee misses out on an important step.
- A well-written and produced video/DVD is generally more thorough and detailed than the personal training provided by individuals in the company. That's because they are usually prepared by the company that, for example, designed the software program or the piece of equipment. I must quickly add that I've come across some wretched productions featuring so-called experts, so the buyer must be wary. A few of

the very best companies will offer a money-back guarantee in the event you are not satisfied for any reason.

The effectiveness of video or DVD as a training tool can and should be tested at the completion of the training cycle. It is at that time when your trainer can handle additional questions and evaluate performance. The trainer should have previewed the video so that he or she can explain any discrepancies between the content of the video and your standard operating procedures.

4. Software—A Source of Invaluable Assistance

I am continually amazed by what computers can do these days. We installed our first office-wide computer system in 1982, and it was little more than a collection of glorified typewriters. They could store written documents on large floppy disks and could print out our mailing list on tractor-fed paper. We were forced to junk the entire system by 1987. The storage capacity, software, and overall capabilities did not meet the growing needs of our business, and the system could not be expanded to meet those needs.

In 1987, we bought everyone a Macintosh computer, set up local area networks, and added color scanners, laser printers, design programs, accounting software, and on and on it went.

Before long, we junked all of that for more, better, faster Macs. Upgrade after upgrade was the story of my life—and it still is.

The level of assistance I can obtain from my desktop and laptop computers is truly amazing. As I'm writing this,

Microsoft Word is checking my spelling and grammar—and making changes (some of them unwanted!) in the background. I can download digital photos on the fly, and edit footage from my mini DV video camera on my laptop computer while still on location. Even the smallest companies can obtain an accounting program for well under $100 that makes it easier and faster to write checks, balance the checkbook, handle general ledger and receivables aging functions, and prepare invoices and statements.

It's worth frequent trips to the computer store or Web site just to explore new options that may enable you to save more time and money. You can also gain valuable information from one or more of the magazines published for your specific computer operating system. Don't forget to sign up for software updates via online downloads.

5. Seminars—A Source for Advice

If you read the right local publications or have made it onto the right mailing lists, you'll learn about a variety of seminars and training programs. Some of these seminars, sadly, are run by hucksters who want to separate you from three or four or five hundred dollars.

Thanks to the attention generated by the Justice Clarence Thomas hearings back in the early 1990s, I was "invited" to a number of seminars "of vital importance" on the topic of sexual harassment. One of them cost $795 for one day. The mailer told us that this was a small price to pay when one considered the possibility of multimillion-dollar lawsuits.

Well, my company had a written policy on sexual

harassment in place for several years prior to the Clarence Thomas hearings. Our policy was based on information we'd gleaned from a *free* seminar offered by a local law firm. We were invited even though we didn't retain this particular group of lawyers.

Many accounting firms, law firms, and investment counselors offer free or low-cost seminars that can be of tremendous value to you and your company. Take advantage of any that are of interest or potential value, as time permits.

6. Trade Associations— Support and Information

You can also obtain free or low-cost information from your trade association. They *want* your business to be successful. Most such associations have publications, information hotlines, and Web sites and offer interactive communications. If these resources are available, take advantage of them. It's one of the best ways to learn from the experiences of others in your industry or profession.

7. Consultants—Your Source of Experience

I've heard consultants described as "any person who used to have a job." While it's true that there are many so-called experts who clearly are not, there are knowledgeable consultants in every field. They can provide you with the one thing you can't gain entirely on your own—because there just isn't enough time in your lifetime. They can give you the benefit of their *experience*.

And they can share what they've learned through their contact with similar companies in similar situations.

This is going to cost you something, though. So it's best to make your needs and expectations very clear, and to gain some assurance that the consultant can meet those needs and expectations.

It's vital that you check out the credentials of every consultant you are considering, so that you don't shell out your hard-earned money for people who can't deliver on their promises.

8. Peers—Support and Advice

Business is so competitive these days that it may be difficult to seek support and advice from peers within your specific field. However, it's quite easy to network with others on your management level through such groups as your chamber of commerce, or through service organizations, such as the Rotary Club.

Some of you may be thinking to yourselves, *Rotary? He has to be kidding! That's nothing but a bunch of old men who sit around and smoke cigars.* I can't speak for every club everywhere, but I have belonged to a local Rotary Club, and it's everything but that. It's comprised of businessmen and -women, both young and old, who are caring, giving, involved people. I lean on and learn from each of them. I could never afford to pay for some of the invaluable advice I've picked up both from the guest speakers at our meetings and from casual conversations with other members.

In the process of expanding my circle of friendships among peers, I did discover one person in my industry who realized that he and I did not have to be cutthroat competitors, because there was enough work for both of us. He happened to be the president and one of the owners of a larger advertising agency in the same office building in which I leased my office space. He was a source of good solid advice, as well as of business leads—he gave me names of companies that he couldn't accept as clients because they competed with other clients of his firm. I, in return, tried to do the same for him.

If you're open to it, you can form some interesting and unexpected alliances that can be of tremendous help to your business.

9. Your Own Team of Advisers—Hands-On Advice

There is a group of people who have a vested interest in your company. They are among those who truly want you to succeed. They are your lawyer, your accountant, your insurance agent, your stockbroker, and your investors or stockholders. Your particular group may not include all of these, but if it encompasses any of them, this is a group to which you could, and should, turn for help.

Some companies formalize the advisory relationship with this group. Others rely on sporadic luncheons and phone calls to glean much helpful advice.

I preferred to follow the formal track. My plan called for quarterly breakfast meetings with my attorney, my CPA, my insurance agent, and my brother, who was a minority stockholder and a vice president of the corporation. (You'll notice that I didn't include a stockbroker or investment counselor in the group. More on that later.)

One significant word of caution: You are going to get differing opinions, advice, and even supporting evidence from different sources. Ultimately, it's your responsibility to sort out all the conflicting ideas to determine the most appropriate course of action.

As you develop the habit of searching for outside resources to help you fill in the missing pieces, you will discover that you will be well served not only in the Implementation Stage, but in all subsequent stages of the business life cycle, as well.

THINKING IT THROUGH

In terms of outside sources of information . . .
What books and magazines would be most helpful?

_____

What Web sites should I check out? _____

_____

What useful training videos/DVDs are available?

_____

What software should I consider? _____

_____

What upcoming seminars am I aware of?_____

_____

What trade associations should I join? _____

_____

Who would provide effective consulting services?

_____

What industry peers do I know?_____

_____

Who should be on my team of advisers? _____

_____

4

The Growth Stage

In the Growth Stage—and in just about every stage of business that follows—competition is a way of life. And the fact is, competition can either immobilize you or inspire you.

The essential thing to remember is that you—your business—will not win 100 percent of the challenges you face. You will not come out on top of your competition all of the time. In our company, we generally competed against three or four other agencies for every piece of business. We considered ourselves very fortunate if we won the account 25 percent of the time.

As a businessperson, you compete in several arenas. You compete for the best employees, against companies that are often larger and may be able to offer bigger salaries, more benefits, and greater opportunity for advancement.

As a buyer of outside services, you compete against

other companies for the best products, terms, and delivery schedules from your vendors.

You compete for clients or customers. Generally, to compete successfully, you must offer the best product in the shortest time frame at the lowest price. That's not a small order to fill. It's called value.

In a sound, growing economy, *value* is judged on the basis of *quality*. In times of recession, *value* is judged more on the basis of *price*—and often price alone. As a result of the last two downturns—the one in the early 1990s and the one that followed September 11, 2001—I believe we are conditioning ourselves to judge value on the basis of price. As Newton theorized, a body in motion tends to stay in motion until some outside force acts upon it.

Applying that principle to the notion of value, it would take a protracted period of good economic times to reverse the trend—for quality to become the primary descriptor of value once again.

In other words, in order to offer value in today's economy, you must have the lowest price on the product or service that can effectively fulfill the needs of the customer. To achieve that end, you have to control costs. You must have:

- Tightly managed overhead.
- The lowest cost or most efficient employees or outside labor force required to produce a quality product.
- The most up-to-date cost-saving technology available.

Cost control takes on less significance only if you can offer the best or most innovative product on the market—one that has no equal at any price—or if you are willing to operate on the lowest margin of profit, which may make you vulnerable to "price wars."

There are two big things that have been happening in the business world.

The first, of course, has to do with "outsourcing" and "off-shoring." I don't know about you, but the last time I called for software tech support, I could understand only about every other word the technician said. I don't know what country the call center was in, but it wasn't the United States.

Yes, the companies that follow this path are saving money. But a lot of consumers are getting fed up. So will this trend reverse? I sure hope so!

The other big thing is that the big players in any industry used to squash the little players. There was a time when the larger well-capitalized companies wanted to grow and did not want the smaller undercapitalized companies to stand in their way. The companies in the strongest financial position would try to weed out those in the weakest position. That's how they gain market share. And that's what United Airlines and American Airlines were trying to do to America West, Continental, Northwest, and the other smaller carriers. They would cut first-class fares by as much as 50 percent, and coach fares by as much as 38 percent, to squeeze the smaller airlines out of competitive markets.

But no more—especially following 9/11. The smaller carriers finally figured out that the big guys were paying all their employees way too much money. They knew they could go to market with lower fares and kill the big guys. And that's exactly what they're doing. (Of course, the landscape could all be different by the time you read this.)

The point is, if you want to grow, as a smaller company, you have to play some aspect of the game smarter than the big guys who might want to squash you.

You have to control overhead. Don't play the "glitz" game that your more flashy competitors may be playing. Stay away from the "Class A" high-rise office buildings with the marble lobbies and the brass doorknobs. You really don't need it. Although image is important in many businesses, most of your clients don't want to get the feeling that they're paying for your expensive tastes. It's possible to achieve a substantial measure of the image you want or need, without paying premium prices.

My business was situated in what was considered a "Class B" ten-story suburban office building. It was clean, well-managed, and well-maintained, the staff provided outstanding service, and the owners were willing to invest enough money in upgrades and updates to keep the building looking sharp. There were plenty of amenities—a convenience store, conference rooms, heated indoor parking, a travel agency, a lunchroom and a fun restaurant—to more than satisfy my needs.

Naturally, I would have loved to move into the premier office building just three blocks away. That building offered bigger windows, spectacular views of a nature preserve and a lake, on-site child care, a shoeshine stand, hair care, lots of gleaming chrome and marble, and one of the finest award-winning restaurants in the Twin Cities.

But if I had relocated to that building, my clients would have sworn that I was "ripping them off." And I'd have paid nearly double the rent, which would have made next to no sense.

You have to find hungry, eager employees. The old saying is, "There's no substitute for experience." But, as much as I would like to employ experienced people, that's not always possible. I had to find another alternative. That alternative was the young worker who was eager to work and prove himself or herself, or the older employee who had perhaps gone through a career change and wanted a new beginning.

Over the years, I found—and hired—people with tremendous abilities and great drive who were being overlooked by other companies because they were too young or too old or too something, and didn't fit the same criteria as the rest of the employees.

When unemployment is high, you can find prospective employees with almost unbelievable knowledge and skills. When unemployment is low, it's more challenging to find good people.

Later on, we'll discuss in detail some ideas on how to gain the most from your employees. We'll talk about ways to reward producers and bring the valuable ideas that your employees have to the surface and build on them. So, stay tuned. . . .

You have to keep your business structure simple. For decades, large corporations have had several layers of management that have cost them billions of dollars, yet those layers have produced little or nothing in terms of a meaningful, measurable return. In order to keep employees happy, top management has promoted them to positions for which they are not qualified, and in which they perform little meaningful work. This phenomenon has not changed since Laurence J. Peter first described it the *Peter Principle*. Those companies that have gained a bit more from middle management have had them "crunch numbers"—making projections, forecasts, and so on.

Shifts in the nature of our economy and in technology are impacting how businesses are run, and, in the process, what people do for an income. In a tight economy, the jobs of those who are marginally productive will be eliminated. In a good economy, there will be increasing hesitancy to add people who do not clearly add value. And the advances in technology will continue to have an impact on the kinds of jobs that are necessary and useful in future businesses.

Do everything you can to protect your company from wasted levels of bureaucracy and middle management that drain profits while returning no measurable benefits. Keep your structure simple. Find ways to push yourself and your employees to the fullest potential.

You have to expect change. Throughout the life of your business, things will change. This has always been the case and will continue to be so.

Since the founding of this nation, we have evolved from an agricultural economy, to an industrial economy, to a service economy. Now we have become an information-based economy with a strong service component. Some project that the "design economy" is next.

Perhaps one of the reasons you started—or are considering starting—your own business is that your job was the victim of the four-horned demon of recession, the computer revolution, off-shoring, and corporate restructuring or downsizing.

During the growth period of your business, you owe it to your employees, as well as to your bottom line, to resist the temptation to create jobs that aren't needed, aren't productive, or could be eliminated as the result of the slightest decline in sales or profits. I believe that if possible, you also owe it to your loyal employees to provide training so that they can take on the new functions that will be the result of advances in technology.

One of the most tragic things happening today is that there are so many hardworking, smart, talented people who do not have jobs simply because they are not trained in new processes. What America desperately needs is meaningful jobs for its unemployed and an educational system that prepares the unemployed to fill those jobs.

On the flip side, since so many technical/informational jobs are being taken over by powerful computers and overseas workers, I believe we need to become an economy that once again produces tangible manufactured products that can hold their own against foreign competitors, or that we must provide services that meet real needs more effectively. Our economy cannot be based on the exchange of dollars that results from the "sue everyone" mentality that seems to have taken over our nation.

You have to make the best use of up-to-date technology. It is entirely possible that the right technologies, properly implemented, can give your company a competitive edge over larger, better-staffed companies. In the best-case scenario, that edge can be maintained, and you will build customer loyalty as a result. In the worst case, your edge won't last, and the cost of keeping up with advances in technology will outstrip profits.

Our company "signed up" for the computer revolution well ahead of most other ad agencies. As a result, we were able to achieve some cost savings in design, typesetting, and printing that others couldn't offer. It was short-lived, though. They caught up. And, ultimately, it was the computer revolution in the area of graphic design that contributed significantly to the company's failure.

My experiences don't mean that I'll ever turn my back on technology. I recognize that I still have to keep pace in a changing world. If I allow myself to drop too far behind, I may never be able to catch up. (So, yes, Karla, I *do* need that faster computer!)

You have to offer the best or most innovative product or service—one that has no equal at any price. Or you must provide some meaningful, measurable, realistic benefit that your larger competitors can't—faster delivery or more personal service, for example.

In some way, you have to be different or better. Your point of difference doesn't necessarily have to be a major one. It can be something as simple as building an easy-to-use Web site, or establishing a memorable toll-free phone number for ordering, or offering to accept every kind of credit card, or staying open later on weekends. It can mean making small product changes that make it easier for the customer to use, transport, or service your product. It can mean a longer warranty or a strong "technical support" department.

Simply look at what your most successful competitors are doing and go one better. Then, let your customers and prospects know what you are doing.

Ultimately, you have to market your product or service effectively. It matters little that you offer the most innovative product at the lowest price or provide service that has no equal anywhere if your potential buyers don't know about you.

All of business is selling. If you can learn how to sell, or find people who can sell, you can succeed.

Part of what led my ad agency (and video division) down the dismal path of destruction was its mass quantities of ineffective salespeople. Over the years, I hired nearly a dozen gung-ho sales types who convinced me that they were the right people at the right time in the right place to make our company grow and prosper. Some of them were with us for nearly two years and never generated a single viable lead. They *appeared* to be busy. They scheduled any number of "wild goose chases" that led to nothing.

I later learned some great secrets by watching my wife, Karla, who is in sales in the cemetery and funeral profession. (Yes, I know that sounds "sick.") I am now finally able to describe the qualities I had been seeking in an effective, winning salesperson:

- A willingness—no, an *eagerness*—to make cold calls.
- A persistent personality, yet one that is not abrasive.
- A bright sense of humor and an outgoing nature.
- Outstanding organizational skills.
- Exacting follow-through.
- Personal integrity—one whose word is as "good as gold."
- A genuine interest in the needs and wishes of the customer.
- A person who is not discouraged by hearing the word "no"—time and time again.
- Someone who is not satisfied with his or her present income.

I'm not saying this because she's my wife, but Karla is the only salesperson I've ever met who possesses all of the qualities I've described. And that's why she's successful!

Your outside sales staff, your on-site sales team, or your telemarketing representatives are your keys to person-to-person or business-to-business direct sales. They are where it all begins . . . and ends. No matter what other sales and marketing tools you employ, they are the ones who actually close the sale or take the order.

For most businesses, though, there are other components that can and should be considered when developing a marketing strategy. I could probably write a book about them, but there appears to be no need. Many such books are available.

Basically, these components can be divided into eight general categories: media advertising, Internet marketing, direct marketing, incentives and premiums, contests and promotions, point-of-purchase materials, public relations, and customer relations (or public contact).

So what are they?

Media advertising includes such things as radio and television, newspaper and magazine, outdoor (billboards) and transit, and yellow pages placements.

Internet marketing involves such things as your Web site, your e-mail list, and your partnerships with other e-marketers (whereby you run banner ads on your partners' Web sites).

Direct marketing covers direct mail, catalogs, and telemarketing—those annoying phone calls that always occur when the baby is crying or dinner is scorching in the oven.

Incentives and premiums comprise a category that encompasses special sales events, discount coupons, "early bird" specials and bonus programs—"Buy this, and get this other thing free." This category can also include free promotional items that are sent to the prospective customer to gain attention or attract the customer to the store. Even matchbooks bearing your company's name are a form of incentive—or specialty—advertising.

Contests and promotions are designed to build traffic by encouraging your prospects and customers to "come in and enter to win our free trip to Wherever." They can also have an important role in encouraging your salespeople to perform beyond your normal expectations. One company we know of enhances superior performance by awarding a bronze eagle—the President's Award of Excellence—to the most deserving employee every year. Sounds kind of silly . . . but it works.

Point-of-purchase is a "salesperson" that is constantly on duty, no matter what. This tool is particularly effective in retail or wholesale businesses that rely on walk-in traffic. P-O-P, as it's called, can be an elaborate, animated floor display supplied by your manufacturer or supplier, or it can be a simple hand-painted window sign or interior banner that calls attention to the "special of the week."

Public relations encompasses all of the activities related to the dissemination of information about the company and its people, products, and services. This information can take the form of news releases, press conferences, and events that are covered by the press. It is considered by many to be "free advertising" because the company does not pay for advertising space or commercial time to get the message out to the public. In truth, effective PR is not free, because a qualified practitioner must prepare news releases and search out contacts in the media. That person may be either a paid staff member or an outside consultant or a member of a public relations firm. In any case, it costs something.

Customer relations/public contact is in your hands, as well as in the hands of every employee—from the person who answers the phone, to the person who fills the order, rings up the sale, or takes the complaint call. The most powerful, memorable, effective advertising campaign in the world can't counter the effects of rude, inconsiderate employees.

My guidelines for anyone who meets the customer are very simple:

- Be clean.
- Smell good.
- Smile.
- Ask "How may I help you?"
- Then help!

As popular as it has become for so many people to malign Wal-Mart recently, they have this stuff down cold!

MEDIA ADVERTISING: MAKING THE BEST CHOICES

The underlying purpose behind any media decision is to **reach as much of your target audience as possible, with as little waste as possible, for the lowest cost**

possible. Obviously, you do not want to pay high rates to reach a huge audience of people who are not likely to be interested in your product or service. Nor do you want to pay low rates simply because they are low, and, as a result, you reach practically nobody.

There's more than pure cost to take into account when determining how and where to advertise. You must consider the advantages and disadvantages of each individual medium and weigh them against your budget considerations.

Television/Cable

The cost of a television or cable commercial is directly related to the size of the audience that is viewing the spot at the time it airs. This can be measured in "cost per thousand" viewers or in "gross rating points" (the total combined rating—or cumulative size of the audience that will see your commercial). If based on cost-per-thousand, the rate charged for your commercial is determined by the audience size for the time slot in which it is broadcast. The size of the audience is *predicted* (not guaranteed) through the use of viewer surveys. *Nielsen* provides survey data on audience size to the television station, as well as to advertising agencies that subscribe to their services.

Using this audience research information, which can be supplied to you by either the station or your advertising agency, you can determine how many men, women, teens, and children are likely to watch each specific show in each time period, and you can buy the appropriate time slots to reach your desired target audience.

Advantages of television/cable: Television and cable offer some of advantages not available with other media:

- You have the possibility of speaking to a very broad audience, while still being able to reach selected groups. (If you need to target your audience even more directly than you can through specific network programs, cable television channels offer an excellent solution.)
- TV is the only available medium that combines color, sound, music, motion, emotion, and demonstration.

Pitfalls of television/cable: Sales reps for local television stations will tell you that they can get you on TV for less than the cost of advertising on local radio, and in many cases, this is true. But the fact remains that you will pay a rate for your spot based on audience size. For example, consider the three Phoenix stations affiliated with the major networks—ABC, CBS, and NBC. You will pay somewhere between $10,000 and $13,000 for a thirty-second spot during their top-rated prime-time programs but as little as $5 to $25 for the same spot during the lowest-rated program airing in the middle of the night. While $20 may seem like a great rate for TV, your spot will probably run at 2:15 A.M. and reach only a couple of hundred viewers. If you're selling a drug-free answer for insomniacs, that may prove to be a good buy in any case!

Companies sometimes run TV spots for the wrong reasons: ego, for example. It sounds good in a conversation to say you advertise on TV. There is something more glamorous about TV, but is it your best investment?

If you're not a trained actor, don't give in to the temptation to appear on camera (or even off camera) yourself, unless you have a lot of public-speaking experience. It's tougher being an actor and developing a smooth delivery than it appears to be. Far better to include the cost of a professional in your budget.

Finally, a professionally produced television commercial is usually going to cost significantly more than a radio spot or print ad. You can easily invest thousands of dollars in creating the spot before it ever gets on the air. The average spot shown on network TV costs $200,000 to produce. The really elaborate ones cost $4 million and up. And if you want "star power" in your commercial, expect the costs to skyrocket.

Of course, there *are* some bargains out there. TV stations will volunteer to produce your spot for you if you sign a contract to run it for an extended period of time. (You may or may not be able to run that spot on other stations.) More often than not, these spots are cheap looking and simply provide the viewing audience with more time to visit the bathroom. You can count on having to pay for the more elaborate things that make a spot effective, including animation, original music, union talent, special effects, and endorsements by personalities.

Radio

Radio can also be used effectively to reach select audiences. Differentiation by age is the easiest task to accomplish. As in the case of television, the makeup of the audience—age, sex, and so on—is determined by reference to audience surveys.

Cost is, again, determined by size of audience. In general, the highest rates for radio commercials are much lower than those for television. One reason is that it costs much less to properly equip, operate, and create programming for radio. An added bonus is that the advertiser can get a short turnaround time on radio. You can be on the air, in many cases, the same day you determine that you need to be.

Radio is more readily and passively accessed than television. By that, I mean that people listen to radio in their cars, while doing dishes or cleaning the garage, or even at their desks at work. Generally, television has to be actively engaged.

Radio offers the combined impact of sound, music, mood, and emotion. It doesn't offer color, motion, or demonstration, although an interesting demonstration effect can be conveyed through the use of sound effects. Radio can capture the imagination of the listener and create powerful images in the mind.

Newspapers

Newspapers offer a number of distinct advantages over the broadcast media. For one, the reader can refer back to your message to note the phone number, address, Web site, and other details of any special offer. In the case of TV or radio, "when it's over, it's over."

Your customers can't tear a coupon out of a TV spot, but they can clip one out of the newspaper.

You can target your demographics based on the section of the paper in which you run your ad. That's why copier and computer ads run in the business section, hotel and restaurant offers run in the travel and leisure section, and sports equipment ads run in the sports section.

Newspaper advertising is cost-effective for purposes of testing special offers and incentives.

Newspapers offer quick turnarounds on deadlines. The lead time can be as short as two or three days, compared, for example, to forty-five days or more for most magazines.

Creative and production costs for a quality ad are much lower than the costs associated with TV and radio.

Newspaper readers actively participate in the selection process. It's not a background medium like radio.

Disadvantages of newspapers: Unless your prospective customers include every segment of society, you could be paying to reach a large audience of nonprospects—an unnecessary waste of money.

The quality of reproduction in newspapers (except for preprinted color sections) is generally very poor. A newspaper is not the best place to show the beautiful sparkle of a diamond ring.

A lot of competing messages often appear on the same page. You can get lost in the clutter. (Of course, that's possible with virtually every medium.)

Newspapers have a short shelf life. They are generally disposed of in a day or two. When the next edition arrives, the previous one is forgotten.

Magazines

Magazines offer the capability to target extremely selective audiences. There are magazines for skiers, boaters, pilots, wrestling fans, Caribbean-cruise lovers, golfers, quilters, home handypersons, moviegoers, musicians, and on and on. If you can think of a topic—no matter how obscure—chances are there's a magazine (or two or three) published on that topic. There are literally thousands of magazines—both consumer and business—published today. Most ad agencies (and possibly your public library) subscribe to the Standard Rate and Data Service (SRDS), which publishes bulky phone-book-like directories that list all of the magazines and newspapers published today, along with their ad rates. SRDS also prints similar volumes for other media, including radio and television. SRDS information is also available by subscription on the Internet at www.srds.com.

The quality of reproduction in magazines is generally far superior to that of newspapers, so you *can* show the sparkle in a diamond ring.

You can make special offers involving coupons, and, if your budget permits, you can create elaborate pre-printed color inserts that can be bound into the magazine. (All of those perfume and cologne samples are an example of preprinted inserts.)

Generally, the shelf life of magazines is longer than that of newspapers—it can be a month or more. Some people save their magazines nearly forever. *National Geographic* and *Architectural Digest* are two of my personal collectibles.

Finally, the pass-along characteristics of magazines are excellent. Readership studies demonstrate that several people usually read a single copy of the typical magazine. This gives you more reach (a larger audience) for your investment.

Outdoor/Transit

Here's an excellent way to reach a large, nontargeted audience. The only audience selection you can make is by paying a premium for a specific billboard site in a certain geographic or demographic area. Several liquor producers and cigarette manufacturers have been taking a lot of flak for running billboards in our nation's inner cities, targeting minorities with messages about the "glamour" associated with smoking and drinking. Without getting into a debate on "freedom of expression," I believe the critics have a point.

Many retail and service establishments have made effective use of outdoor advertising by purchasing a board near their places of business. Perhaps it offers "where to exit" instructions or other helpful information.

In any form of outdoor or transit advertising, the sales message must be extremely short, concise, and clear, because the exposure time is very brief.

Yellow Pages Advertising

If you sell impulse items or need to generate a lot of walk-in traffic or phone inquiries, put together a great yellow pages ad. It's out there doing its job for a full year.

In fact, I would never consider operating a tire store, pizza-delivery service, or limousine company without a great yellow pages ad.

One pitfall of yellow pages advertising is the tendency that certain industries have to try to outdo each other in terms of the size of their ads and the addition of a second color or full color. The result is a lot of full-page ads screaming to attract attention at a cost that can become outlandish. Yellow pages ads are not cheap.

INTERNET MARKETING: IT'S HERE, IT'S NOW

The Internet has opened up exciting avenues for marketers.

Yes, your new business venture more than likely needs an Internet presence.

But just because you build such a Web site does not mean they will come.

Creating a successful Web site that generates income is dependent on several factors:

- There need to be reasons for people to go to your site.

  Coupons.
  Special offers/discounts/deals.
  Important news.

- The site needs to be updated frequently, or people will stop going back to it.
- It needs to be promoted heavily.

  Opt-in e-mails.
  On letterheads, delivery trucks, business cards.
  In all media advertising, direct mail, printed catalogs.

- Your Webmaster must know how to incorporate codes and search words to make certain that your site appears at or near the top of the list in various search engines (Google, Yahoo!, and many others). You need to know that if your competitors pay to be sponsors, their information will appear above yours, no matter what.

· Your site must be easy to navigate—not confusing.

· You must make it extremely easy to order. Make sure *all* ordering information (online order form, toll-free number, and actual mailing address) is easy to find. There should be a clear link on *every* page.

· Creativity helps, too. Make your site fun to look at . . . and a pleasure to read! Hire professional photographers to shoot your product photos and experienced copywriters to weave the words around those photos.

· Avoid excessive glitz (animations, big audio or video files, and so on). You may love 'em, but most customers are in a hurry and don't want to be forced to download the latest version of some special program just to view your clever content.

· And, yes, it's vital that you deliver on your promises.

Fast shipping.
Meaningful guarantees.
A clearly stated return policy.

Advantages of a Web site:
    Your Web site offers several potential benefits:

· It can be revised and updated quickly—usually the same day, if your Webmaster works as quickly as the ones I've found.

· Web sites are generally less expensive than media advertising, direct mail, printed catalogs, and so on.

· Your potential "reach" is the entire world—anyone who has a computer.

- You have the ability, if you choose, to add motion, music, and demonstration.

Disadvantages of a Web site:

- Your prospective customer actually has to log on and look for your site. If you don't promote it effectively, no one will see your site.
- If you don't appear among the first listings on the search engines, your competitors may get your business.
- A poorly designed site may work against you. If the links are not clear and ordering processes are not smooth, people will jump to someone else's site.
- Some so-called "experts" in the field of Web development may be nothing more than high-tech con artists. Choose your vendors carefully. A good Web design firm knows something about sales and marketing in addition to the basics of design.

DIRECT MARKETING: MAKING THE CONNECTION

There are still billions of dollars moving through the direct sales system—Avon, Mary Kay cosmetics, Amway, and Herbalife are some of the dominant players. And still the only way you can purchase a Kirby vacuum cleaner is through an in-home demonstration.

In more recent times, the definition of direct marketing has been expanded to include direct mail, catalog outlets, telemarketing, fax marketing, "home shopping" channels on cable TV, and e-mail blasts.

Direct Mail

Direct mail can be an extremely effective way to target your message to specific geographic or demographic markets. Your selection of mailing lists can be made by using a wide range of criteria, including zip code, specific industries or professions, likely purchasers (based on past purchasing habits), and so on.

The following examples should spark your imagination regarding possible uses of direct mail:

- A sheet metal fabricator that manufactures metal frames for PC computers direct-mailed an actual fabricated part (with the sales message printed on it) to 2,000 manufacturers of products that incorporate fabricated parts. The result was a dramatic increase in sales. The use of television spots, radio, or outdoor billboards would have been a complete waste, because, as pointed out earlier, the objective of cost-efficient marketing is to **reach as much of your target audience as possible, with as little waste as possible, for the lowest cost possible.** Mass media would reach great numbers of people at great cost but would not reach the target audience without tremendous waste.
- A company that sells and installs replacement combination windows, screens, and doors direct-mails to neighborhoods in which the houses are at least twenty years old. They realize that it would be a waste to mail to growing suburban neighborhoods in which the houses are relatively new, because those homeowners do not need replacement windows.

- A manufacturer of lawn mowers that are sold at the retail level has maintained a database of past purchasers and has done research to measure customer satisfaction. They mail coupons, valid for discounts on other products in their line, to current owners, because they realize that the satisfied owner of one product is likely to buy other lawn and garden products of the same brand.
- A dry-cleaning service that is situated on a well-traveled road has, since its opening, done a brisk business with people who live in the immediate neighborhood. They realized that their location made it easy for people living in a number of adjacent neighborhoods to use their service, so they mailed introductory discount coupons to those prospects. Business soared.
- The publisher of a unique line of children's books purchased the subscriber lists of publications aimed at both parents and children, as well as the mailing lists of companies that successfully market to the target group by direct mail. They tested a small random portion of each list to determine which ones pulled the best response, and then rolled out a massive mailing to those lists. They sold hundreds of thousands of books.
- A small video company that specializes in taping weddings checks all of the area newspapers for engagement announcements and mails a sample video with a letter of introduction to every couple. They are booked up several months in advance.

Direct mail doesn't have to be a two-dimensional envelope containing a letter, a brochure, or an order card and a reply envelope. It can be strikingly creative, even three-dimensional, for added impact.

You probably wouldn't believe some of the strange things my ad agency mailed on behalf of our various clients—4,000 slices of real toast in imprinted corrugated boxes, 1,000 regulation tennis balls attached to miniature cardboard "tennis courts" in boxes, 20,000 packages of wildflower seeds in specially printed seed packets (and this wasn't for a seed company), 5,000 balsa wood glider airplanes, 1,000 cassettes of original piano music, 75,000 printed pieces that contained a dozen little "windows" to pull open (each with a message behind it), 500 imprinted miniature basketballs, and 5,000 packages of gummi bears. Each mailing was to a select market, and each generated an outstanding response.

The key to every successful direct mail program is to select the right lists. There are companies—direct mail list brokers—that specialize in pulling together lists covering a wide range of categories. You can mail to doctors, dentists, lawyers, teachers, physicists, computer owners, fertilizer manufacturers, farmers—you name it. In most cases, brokers will sell you a portion of the list to test, before you commit to the entire list.

When developing a direct mail plan, make certain that the pro forma works. Given the cost of creating and producing the mailing and purchasing mailing labels and postage, can you sell an adequate quantity of your product at a high enough price to pay for the product and the mailing, while still returning a profit?

The most profitable direct mail strategies are clubs and continuity programs, which secure repeat or ongoing orders from customers.

Clubs—book clubs, record clubs, and video clubs—generally make a wonderful initial offer ("Choose any 5 for $1") and rely on members to order a minimum number of products over a given time period at slightly higher than street prices.

The purpose of continuity programs is to get the customer to purchase the first item in a set, with the promise that they can "cancel at any time." Continuity offers can cover anything from leather-bound classic books or DVD libraries to model cars or porcelain dolls.

Catalog Outlets

A number of successful businesses have been built through the use of catalog marketing. You're familiar with many of them: L.L. Bean, Lands' End, The Sharper Image, Brookstone, Sporty's Pilot Shop, Spiegel, and iGo, among others.

New specialized catalogs are cropping up continually. As a Macintosh computer owner, I receive several catalogs from marketers of Mac-related products, and I order from them. If you offer a specialized product line, you may want to add catalog marketing to your menu of sales tactics.

Telemarketing

The two forms of telemarketing are outbound and inbound. Outbound calls are unsolicited calls placed to selected prospects by the marketer—or what I call "dinner calls." If you are inclined to want to market using this technique, please observe the following:

1. Train your callers to sound like real people, instead of robots reading scripts. To make sure the training is working, "plant" the phone numbers of friends and associates in the call list. (To verify the skills of inbound telemarketers, have people you know call them to spot-check how they sound.)

2. Tell your callers to be courteous and to allow the person called to interrupt and end the call. This suggestion violates some time-tested practices, but your goal as a telemarketer is *not* to have prospects hate you and your company.

3. Prepare your callers to be severely abused by some of the people they call.

4. *Above all*, respect "Do Not Call" lists as well as specific requests from those your telemarketers call to be deleted from your call list.

I hate to admit that something that I personally find to be so obnoxious and invading can be an effective sales method, but it is. And I'm actually nice to those callers who respect my time and my privacy—and sound like thinking human beings.

Inbound telemarketing relies on an outbound advertising message to be successful. The marketer operates a direct mail program or runs print or broadcast ads that tell the prospect, "Operators are standing by; call toll-free, 1–800. . . ." Most consumers respond more favorably to this approach. I have ordered dozens of products through 800 numbers. (If *Rich Dad, Poor Dad* is selling it, chances are I'll be buying it.)

Fax Marketing

Fax marketing is a more "noticed" medium than most typical direct mail, and it is less offensive (at least to me) than telemarketing calls. Despite the fact that inbound faxes consume paper and toner, I don't associate any real costs with incoming faxes, although this is one criticism that has been leveled at fax marketers. Some people simply don't appreciate arriving at work in the morning and discovering that the "in bin" is stuffed with marketing messages and the paper bin is empty.

If you use faxes to market your products or services, *please* give recipients an easy way to "opt out." And don't charge them $3.95 per minute to call you to do so. (I never call anyone to opt out. . . . It's a waste of time and far cheaper—because time really is money—to just let the faxes roll in.)

"Home Shopping" Channels

My television is never tuned to a cable "home shopping" channel for more than two seconds, as I'm clicking onward to something I really want to watch. But the growth of this marketing segment is obvious testimony to its success. Because "home shopping" channels are businesses unto themselves, they won't be discussed here as a viable marketing alternative. If, however, you have a hot new product or you are eager to "close out" some product or product line at rock-bottom prices, you may want to talk to the people who operate this medium.

INCENTIVES AND PREMIUMS

There are two tracks that can be followed: incentives or premiums for your sales staff, or for your direct customer. This tactic covers everything from "Buy one, get one free," or "Buy A, and get B as a bonus," to "Buy the product, mail in the proof-of-purchase, and get money back."

My childhood was spent in the pursuit of "magic spy decoder rings" and other plastic goodies offered by cereal manufacturers. I would empty the whole box into a huge bowl just to get to the free prize inside.

The modern equivalents are the grocery store coupons found in newspaper inserts, magazines, and direct mailers. On the upper end, they can include such things as the "bundling" of software, PDAs, or printers with computers.

The use of incentives and premiums should be one of the first things considered in connection with the introduction of a new consumer product—especially if the product requires a change in consumer brand loyalty.

CONTESTS AND PROMOTIONS

Whereas incentives and premiums generally involve a sale to the customer (or, in the case of sales staff, increased sales on their part), contests and promotions are traffic-builders and are not tied directly to a purchase. The goal may be to elicit the sale, but a purchase is not mandatory. In fact, there are strict laws that prevent this direct connection in most cases.

One of the most common uses of contests is to sell magazine subscriptions. Another popular variety is the "Come on in and register to win a free trip" contest.

Promotions can be as varied as the imaginations of the businesspeople who create them. For decades, both small communities and large shopping malls have relied on visits from Santa Claus to draw children and their parents to the stores. (As a child, I could never understand why Santa came to *our* town on a fire truck. My parents claimed it was because the reindeer were resting up for the big day.) Retailers use sidewalk sales, white sales, midnight sales, and every other kind of sale to generate excitement. Macy's parades giant balloons through the streets of New York on Thanksgiving Day. And companies that sell business-to-business often hold open houses and new product expos or offer free seminars to their customers and prospects.

In addition to building traffic, contests and promotions are effective in acquiring names to add to a prospect file, direct mail list or email list.

POINT-OF-PURCHASE

Both business owners and product manufacturers have answered the question "How are we going to capture their attention, get them in the door, and keep their attention once they've walked in?" by using point-of-purchase materials.

In reality, the selling process begins when the customer walks or drives up to the store or enters the lobby of the business. First impressions have a significant impact on whether or not the customer will feel comfortable doing business with the company.

On the retail side, the storefront, the signs, and the window displays or posters are all part of point-of-purchase selling. In the manufacturing segment, the actual plant and its equipment are selling tools. In service business, the lobby plays that role. That's why green marble, mahogany reception desks, and overstuffed leather chairs are so popular with law firms, ad agencies, and investment/financial-planning companies.

In the typical retail environment, point-of-purchase is a mixture of floor displays, counter displays, shelf-talkers, suspended banners, video sales messages, end cap displays, and live product demonstrations. These tools are all variations of the famous "blue light special." They are all competing for the customer's attention, often in a cluttered environment. As a result, the creation of effective point-of-purchase materials has become both art and science, practiced by experts in copy writing and design, and in the use of color, light, sound, motion, and unique materials.

A key point to remember is that if everything stands out, nothing stands out. In a crowded theater, no one thinks it's strange if everyone laughs at the same time, but if one person laughs while everyone else is quiet, that person stands out. Every designer of point-of-purchase materials wants his or her design to be "the one person who laughs when all others are silent."

PUBLIC RELATIONS

Over the years, I've had a number of clients who have announced their intentions to cut their advertising budgets, with the words, "We're going to focus more on public relations."

For some of them, that decision was a sound one. They were often the beneficiaries of positive front-page articles in newspapers and glowing coverage in trade publications. They got the kind of press—and prominent placement—that advertising money just can't buy. They were always, it seemed, doing the right thing at the right time to capture the attention of the media.

Other companies weren't quite so fortunate. Their news releases were seldom published. Their press conferences were seldom attended. And when they were, the resulting coverage somehow turned negative and their reputations were damaged.

Public relations efforts pay off, you see, when the "news" is both positive and newsworthy. When the company is prospering, when the stock is climbing, when the new products are wonderful beyond human description, when the humanitarian needs of the public are being met, you can almost count on good press. But if you're simply operating a good, decent company; making a good, dependable product; and providing good, timely service, you're not making news.

With an advertising campaign, you have a substantial amount of control. You can determine *when* your message will appear, *where* it will appear, exactly *what* it will say, and *what size* (or, in radio and TV, *what length*) it will be. You have control over *how often* it is repeated.

With a public relations campaign, you lose that control. You don't know in advance if your message will appear, when it will appear, where it will appear, how often it will run, or even whether or not it will have a positive tone when it does appear.

What you do gain from an effective public relations

campaign is perceived credibility. People generally trust news reports, articles, and reviews more than they trust paid advertising.

CUSTOMER RELATIONS/PUBLIC CONTACT

The entire matter of customer relations can be distilled into a set of simple rules that should be nailed to the restroom walls, taped to the cash register, printed on every telephone, and sewn inside every employee's clothing:

> Smile, be clean, smell good, dress appropriately, give the customers your undivided attention, move quickly, be considerate of their time, respect their opinions, don't argue with them, and don't hang up the phone until after the customer does.

If you and all of your employees follow these guidelines exactly, your company will never be justly criticized for poor customer relations, and you will have the power of positive public contact working on your behalf.

WHY ADVERTISE?

In spite of the fact that most of the people who create ads—whether they are business owners or the advertising agencies hired by business owners—are egotists who believe that every photo they take, every word they write, and every second of film or video they shoot is both brilliantly conceived and intensely interesting, in general, people do not want to see or hear advertising—they view it as an intrusion.

That's why car radios have push buttons and why people go to the bathroom during TV commercial breaks.

That's why they flip past magazine ads that don't interest them, rather than reading and pondering every word. They're not sitting around hoping your ad will come along and make their lives complete.

So why is advertising the multibillion-dollar industry that it is? Because people **are** hoping there is a *product or service* out there that will make their lives complete. They are willing to be told how to best meet their wants and needs . . . if the telling takes a unique path. (Have you ever noticed how sometimes a commercial seems to be more interesting or entertaining than the program it's on?)

People **will** watch television or read through ads looking for someone who can supply their needs and wants. When they find those suppliers, they will discriminate among the many messages they see or hear based on such factors as:

- Price.
- Coupons.
- Perceived value/product integrity.
- Quality.
- Uniqueness of the message (approach, visual appeal, creativity).

Your objective, as an advertiser, is to demonstrate to the prospect that your product or service will meet a perceived need, and that it will meet that need better, longer, or at a lower cost. It's called product benefit. In telling the story of those benefits, you must *capture* their attention, *hold* their attention, and *convince* them.

There are three reasons why companies work with advertising agencies.

First, a good creative team knows how to capture, hold, and convince—how to create messages that cut through the clutter, to convey a sales message that will help their clients achieve a competitive edge.

Second, companies can gain the experience and advice of a solid team with a variety of skills, so they don't have to employ their own full-time people and add to their overhead. They pay only for the services they need and use.

Third, because an ad agency is *not* a part of the day-to-day operation of the company, it can bring a fresh perspective to the problem or situation. It's the same reason people go to the doctor when they're sick. They know they're sick, they know how to describe how they feel, but they are unable to prescribe the cure.

HOW DO YOU GET THE MOST FROM AN AD AGENCY?

If you choose to work with an advertising agency, public relations firm, or outside marketing counselor, there are some steps to follow to make the relationship more productive.

- Listen to them. They *want* your advertising to work. Their success is directly related to yours.
- View them as partners, not adversaries. Give them the information they need to do the job. They will respect your need for confidentiality with regard to industry-sensitive information, and you'll get better advice and

more effective advertising if you don't keep them in the dark.

- Respect the fresh point of view. An ad agency won't necessarily do things the way you would do them. But they're going to look at things from the perspective of your potential customers, and design the message to speak to them.

- Don't discourage them from bringing a wide range of ideas to you. Sometimes the idea that seems a little too far out is the one that will work. But if your agency feels they can't bring you ideas without being ridiculed, you'll see nothing more than typical, maybe even flat, ideas. Remember that one of the things you're paying them for is their creativity.

- Don't beat them up on price. A good relationship has to be a win-win situation. An agency that is giving away the work won't be around to do more of it, and you will lose everything you've invested to get them up to speed on your company and your products.

- If you have asked for an estimate on a job, you are partially responsible for making sure that estimate is not exceeded. Don't make minor or unnecessary subjective changes. On the other hand, don't cut costs on a great idea, because that will likely reduce its effectiveness.

- It's vital that we all understand and agree on the fact that advertising is—in spite of all the research, testing, good books on the subject, and so on—still an inexact science. Some of the most expensive, creative, thoroughly researched advertising campaigns in history have been total bombs. "It's not your father's Oldsmobile" is one example from a few years ago. Now it's not *anyone's* Oldsmobile. The brand is gone.

- You will make mistakes. Your agency will make mistakes. So take a look at the overall relationship, and answer these questions before you drop the agency:

  1. Given an adjustment based on the state of the economy, are you better off or worse off as a result of working with this agency?
  2. Are you keeping pace with the competition in terms of sales, product development, creativity of the message, cost-effectiveness of your advertising?
  3. Are you doing everything you can to help the agency do their job?
  4. If you are being approached by another agency, do you have solid reasons to believe they could do a better job, or are they simply slick presenters of their own services?
  5. Are you getting the attention and service you need?

HOW DO YOU DETERMINE YOUR OBJECTIVES AND BUDGET?

There is no magic formula for determining your advertising budget. It's not set by calculating 1 percent or 3 percent or 10 percent of sales, or gross profit or net profit. It's also not determined by spending part of what's left.

The only way to determine budget is to decide what you want to accomplish, and then determine what you need to do to achieve that objective.

Always bear in mind that **the purpose of advertising is to sell.** Obviously, you can't spend more money to sell your product or service than you would raise in income in the process, so the definition has to be expanded: **The purpose of advertising is to sell more of your product or service to a larger market at a greater profit.** (Does this statement sound familiar? It's from the mission statement for my former company.)

More, Larger, and Greater should all be components of the marketing objective. But there may be conditions under which selling less product to a smaller market at a higher profit may be the most prudent approach. The opposite may also be true. Perhaps selling more product at lower margins will increase the overall size of your market, and ultimately increase your profits.

Advertising should not cost—it should pay. If you are spending more money on advertising without seeing a corresponding increase in sales, there is either something wrong with your advertising or something wrong with your "product," whether it's price, quality, utility, or even the location of your business. If you are unable to discern the underlying reasons, turn to specialists outside your company for help.

THE HAZARDS OF GROWTH

There's a great deal of excitement and personal gratification that result from watching your company grow. But I have seen many companies go under as the result of too rapid growth—growth for which they were not adequately prepared.

The first problem they encounter is that cash flow lags behind, and, as a result, current obligations cannot be met, and payments on long-term debt cannot be made.

The second problem is that they cannot service their customers at a satisfactory level, and their reputation is tarnished.

The third problem is that they have increased their costs by adding staff, space, inventory, or machinery to meet the surge in demand. When the inevitable downturn occurs, they find themselves saddled with the burden of high overhead.

While it's exciting to take risks to grow—and every small businessperson has to do so—there is one risk that I believe is not worth taking. That's putting all the eggs in one basket.

That huge new account—that grand customer that accounts for 70, 80, or 90 percent of all sales—looks good at first. But when they go away, as they all do eventually, your company could easily become history.

Several years ago, we signed on a client that was a vendor for one of the largest high-tech companies in the Twin Cities . . . a corporate giant that, at its peak, employed 35,000 people. A combination of recession, questionable management decisions, and dramatic changes in the industry struck down this Goliath, and their employee force has, thus far, tumbled to less than 7,000. As a result, our client's largest customer was no longer placing orders with them.

We worked together to develop a strategy to obtain new business from a wider range of smaller customers, and, fortunately, it worked quickly enough to save our client's business.

The corollary to the "all-in-one" customer is the all-in-one vendor.

One local company was built on a foundation as the exclusive distributor for a certain product line. Those products accounted for well over 85 percent of the company's sales. When the manufacturer pulled the sales and distribution contract and awarded it to a competitor . . . well, you can guess what happened.

The obvious point I'm making is to be patient about growth. Take small, deliberate steps toward your goals. Work tirelessly to retain your current customers as well as to increase your customer base. And have a plan that does not leave you vulnerable as the result of increased overhead, inadequate cash flow, or the loss of a major client or supplier.

STRATEGIES FOR GROWTH

If you are impatient about growth—or in the financial position to grow quickly—there are a variety of strategies that can be employed.

The first, and perhaps most obvious is *merger*. In its ideal form, two or more companies with exactly the same structure, sales, and assets join together in a deal that is easily executed because of their similarity. This situation is nearly perfect, because it will not require any form of cash or stock transaction, since both (or all) parties are bringing exactly the same value to the table. When one company has more net worth or higher annual sales or profits than the other(s), the deal becomes more complicated.

In a merger, the companies are united into a new company that may or may not have a new name. From a marketing standpoint, it is advisable to retain the name of the company with the strongest image and market presence. Take advantage of the cumulative effect of all of the advertising, signage or visibility, and customer loyalty that were in place before the merger.

The second strategy for growth is *acquisition*. In this case, one individual or company is purchasing the assets, customer base, and goodwill of another company. The owner of the acquired company more than likely will have no day-to-day involvement in the acquiring company and will receive cash or stock as the result of the transaction. The worst-case scenario is that the former owner receives no cash but simply has his or her debt assumed by the new owner. In any case, the former owner is essentially "cashing out" of the business he or she built, and the new owner is counting on the continued loyalty of the company's customer base.

The company that emerges as the result of acquisition will usually retain the name of the acquiring company, although occasionally the names of the companies are blended.

For the business owner who is considering either retirement or new and different business pursuits, making the business available to companies interested in growth by acquisition can be an attractive option.

The third strategy for growth is to add *new locations*. This approach is particularly effective in growing a retail business. If you are successful and profitable in one geographic area or one shopping mall, for example, adding new locations in new areas or in additional malls can be the key to growth.

Can you imagine the Walton family being among the wealthiest people in America had Sam Walton had the vision to open only one Wal-Mart? If you have a good business idea, and it's generating a healthy profit, weigh carefully the advantages that opening additional locations may offer. But don't continue to pour unreasonable amounts of money into unprofitable locations hoping they'll turn around. That kind of wishful thinking has taken down many a company that could have survived on a single location.

The fourth strategy for growth is to *franchise* your business. This tactic presumes that the idea is, indeed, franchisable. I am aware of a number of business concepts that were offered as franchises, but the need was so localized or the franchise plan was so poorly constructed that the few operations that did open up failed miserably. The ideas died before they got off the ground.

The advantage of franchising your business concept is that you do not have to assume the financial risks associated with opening new locations. Further, if the plan is successful, you can achieve a long-term, steady cash flow. But, then, you're an entrepreneur and you already knew that!

The fifth strategy for growth is to offer *expanded products or services.* The most obvious things are often overlooked; for example, adding service to a sales operation, or sales to a service-based company. I have been told that in most automobile dealerships, the profits generated by the service department exceed those of both new and used car sales combined. If that's true in the automobile business, it could be a factor in your business as well.

In the mid-1970s, we discovered that we were paying an outside service (and charging our clients) thousands of dollars annually for the relatively simple task of shooting photo-stats (black-and-white enlargements and reductions of artwork) on a large camera. We saw this as an opportunity to generate more profit for ourselves and simply bought a stat camera and converted a small storage room into a photo darkroom. The investment was small, the return was significant, and the improved turnaround meant that we could service our clients better. That revenue stream was short-lived, however, because computer graphics made stat cameras irrelevant. But it was good while it lasted!

There are, I'm sure, opportunities to expand your services and increase your profits right in front of you, waiting to be discovered. Look for them. And don't send cash to outside services if you can keep that cash in your company.

The sixth strategy for growth is to fully *develop both horizontal and vertical markets*. If you sell computers and you discover, as the result of an isolated sale, that your computers are ideally suited to, say, medical clinics, you should work to develop that vertical market, and target your sales and marketing efforts to that field. If you sell computers that, for example, by virtue of price, are well suited to a broad spectrum of business, develop that horizontal market. Don't just sell computers. Sell them to specific markets. Discover who needs them, who wants them, and who will buy them.

I once heard the story of a woman who manufactured greeting cards that contained lots of interesting "sparkles"—sequins, gemstones, and the like. She discovered that what her customers wanted were not her cards, but all the glitter she put on them. She now does a booming business in selling bags of this stuff to handicraft types.

The seventh strategy for growth—one that may serve as the foundation for all of the others—is to *find sources of new capital.* Bring in new investors so that you can move ahead with the other elements of your plan for growth.

One of the sources of new capital can be an ESOP—an Employee Stock Ownership Plan. Through a leveraged ESOP, your employees are able to buy a part of your company using someone else's money. Through this plan, the ESOP borrows money from an outside lender to buy stock in the company. The company makes pretax contributions to the ESOP over the long term, and the ESOP uses those contributions to repay the loan.

An ESOP is, in effect, a profit-sharing plan with special nuances. Normally, the participants in a 401(K) plan can't buy and hold the employer's stock. But an ESOP can. And the result of such "vested interest" in the company is usually heightened morale and increased performance.

There is a tendency on the part of some owners to seek new money for the purpose of covering up or rectifying past management mistakes. Investors are quick to spot this ploy, and if they are willing to invest at all, it will be because they see a bright future for the company in spite of the problems, and they will often invest with the stipulation that they take control of the company.

My friend, Young Pup, had quite the desire for rapid

growth and spent all his time putting together a plan for potential investors, when he should have been out selling. As a result, he found himself in a fairly large financial jam. This diminished the interest on the part of his potential investors in getting involved, and anyone who still had an interest in investing wanted control. Young Pup decided it would be in his best interests to grow more slowly and deliberately. That is the course he charted for his company, and it worked. He got out of debt through a combination of hard work, a sound pricing strategy, and excellent customer service. It's "in-the-trenches" warfare, and he continues to win!

Growth for the sake of growth is not a sound idea. There has to be a valid business basis for growth. As the result of "diversification mania" that was running rampant in the 1980s, large corporations found themselves running unprofitable divisions in areas in which they had no prior experience. In the 1990s, these same corporations sold off the divisions that were not related to the primary focus of their businesses. Companies today are far more focused on the core of their businesses. That's proving to be a good thing.

No matter how carefully planned or diverse your strategy for growth may be, no matter how solid your marketing plan or effective your advertising, no matter how experienced your sales team, remember this one crucial statement. In order to be a successful, growing company, you must offer a meaningful product, supported by timely delivery, backed by competent service, and sold at a competitive price. If you do, you will be able to build on your reputation. If you don't, word-of-mouth will kill you.

THINKING IT THROUGH

In the "growth years" of my company:

What are some ways I can control overhead and increase

profit? _____

_____

_____

How can I simplify my structure? _____

_____

_____

What changes in my industry should I anticipate?

_____

_____

_____

What growth strategies should I consider? _____

_____

_____

_____

5

The Preservation and Evolution Stages

When things are going well—business is moving along—the tendency is to pull back, become more conservative, and protect what one already has.

Perhaps inventory can be cut a bit. Perhaps that new piece of equipment can wait. No need to hire someone to fill a specific need. It can wait. Why not save some money and cut back on advertising and marketing?

But the fact is, just "holding on" isn't going to make it any easier to earn a profit. Now is the time to take some calculated risks—to embrace new ideas about how to perform the old tasks—to explore new technologies. To put FANAFI to work!

If your only goal is to continue business as usual, you'll discover that your employees will become stagnant, uninspired, and lackluster. Your business will be like a swamp—nothing fresh will ever flow into it, and the stale water will never flow out.

Businesses that want to survive will change because needs change. To apply the FANAFI Principle, you have to ask—and answer—some tough questions. Is your business still in tune with your customer's valid needs and are you filling them? Are you willing to move ahead to the next inevitable stage in the business life cycle? Is your business ready, willing, and able to evolve?

WILLINGNESS TO EVOLVE

If you are not prepared to accept the fact that your business must change with the passage of time, you shouldn't be in business.

Imagine trying to open an upscale health club but refusing to install aero bicycles, stair climbers, rowing machines, or Nautilus or Cybex equipment. Just you, your free weights, your punching bag, and eight or ten paying customers.

Imagine operating a music store that sold only eight-track tapes and long-playing record albums—and no CDs. Lo-fi, and low sales.

Imagine opening a one-screen movie theater. And telling Dolby® sound systems and THX® to take a hike. You don't need to offer variety . . . and who cares about room-filling sound anyway? The old tinny speakers at drive-ins were good enough for you!

Imagine failing to embrace the latest manufacturing techniques. Forget robotic welders. Forget moving assembly lines. Just do it the old way.

The key to ongoing success in business is the willingness to evolve—to be alert to changes in needs, interests, and tastes, and to change with them.

There are a number of ways to maintain your awareness of change. Watch the news. Read trade journals. Pay particularly close attention to technology. And put together a group of your most aware people and call it **"The Focus Committee."**

The reason to form a focus committee is that it is impossible for you to keep on top of all of the changes in your industry, and the changes in technology that affect your industry.

How does it work? First, select two or three people (if you have that many employees) to be permanent members of the group. They will provide the continuity you'll need. Then, select one or two other people to serve as "members of the month." In advance of the meeting, give each participant two pages of general questions to ponder. Leave space under each question for your committee members to make notes or offer answers. Some typical points to consider are:

1. **Industry trends that could or will affect us.**
2. **Technical developments that could or will affect us.**
3. **Investments we need to make to maintain leadership in our field.**
4. **Departmental operation review.**
5. **Projection of departmental needs and changes.**
6. **Departmental troubleshooting/problem solving.**
7. **New business/clients/markets to pursue.**
8. **Time use and efficiency/scheduling issues.**
9. **Evaluation of the products or services we offer.**
10. **Critique of our service levels.**

11. Personal career goals and aspirations.
12. Other topics of interest or concern.

Through focus meetings, you'll develop new products and services to offer, you'll explore new markets, you'll find ways to improve cash flow, and you'll spot potential problems before they can have a negative impact on your business.

Evolution may require major changes in the way you do business—in what products and services you offer and how—and at what price—you deliver them. It may require significant investments in equipment that could be worthless in an unreasonably short time—in technology that could quickly become as extinct as the dinosaur.

I want to insert a word of caution, though. There are some business owners who try to force their businesses to become something they aren't—and shouldn't be. They try to redefine their niche—for reasons of ego or whatever—and, as a result, "fix something that ain't broke."

Here's an example: A company I've watched evolve for several years began operation in a slightly run-down (but not unsafe) warehouse building, selling furniture and mattresses at a discount. Throughout the years, they invested a fortune telling the market that they were discounters—had the best prices and sold low because of low overhead. And the market believed them. They sold great volumes and opened more "warehouse" locations.

But somewhere along the line, someone in the upper levels of management decided they could sell more if they built fancy new buildings with wonderful lighting and beautiful display spaces. Naturally, their prices had to be increased to pay for the added "high-class" overhead.

So, I was not too surprised when I visited one of their stores and discovered that their "sale" prices were higher than those of a well-reputed major department store, that their parking lot was empty, and that it was easy to get the attention of a salesperson, because I was one of only two customers in the store. Now, I don't have access to this company's private financial information, and they may be "doing just fine, thank you." But it doesn't appear that way, and it could likely be that their redefinition of themselves and their market has hurt them.

The point is this: If you are operating a business that is successfully filling a need at a profit, don't tamper with the formula for no real reason. It could backfire on you.

This said, I still can't overemphasize that the key to continued success throughout the life of every business is simply FANAFI: Find a need and fill it. If needs change, the products and services businesses must provide to fulfill them must change as well. You are likely to find that the business of your dreams, the business you operate the day you open it, and your business of tomorrow are three totally distinct things. Don't fight market-driven evolution. And don't evolve unless that evolution is market driven. Use change to your advantage. Maximize every opportunity!

THINKING IT THROUGH

Action Plan

I will start a focus committee by: _____

_____

_____

The schedule for the meetings will be: _____

_____

_____

The "permanent" members of the committee will be:

_____

_____

_____

In addition to (or instead of) the list of topics suggested

above, I will include the following: _____

_____

_____

_____

6

The Selling/
Divesting Stage

There will come a day when you've had enough. You'll be older. You'll be tired. You'll have grown weary of competition, and you'll want out.

It will be time to sell the company—to let someone else take over the reins—or to cease operations altogether. As you march toward that day, it becomes vital that you are psychologically prepared—that you are emotionally ready—for the accompanying trauma. To leave your life-long business without an alternate plan that fulfills your mental, social, and even spiritual needs could be devastating.

It is also crucial that you have made adequate advance preparations from a tax standpoint. There are a variety of tax consequences that result from the sale of a business. It would be impossible to delineate them all here, because they vary from state to state, and from congressional term to congressional term. To avoid unpleasant surprises, obtain sound tax advice from your accountant and legal counsel from your lawyer before you are faced with the realities of this stage of the business life cycle.

SEVEN WAYS TO LEAVE YOUR BUSINESS

There are seven basic ways to bring your involvement with your business to a conclusion.

The first is to simply close the doors—to sell off your assets and pocket the money, minus taxes, of course. This may become your only option if you are among those optimistic souls who believe that their lives will go on forever. As the result of this belief, you may be tempted to hold on to your business too long and sell too late. Liquidation may become your only choice.

There are some advantages to this approach, however. You don't have to worry about what's going to happen to your business after you're gone. There won't be any fighting over who gains control—or how.

But the disadvantages, in most cases, clearly outweigh the advantages. You won't realize the equity of all the sweat you've put into your business—the value of your name and reputation, for example. The cash you receive won't be based on true market value. You'll simply get a few dollars for the current market value of your buildings, fixtures, inventory, and equipment. And you'll be watching your dream dissolve right in front of your eyes.

The second way to conclude your business is through bankruptcy—an unpleasant alternative that is discussed in some greater detail in the next section of this book, titled "The Alternate Route."

The third way is to sell it outright—perhaps through a banker, lawyer, accountant, or business broker. In this case, you have very little real say in determining who takes over your good name. You won't know how honest, competent, or well intentioned they are. But, at least by following this path, you should be able to benefit financially from the goodwill you've created over the years.

The fourth option is to sell your business to your partners (if a partnership) *or to your key employees.* This plan offers a way to place your business in the hands of people you know, value, and trust. It is also a great way to repay them for years of dedicated service and should provide your faithful employees with greater job security than they would have if you simply sold your business to strangers.

In the case of a partnership, you will have wanted to preplan for this possibility. At the inception of your business, you should have drafted a "buy/sell" agreement so that the transfer of your equity could be orderly and could take place without misunderstanding or dispute.

The fifth approach is to bring your company public. This option assumes that your company is profitable and growing and is in an industry with a bright future. Depending on how the public offering is structured, you can maintain control by owning the majority of the stock or you can put your control at risk by selling the majority of the stock to investors. As long as your company remains profitable, your shareholders and board of directors will likely realize the value of supporting your role as the CEO/president, even if you no longer maintain your position as majority shareholder. At the first signs of distress, however, you could be gone. You would still have the equity in the stock you do own, of course.

According to Richard Young of Bayfields, Inc., who has helped a great number of companies go public, if you want to follow this path, you must be willing to undergo a considerable amount of open scrutiny. Every aspect of your business will be investigated, probed, and explored. You must have a substantiated record of three to five years of growth in earnings.

Young also cautions that you must also be prepared to wait to fully "cash out." Underwriters will not likely sell the founder's stock until the second to third round of financing has been completed and proven replacement management is in place.

The sixth strategy is to turn your company over to your children or other heirs. One of the most prevalent problems with this tactic is that your children, love them as you do, may be totally incompetent and unable to effectively run the business. The other problem is that your longtime employees may resent the fact that there's nothing in this plan for them, and they may not willingly or eagerly pledge their allegiance to your beloved offspring.

If you have preplanned the course your business will take—and that plan involves your children—you may want to begin early. You can slowly "gift" your business to your children at the current rate of $11,000 per year per child ($22,000 per year if your spouse is part of the plan). In aggregate, you can gift up to $1,500,000 of your estate tax free, and your heirs can realize the benefits of the appreciation of those assets without additional tax liabilities. If you wait until your "last will and testament" kicks in, your heirs will be subject to the taxes on the market value at that time, less the (current) $1,500,000 exemption.

Another sound plan is to create a revocable trust and place all of your assets in the trust. Karla and I created a trust several years ago, with the help of an attorney who specialized in trusts and other ways of dealing with assets over the long term.

Be sure to watch your newspapers and business magazines—and talk to both your accountant and your attorney. These numbers—and the rules—could change with the next congressional session.

The *seventh, and last, plan* generally involves several years of deliberate preplanning on your part. It is the *Employee Stock Ownership Plan, or ESOP.* ESOPs provide a method of turning the ownership of your company over to your employees on a bit-by-bit basis.

If you respect and appreciate your employees, an ESOP is an excellent exit vehicle. You must make sure you have a willing and capable leader to replace yourself, and your company's long-term debt level must be relatively low and under control. You can generally assume that it will take five to ten years until you receive your last check.

There are a number of combinations of these plans that can be considered. You can combine a public offering with an ESOP, or an ESOP with gifting to your children.

No matter which path you choose to follow, the divestiture of your company will necessarily involve some advance planning. You will need the help of your accountant to plan a suitable tax strategy, and you will need the assistance of both your accountant and an outside business counselor to determine the fair market value of your company, its goodwill, and its assets.

Early in the process, you will also want to get your attorney involved. Whatever plan you choose, a thick stack of complex legal documents will be part of the picture.

As you turn your business over to others, my hope for you is that you will realize the full fruits of your labor of love, and that you will have a long and healthy life in which you enjoy the rewards of all that hard work! You certainly will deserve it!

THINKING IT THROUGH

What do I believe to be the fair market value of my company right now? _____

_____

What could I do to add more value to my company before I exit? _____

_____

Am I aware of any individual, investment group, or competitor who would be interested in buying my company? _____ Who? _____

Would my employees be interested in an ESOP? _____

Why should I or shouldn't I consider an ESOP? _____

_____

_____

Based on what I know right now, my best exit strategy

will be: _____

_____

_____

My team of advisers will include: _____

_____

_____

My plan after I leave my business is:_____

_____

_____

_____

The
Alternate
Route

7

Downsizing—Voluntary and Involuntary

Back in the 1990s, I was enjoying what I considered to be the good life to the fullest! My businesses—both the advertising agency and the video production company—were racing along. Even throughout fiscal year 1991, which ended February 29, 1992, we showed steady profits. The recession was both deep and widespread at that time, and we weren't really feeling its impact at all.

In fact, sales activity and billings throughout March 1992—the first month of our new fiscal year—were very high, and the reports were good. With confidence in our ongoing success, and a firm belief that our nation's economy was entering recovery, Karla and I left the blustery winter weather of Minneapolis for the warmth and sunshine of Palm Springs, California, to enjoy some sunny weather and time out by the pool.

Upon our return from California, one of the first

things I did was take a close look at our job list—the weekly record of new and existing assignments. I noticed that this list was rather slim. But considering how busy we had been over the past couple of years, I welcomed this as an opportunity to take a "short breather." After all, I reasoned, people cannot operate at peak efficiency under tremendous deadline pressure forever.

As the days and weeks passed, however, this "short breather" had the appearance of becoming a "long dry spell." As I reviewed the weekly time reports, it was clear that we were generating less revenue than it cost to operate the business. New sales were slow to come in, and the job list continued to shrink.

To make matters worse, one of our major clients had eliminated its Minneapolis office, consolidated its operations in Chicago, and shifted the person with whom we had worked to another area of responsibility. Our new contact person believed that advertising and marketing were unnecessary expenses, and, as a result, nearly 10 percent of our business was lost to that belief.

More bad news followed. Another client—part of a huge conglomerate—was told by corporate headquarters to cut $400,000 from their already-approved budget immediately. We were $330,000 of that cut.

Another client received their own bad news. The product for which we did advertising was banned by the Food and Drug Administration. With no product, there would be no advertising.

I was nothing short of devastated. But with over two decades invested in my business—and little interest in doing anything else—I realized I had to do whatever I could to save my company.

Trouble was, I had no idea what to do next. So I stumbled through the next several months, losing an unimaginable amount of money.

Over time, I've come to realize that there were seven crucial steps I should have taken to keep my business alive. It's too late for The Gottry Communications Group, but if you find yourself going through a similar situation, I believe these seven steps will save you.

1. Acknowledge the problem.

When things have been going well for a long time, most business owners typically assume that they will continue to go well. They ignore any evidence to the contrary. They don't want to acknowledge that there's something wrong, and that something has to be done to fix it. Maybe it's ego. None of us likes to admit to failure, whether we caused it ourselves or it was thrust upon us.

In order to make the changes necessary to stay in business, you must first face the unpleasant news that you have a very real problem, and that the problem could be big enough to destroy your business. Only then can you draw from your resources and make the tough decisions that have to be made.

2. Cut quickly and deeply.

The most dreadful responsibility the owner of any business—large or small—ever faces is that of laying off good, loyal employees.

I'd read reports of companies that had been forced to lay off 5,000 or 20,000 or even 75,000 employees. In my case, I initially decided to lay off only two employees. But, judging from the way I felt, it might as well have been 75,000. It was extremely painful for me.

One was a man whose wife was pregnant—and due just three months later. He had recently sold his house and bought another one, but that deal failed to close at the last minute due to an unfortunate legal technicality. For all practical purposes, he and his expecting wife were homeless. Yet I had no choice. . . .

The other was a woman who was getting married five weeks after the date of her layoff. Both she and her fiancé were young—and just getting a start in their chosen careers.

I hurt for both of them. My heart ached. I wanted to say, "Don't worry, we'll make it work somehow. We'll find a way for you to stay with the company."

In business, one does what has to be done.

I made numerous other cuts. I slashed travel and entertainment expenses, dropped my club memberships, eliminated 25 percent of my leased office space, canceled my indoor heated garage space (a real sacrifice in Minnesota, where the temperatures can drop to minus thirty degrees in the winter), and made dozens of other adjustments in the way I spent money.

"Hope," they say, "springs eternal." And hope delayed these and many more tough decisions beyond when they should have been made. I did too little, too late.

3. Renegotiate debt.

As the result of my "economic downturn," my payments to my creditors were delayed well beyond terms. Many of them became nervous. *I* became nervous. Then I asked myself this question: *Do any of my creditors, being of sound mind (hopefully), want to force me to go under? What would they get then? Wouldn't I—and they—be much better off if we worked together to renegotiate the debt?*

The loss of certain clients meant that we would no longer need the services of certain vendors. Specifically, we wouldn't be advertising in certain publications that were targeted to industries in which we no longer worked. These were the first vendors with whom we renegotiated our outstanding debt. This was fairly simple and straightforward. I promised to send them *something*, no matter how small an amount, every week or every month until the debt was paid. They agreed to the plan. Because I established credibility with them as a result, and did what I said, all of the debts were paid off.

Other vendors—the ones with whom we needed to maintain an ongoing relationship in order to meet our clients' needs—provided a different challenge. They wanted to make sure we weren't adding new debt faster than we were paying off old invoices. Fortunately, our drastic reductions in our overhead enabled us to "get ahead of the curve."

Then we looked at long-term debt—equipment payments and the like. We calculated that by selling one asset, we could eliminate three debts and consolidate two others, cutting our overhead by another $1,400 per month. Not a lot of money to most businesses, but in the midst of our struggle for survival, it may as well have been $14 million.

Finally, we reviewed our office lease and decided that since we were within eighteen months of renewal, we could approach our landlord to negotiate a rate that reflected the declines in rental rates that had impacted the commercial real estate market at that time. They knew as well as we did that there was a huge amount of empty office space in the Twin Cities, so they cooperated.

4. Do away with the toys.

The Mercedes and the Fiat convertible were among the first things out the door. Then the airplane and hangar went up for sale, along with some of the older computers that were sitting around idle.

As we walked from office to office, we discovered that much of what we owned fell into the "toy" category. These things didn't do anything for our growth or profitability. Really, did we actually *need* an air hockey table or video games to create effective advertising?

We were careful not to sell things that still had reasonable utility, or that we would need to repurchase later. We also fought the temptation to "fire sale" some of the items just to get some fast cash.

But the toys had to go, and go they did.

5. Get good advice.

"Going it alone" in times of economic hardship and business restructuring is not a good idea. No matter where you stand, you cannot get a clear view of the entire problem—nor can you see all of the possible solutions. I relied heavily on my support system, a concept I will discuss in detail in Part Two, "Building on Your Assets."

My best advice during this period came from a man who had been through a major downsizing in the past, as well as the head of another ad agency that had experienced recent problems similar to mine. If you are ever faced with the pain of downsizing, it will surprise you to discover how many sources of helpful advice will become available to you—if you are open to them.

6. Focus on areas of proven expertise and success.

My ad agency friend's advice during this period was to focus on areas in which we had knowledge and experience. In seeking new clients to replace the dear departed, it was easier to demonstrate what we had accomplished in a particular field to others in the same field, rather than to head off in new directions in which we had limited expertise.

We decided to build on the fact that we had achieved success in the areas of book marketing, real estate, home building and home improvements, medical research, tourism and hospitality, and college marketing. We went after clients in those fields. But getting new clients quickly enough to make a difference is a daunting task. We did have some success, but because we did not have active prospects, we were able to hang on only for an additional seventeen months.

7. Draft a plan for recovery.

If you ever find yourself in our situation, it's vital to formulate a plan, write it down, and stick with it. We were faced with precious little time to think about and draft an elaborate, detailed plan for recovery. But we realized that a plan, no matter how simple, was a crucial key to our future as a company.

Our plan incorporated these few straightforward points:

- Our number one job would be *sales*. Everyone on the team would be expected to keep alert for possibilities, prospect individually, and participate in proposals and presentations. Sales would be viewed as a cooperative team effort, with "team calling" done on an as-advisable-and-needed basis. The goal in all cases would be to actively and aggressively ask for and seek the sale. Sales activity was to be carefully tracked.
- Our number two job would be to cut expenses everywhere we could. We attempted to streamline our support staff to the point where one highly competent full-time person could handle phones, media, computer input, general ledgers, invoice preparation, bill paying, mailing list management, proofreading, assistance in traffic, filing, and general sales support services. Wow! That's some kind of person!
- We would set up, once and for all, any systems that could or should be handled on computer. When operational, these systems would not be tinkered with, nor would any programs be changed, except by virtue of upgrades that did not require major adjustments to operating procedures. We could not afford to invest time to rethink systems and procedures at the expense of sales and billings for creative time.
- We would handle immediate overload situations by developing a strong network of freelancers for both video and advertising/graphic design.
- We would invoice as quickly as possible upon comple-

tion of jobs, so that cash would be available to meet urgent needs.

- We decided to suspend all equipment purchases until such time as profits allowed them and real needs demanded them.
- We continued to evaluate our sales, cash, and receivables position on a weekly basis, and made necessary cuts and adjustments as rapidly as possible.
- Over the long term, we would employ new people with an upgraded level of creative competence—we would try to find people who were better at this business than we were.
- We would be quicker to terminate those employees who did not measure up to our standards or the standards of our clients. There would be no "free rides" for anyone.
- *Those who said "It can't be done" would have to get out of the way of those who were doing it—or were willing to do it!*
- We would explore every way possible to keep more of our billed dollars in-house, while sending fewer dollars to outside vendors, by hiring people with multiple skills—to prepare realistic layouts, do illustrations, shoot photographs, and perform other vital functions.
- We would work diligently to reduce current debt over the long term and would do everything possible to avoid taking on new debt.
- We would not add new programs, benefits, equipment, or people until we could readily afford to do so.
- We would still do what we could to provide for the futures of key employees through benefits, including a retirement program that would be available to all

employees. We knew it would be costly, but it would help build loyalty.

· We would sell hard, work smart, and practice patience, understanding, and tolerance. We would always keep our senses of humor alive.

· We would balance the demands of work with the needs of our families and our personal needs for various escapes from the pressures of our jobs.

Lofty goals, right? This sounded as though it should have worked, right? The fact is, though, that my company—the ad agency that I had built for more than twenty years—was about to go under. A major part of the problem was that I didn't move quickly enough during any stage of the recovery plan. I still had a boat, an airplane, and a hangar during an extended period when I was losing tens of thousands of dollars every month. I was unrealistic in my assessment of where we were and where we were going. **If you ever go through this, be totally honest with yourself. Understand the numbers and what they are telling you.**

As I've tried to illustrate throughout this book, often it's not the big blunders that put companies under; it's the little day-to-day slipups and oversights that lead to disaster.

Downsizing can be the first crucial step toward correcting the slipups. But without acknowledging the problem, reacting quickly, making deep cuts, getting good advice, and drafting a sound new plan, the slipups will end the life of a beloved company. You will come face-to-face with the most dreaded of all of the stages in the business life cycle.

THINKING IT THROUGH

Have I noticed any trends that could indicate a problem? If

so, what are they? _____

_____

_____

What cuts could I make quickly? _____

_____

_____

What would be the financial impact of those cuts?

_____

_____

What debts could I renegotiate? _____

_____

_____

To whom could I turn for advice? _____

_____

_____

In what areas (products/services) are we the most suc-

cessful?_____

_____

_____

How can I build on that success? _____

_____

_____

Am I being completely honest with myself about what

the numbers are telling me? _____   What *are* they

telling me? _____

_____

_____

8

Bankruptcy

The curtain could have—maybe should have—been lowered on my fledgling business in the fall of 1971. At the time, I had a small two-room office in a dilapidated old building in south Minneapolis. My rent was a whopping $120 per month. I had one employee in addition to myself. And I had two clients.

One of them was World Wide Pictures, the motion picture division of Billy Graham's organization. These people were nothing but wonderful—they liked my work, paid their bills on time, and were positive, uplifting people with tremendous integrity.

The other was a company based in Detroit. These people were an absolute nightmare. They were demanding, paid slowly, and beat me up on price. Eventually, they went away, but not before they stuck me for $22,000.

That, friends, was a real problem for a dinky little two-person operation that was started with $125 in the bank and had no investors behind it. I took a quick look at my payables, and discovered that I owed two printers a total of nearly $14,000. I didn't have that kind of money, and I didn't know where I could ever get it.

I had two choices. I could let my dream slip away from me and declare bankruptcy. Or I could call the printers, tell them what had happened, and arrange a payment plan. I chose the latter.

To my surprise, the owners of both companies said that they would be happy to work with me, and that I should simply send them whatever I could afford every month. One of them refused to do any additional work for me. The other said he'd gladly continue to work with me, so long as I did not get deeper in debt.

Every month, for nearly three years, I sent a payment to each of them. I delivered my final payment—in person—to the one who had agreed to continue to work with me. He commemorated the occasion by taking me to dinner at a wonderful steak house, followed by an NHL hockey game, where we enjoyed a great night of hockey from superb seats right behind the goal.

I continued to contract the services of Custom Craftsman Printing over the next couple of decades, simply because its owner, LeRoy Undis, was patient and understanding, and he had earned my loyalty and respect.

Had I declared bankruptcy in 1971, I would not have had the satisfaction of personally delivering that hardearned final payment on my debt. And I would not have had a valued friend in LeRoy for all these years.

In 1992–93, I woke up from a comfortable "sleep" as the result of the same nightmare. When I sorted everything out—and put the bills I owed in one pile and my receivables in another—the news simply was not good.

Most of my advisers and interested onlookers said, "C'mon, Steve. Bite the bullet and shut this thing down. Your debt outruns your receivables by a ratio of three to one. Save yourself the headaches, worries, and sleepless nights—and go bankrupt. You can always start over."

They were right. I *could* start over. I could wipe the slate clean. I could "stick" it to the suppliers I'd had relationships with for several years. For what? To save myself the "sleepless nights"? Thank you, but I knew I'd sleep better knowing I did everything possible to pay off my debts.

One of my largest outstanding debts was with my landlord. I was three months behind in my rent. And he was, justifiably, getting impatient. During the downsizing of my office, I began to sell off my excess furniture and equipment. I would immediately write a check for the amount of each sale, and I'd hand-carry the check to the building owner's management office. The landlord couldn't believe it. He said, "Most people would just vacate the building and leave us hanging." Well, readers, I honestly like to think that I'm not "most people."

The point I'm trying to make should be clear. If you and I, as businesspeople, have even the slightest hope of living up to our commitments—of meeting our obligations— we should do everything within our power to fulfill them. Bankruptcy shouldn't be viewed as an easy "out."

I recognize that there are circumstances under which bankruptcy is clearly unavoidable. There comes a time in the life of some businesses when there simply is no alternative. The debt load is staggering, and the prospects for new sales, followed by sufficient profits, are bleak. There are few assets to liquidate for cash.

It's important, in such cases, to know when to call it

quits. Lock the door before incurring even more debt and hurting even more creditors. And minimize your personal exposure as much as possible.

If you have kept a close watch on your finances—sales, expenses, receivables—you will know when a monster hurricane is brewing, and where its track will take it. If at all possible, try to anticipate your bankruptcy and plan for it at least three months in advance. This will give you an opportunity to retain and work with a competent attorney—in conjunction with your accountant—to chart the proper course of action.

Your accountant will be able to present a clear picture of your current situation—including a detail of your assets and liabilities—as well as an overview of the tax implications of any moves you are contemplating.

Your attorney will use that information to make a recommendation with regard to whether you should file Chapter 11 or Chapter 7 bankruptcy. Chapter 11 provides for a court-ordered plan for reorganization and payment of your creditors, while offering you enough protection to operate your business with rebuilding it as your objective. Chapter 7 is the statement, "I am closing the doors, and the spoils will be divided among all those who have a legitimate claim against the business, based on how those claims are secured."

Generally, the government has first claim for any back taxes owed, followed by payroll due to employees, then by secured creditors, then by unsecured creditors, who may receive ten cents on the dollar—or less.

About the only hope you have is that your attorney may be able to devise a plan, in advance, under which you are one of the employees to whom payroll may be due, or under which you may be a secured creditor. Again, I want to emphasize that the purpose of such a plan should not be to cheat your creditors out of any money that is due to them.

If you have gone through—or will soon submit yourself to—bankruptcy, you must immediately move ahead to the next phase of your business career. **Do not dwell on it.** Do not think of yourself as a failure. You will have another opportunity for success. Colonel Harlan Sanders was well into his sixties when he came up with the notion of Kentucky Fried Chicken. It's never too late to make another start in business!

THINKING IT THROUGH

Is my accountant fully aware of my situation? _____

_____

_____

_____

Is bankruptcy my best option given my situation? _____

_____

_____

_____

Could I pay off my debts without declaring bankruptcy?

_____

_____

_____

What lawyer should I retain?   _____

_____

_____

9

The Second Start-Up

Despite my bleak situation, I decided not to file for bankruptcy. I closed my large office in July of 1993 and moved into a small two-office suite next to a dental office. One loyal employee and friend came with me. He was the graphic designer and I was the copywriter.

We hung on—barely—until December of 1994. The loss of another large client ended it. I helped my friend find a job with a former client, and I accepted a position as the marketing director for one of my longtime clients.

By the time I finally closed the doors on The Gottry Communications Group, Inc., I had managed to lose $880,000 in assets, cash, savings, and receivables. (And, when they discovered I was in trouble, two clients "stuck me" for a total of $31,000.) At the time I first downsized, I had a negative cash position of $168,000. That's what I owed to my suppliers. When I shut down for good in December 1994, I owed less than $90,000.

I was very fortunate to have worked with vendors who agreed to forgo interest charges and let me pay what I could every month. Some of them hired me to do creative work on their behalf as a way of paying off my debt.

My new job with the former client—the first time I had been an employee of someone else since 1970—went well. The owners of the business are two great guys who came to my rescue and provided support and encouragement during very dark days. I stayed with them only six months but accomplished a lot of good things on their behalf during that brief time.

But I'm not cut out to work for someone else. When I was in business, I asked myself the following question hundreds—possibly even thousands—of times: *What happens if my business goes under? If it fails? What will I do then? Will I go to work for someone else?*

The answer always was, *I will regroup, begin again, and start a new business. I will not work for someone else—at least not for very long. I am an entrepreneur. I want to do my own thing, captain my own company, forge my own future, chart my own destiny.*

Any businessperson who is fueled by desire and fired by determination will never settle for anything less. There will be no doubts or hesitations—a new business will be born.

True to my own gut feelings and desires, in July 1995, I formed a new corporation—Priority Multimedia Group, Inc.—with a new mission, a new approach, a new marketing strategy, and a new way of doing business.

My company is involved in "content creation." We write and produce videos and develop marketing materials for a variety of clients (just as Gottry Communications Group did), but we also develop Web sites, ghost-write books, package those books for publishers, and write videos/DVDs for children. All of this explains why the copyright for this book is held by Priority Multimedia Group. My company paid me to write it! I love it!

Karla and I moved our family to Arizona in 1996 to build our new venture. I mailed the last checks to my vendors in September 2001. I thought I'd hear cheering from 1,800 miles away, but I didn't! I did receive calls of congratulations from them. One said, "I knew you'd do it!" Another offered to take me to lunch on a return visit to Minnesota.

So how do I get things done these days? First, I have invested in up-to-date computers, software, digital cameras, and video equipment. My small office-for-two holds four computers and two printers, and I can keep all of them busy at the same time doing various tasks.

I keep eight or nine people fairly busy, too, but I don't have any employees. I have independent contractors who perform a variety of functions for me—on their own time, in their own facilities, using their own equipment. They edit video, serve as video crews, do graphic design, proofread my writing, and do research. I don't have to pay benefits, I don't have to guarantee a certain amount of work, and I don't have to fire a nonperformer. I simply stop using that person.

(Before you rush out and find contract workers, please check the IRS guidelines and rulings on this matter. If you ask someone to come to your place of business, use your equipment, and work from eight to five, the IRS will classify that person as an employee and you could end up owing buckets of taxes and penalties. My independent contractors truly are independent.)

Hopefully, I have learned enough from my Gottry Communications Group experiences—triumphs, mistakes, omissions, and miscalculations—to do a better job of it the second time around.

WHAT IS A SECOND START-UP?

The most common definition of "second start-up" would be that of a new business that is begun after an entrepreneur's first business has gone away completely—after it has failed. He or she then dreams a new dream, drafts a new plan, and starts over. That's what I've just described.

But from another perspective, a second start-up can take place when an owner sells a successful business and reinvests the proceeds to begin another one. There's no business failure involved.

A third view is that a second start-up can be the opening of a new location, the formation of a subsidiary division, or the establishment of a business unrelated to, yet operated concurrently with, the first. I had some experience in this area as the result of the start-up of the video division, some seventeen years after I first opened the advertising agency.

But the perspective from which I can share the most relevant insights is that of a businessperson who watched his successful business crumble and did everything possible to rebuild it. That's probably the toughest form of a second start-up.

MORE OF MY STORY

I already shared how we lost most of our clients over a very brief time.

But what I haven't told you is that most of my employees—those who were still with me following that excruciatingly painful Friday when I had to lay some of them off—decided to bail out of what they saw as a rapidly sinking ship. Many of them had been with me for three or five or eight years or more, but they concluded that although the captain may choose to go down with the ship, they had no desire to join him. Two of them left to form their own competing agency in the basement of one of the partner's homes. Two left for other jobs. One left for unemployment.

And one stuck with me. Good ol' Eric Walljasper. I'm the president of his fan club. Even after I had laid him off, he was willing to come back to try to make the agency succeed. The president of *my* fan club stuck with me, too. She had to. She is my wife. As she says so frequently, "It's in my job description."

So, what do you do if you are ever faced with the prospect of a second start-up? What have I learned? What am I doing today that I didn't do before? What will you need to do?

1. You'll need to do things differently. "More, better, differently!" is the mantra of the successful businessperson. Become a stickler for the details that spell a difference in the real world of business, and, at the same time, turn your back on the meaningless drivel that doesn't produce much of anything for

the bottom line. (Example: I now watch my receivables more closely—the detail—and I *don't* have an airplane—the drivel!)

2. You'll need to learn from your mistakes. Work smart, service your clients better, compete more effectively on price, watch financial trends, hire good people, cut expenses quickly and deeply if you have to. Don't lag behind the urgent demands.

3. You'll need to take different risks. If what you were doing didn't work, you need to do something else. The same flawed actions will usually produce the same flawed results.

4. You'll need to invest your profits wisely. Resist temptation! No expensive toys, flashy cars, or five-star hotels. If it doesn't add to your bottom line, you don't really need it.

5. You'll need to fill in the pieces that were missing last time. Start by listening to the advice of people you trust.

6. Don't delay important decisions. Make key decisions more quickly—especially those related to hiring and firing. If you want a lean, mean, profitable business, don't put up with "deadwood."

7. You'll need to build a *team*. Team building is one of the greatest skills a business owner or manager can possess. There can be no room for jealousy, bickering, or hotshot loners. If you're successful, it will be because you and your team all had a hand in it.

I believe that common sense in business *does* work—in both good and bad economic times. Follow this plan in your next venture, and you'll be proof of the statement!

THINKING IT THROUGH

What new business would I like to start? _____

_____

_____

What existing business would I like to buy? _____

_____

_____

What new locations should I consider? _____

_____

_____

What new subsidiary could I add? _____

_____

_____

What new risks should I take? _____

_____

_____

What are my "missing pieces?"_____

_____

_____

How can I build stronger teams?_____

_____

_____

PART TWO

Building on Your Assets

10

Yourself

You, as an entrepreneur, are the greatest single asset your company has. It was your drive and your dream that created your company, probably out of little or nothing—if your company is like so many other self-made ventures.

What are the attributes that you bring to your company, and how can you make the most of them—to build a better future for you and your employees?

YOUR ENTHUSIASM

No one can be a rah-rah cheerleader all the time. But enthusiasm, or the lack of it, is catching. As the owner of your business, your attitude sets the tone for the entire company.

When you arrive in the morning, smile. When you talk to employees, smile and look them in the eyes. If you offer praise for a job well done (a habit you should get into), smile, look them in the eyes, and shake their hands. Note the recurring theme: "Smile."

Enthusiasm is like a dose of multivitamins. It's needed daily. Without that dose, your company will become sluggish and lackluster.

YOUR ATTITUDES

I believe that people can have only one of two attitudes— positive or negative. And we have the opportunity, independent of our circumstances, to deliberately choose under which of those attitudes we live the days of our lives.

It's easy to make that choice—to say "I will not dwell on the negative. I will believe what I've heard from Norman Vincent Peale, and Dr. Robert Schuller, and all those other advocates of positive thinking, and I will live a life of positive attitudes."

It's far more difficult to *live* that choice—to practice what they preach and actually approach each day with a positive attitude.

One of the first things you see every morning plants negative thoughts in your mind. No, not your face in the mirror! It's your morning newspaper. The headlines blast you with news of war, crime, earthquakes—like the devastation of the tsunami in the Indian Ocean—hurricanes, drugs, the homeless, unemployment, business failures, strikes, layoffs, environmental pollution, the deficit, and another loss by your favorite team. You turn to the business section only to discover that every stock you own went down at least a point.

And now you're expected to go to work with a smile on your face?

Well, you do your best. Then, your employee who has a key new business proposal due today calls in sick. (Probably from reading the morning newspaper.) There are no checks in the mail—only bills. And the client you thought you had "in the bag" calls to tell you that your competitor made a better offer. You have a five-minute lunch of some yucky fruit yogurt at your desk because things are piling up on you. There's a brief power failure in the afternoon, and everything that wasn't just backed up on your computers is lost.

At the end of your day, you realize you can't face the long lines waiting for the aero bicycle at your health club, so you decide to face the long lines of traffic on the freeway instead. You arrive home to the news that your ninth grader got a D in Spanish and an F in physical education. You didn't realize it was even possible to flunk P.E.

How do you maintain a positive attitude through all that?

You do it by viewing the great tapestry of your life from a distance, rather than focusing on the small threads that are out of place, or the slight frays around the edges, or that little rip that really doesn't have an impact on the beauty of the work.

You can gain that perspective by following a few simple strategies.

The first is to visualize yourself, your business, and the day just ahead of you as successes. Start each day recalling three positive things that happened the previous day. Note in your mind or on paper three positive goals you know you can meet today. It doesn't matter how big they are, how small they are, or whether or not you accomplish anything else in your day. As long as you meet your three goals, you can go to sleep believing you had a positive day.

Visualize yourself as a success by creating a notebook in which you list the good things about your life. It's called a "Personal Book of Affirmation," and it's a wonderful idea I picked up from Peter J. Daniels's book, *How to Be Happy Though Rich.*

To affirm myself, in my Personal Book, I've written brief observations and memories under a variety of topical headings, including accomplishments way back in high school, in college, and in business; the good feelings about marriage, children, and extended family; personal achievements such as earning my pilot's license and instrument rating; being named to various Who's Who publications; and winning awards such as "Bloomington Small Company of the Year," "Small Business Advocate of the Year," and "New Rotarian of the Year." I've even included recollections about some of the notable people I've met, including Vice President Hubert Humphrey, all four of The Beatles, Bob Dylan, Dr. Billy Graham, and one of the most remarkable people I've ever been privileged to meet—Corrie ten Boom, a Dutch watchmaker who, along with her family, was responsible for saving hundreds of Jews from Hitler's insanity during World War II.

When I begin to think that nothing is going my way, I read a few of my handwritten pages of affirmation. It's amazing what a difference that makes!

The second way to build and maintain positive attitudes is to read positive and uplifting books—books by Zig Ziglar, Dr. Robert Schuller, and Norman Vincent Peale.

Some people think of these books as tools for sanguine personality types written by other sanguine types. "Happy Joe gives Happy Bob a little boost." But it's the melancholy personality type that needs them more than anyone.

The third tip is really simple. If you've had a bad day, don't watch the news on television before you go to bed. End your day on positive thoughts, sounds, and images. Every night before we go to bed, we turn on our Sharper Image Sound Soother and set it to play Caribbean surf sounds. Our Caribbean cruises and vacations have been some of our more enjoyable ones, so these sounds give us pleasant thoughts as we drift off to sleep.

The fourth tip is a crucial one. Don't hold hatred in your heart. Hate will clog your arteries and elevate your blood pressure worse than the cholesterol contained in a trainload of cheeseburgers. Medically, I have no authority to make this statement, but I know people whom hatred has destroyed.

There should be no room in your life for racism or anti-Semitism. There should be no time in your day for gay bashing, Arab bashing, and Japanese bashing. (Or, if you're a member of a minority group, "white bashing.") All of us—African Americans, Caucasians, Asians, Hispanics, Native Americans, Arabs, and Jews, straight or gay—are simply people who are trying to find opportunity for ourselves and create a future for our families.

I can't believe that it's even necessary to write about this topic in the twenty-first century. I thought that—as thinking and feeling human beings—we would realize how stupid and out-of-place any form of bigotry really is. But we seem to be regressing in this area. The television news programs carry reports of senseless ethnically related violence nearly every day.

My concern is that it seems to have become *so easy* to fuel the fires of hatred and keep them burning from generation to generation. Because your employees (and your children) may take their lead from you, even the most "harmless" racist joke or casual comment goes a long way toward keeping these attitudes alive in America.

Too many of my fellow white Americans have forgotten that they are here because their ancestors were despised, or persecuted, or downtrodden, or poor. They've "made it," they believe they *deserve* it, but they appear to have little time for the needs or concerns of others.

I believe that it is the responsibility of businesspeople to create opportunity and to help erase hatred and racism.

Think about it. And do something about it. Hire the qualified minority applicant. Make your work environment a healthy and positive place for women, for persons of color, for religious minorities, and for people who don't share your view of human sexuality. Treat all people fairly in terms of raises, benefits, and promotions. I believe that I have always been tolerant and have followed this practice to the best of my ability. In fact, there are only four traits I won't tolerate in employees: laziness, sloppiness, stupidity, and dishonesty.

The fifth tip to help you build positive attitudes is to be a forgiving person. Don't hold grudges. They'll eat away at you and immobilize you. Several times over the years, I sustained significant financial losses from clients who didn't pay their bills. They stuck me for tens of thousands of dollars. Later, I came in contact with these people again. And because I had determined to be a forgiving person, I found that I could look them in the eye, offer a warm handshake, smile, and mean it. They, on the other hand, had some difficulty with the encounter. It could have been a little problem with guilt.

Forgiveness is not easy. It means that you have to recognize and accept that people aren't perfect, that they go back on their word, and that they may not even care about you and your needs. But as the result of being able to forgive, you will be able to focus on the concerns of your business without clogging your mind with useless thoughts and emotions.

The final tip may not apply to every reader, but if it does apply to you, I urge you to follow it. If you are a person of faith, draw upon that strength. It can help you become a forgiving person. It can give you the impetus to care more deeply about others.

If you are a religious person, particularly of the Jewish or Christian faiths, you can't do better than to meditate on the Psalms of King David and his contemporaries. If you read five chapters each day, you'll be able to get through them all in a month. Add to that one chapter of the Proverbs of Solomon each day, and you'll have what Billy Graham once described as "the keys to understanding God and getting along with your fellow human beings."

During those times when I go to bed at night bearing the burdens of my business day, I find it helpful to recall a positive verse from Scripture and turn it over and over in my mind, to discover its meaning and application in my life. It's truly remarkable how much better I sleep.

There will be days when you are so discouraged that these strategies won't help at all. But remember, days are only days; they're not lifetimes. Tomorrow is likely to dawn brighter.

YOUR KNOWLEDGE

"A little learning is a dangerous thing," according to Alexander Pope, who wrote those words way back in 1711. The fact is, the graduates of today's high schools and colleges have no more than "a little learning." Education is an ongoing process that must continue long beyond the days of formal schooling if we are to be competitors in the world of business, as well as in the global economy.

One of my objectives in my life is to learn something new every day. It doesn't matter whether my education takes place through reading newspapers, books, or magazines; through watching videos or television; through listening to CDs or the radio; or as the result of checking out a Web site or engaging in stimulating conversation. I want to come to the end of each day with the realization that I have added to my mental library of useful knowledge. I need to know that I have increased my understanding of how my life, my relationships, my business, and the world at large really work.

One of the wonders of the "information age" is that we all have access to a tremendous volume of data. The task we all face is to sort through all of this knowledge to find those nuggets that will prove to be of value to us on both a personal and a business level.

I've discovered that it's helpful to carry a small tape recorder or a notebook with me wherever I go. (The tape recorder is particularly useful in the car, because the act of writing notes while driving could lead to sudden and unexpected air-bag deployment.) This book had its beginnings on a mini-cassette recorder that I've carried with me for years.

Another path I've followed is to clip relevant articles from newspapers or magazines, photocopy them, and place them in a ring binder labeled "Food for Thought."

It doesn't really matter how you acquire, sort, or store valuable information. Learning is always an adventure. Become an "Indiana Jones" on the quest for knowledge. Live the adventure every day!

YOUR SKILLS

The world is in a state of constant change. The skills of yesterday won't meet the demands of tomorrow. That's why it's so vital to improve them—to keep pace with expanding technologies.

Just as the arc welder of yesterday must learn how to operate the computer-programmed robotic welders of today, the businessperson of today must learn how to take advantage of the advances that will lead all of us into the future.

If you want to increase your computer skills, enroll in a class. If you're a little short on management skills, sign up for a good course. If you need to sharpen your writing skills, turn to a community college or nearby university. If you want to become a more effective speaker, join a nearby Toastmasters International Club.

You can take classes purely for fun, too. Take a photography or videography class. Learn how to paint, sculpt, or throw pots. (Why on earth do they call it that!) Pay a visit to Arthur Murray and learn to dance.

Go to culinary school. The point is, *all* learning is fun!

The development of skills is simply the application of new knowledge. First learn, then understand, then *do*. A growing, prospering business could be the result . . . even if you're just taking classes for fun.

YOUR COURAGE

Although you may not think about it in this light, you had to have courage to start your own business. Many business owners leave the security of a steady paycheck to start their own companies. I did. Not only did I quit my job, but, as you know, I turned down another offer with a starting salary that I knew was substantially more than what I would make in my own business. In fact, it took me almost three years in business to equal that starting salary on a regular basis.

Courage involves making decisions, even though you could be wrong. My belief is that anyone who is confident that 51 percent of the decisions he or she makes will invariably be the right ones could easily become a multibillionaire and could probably rule the world without much resistance from the masses.

Every day of your business life, draw from the fountain of courage you drank from when you first began your company, and you will be refreshed and invigorated!

YOUR PAST

Many people I know have had difficulty dealing with their pasts. They have blamed their pasts for the problems they are experiencing in the present.

If not for your past, you wouldn't be where you are today. *Something* about your past provided you with the drive, the desire, the education, and the experiences necessary to be in business—or to dream of being in business—for yourself.

Naturally, the easiest path to success and prosperity would be to attain substantial wealth through inheritance. Fortunately, that seldom happens in real life. If we all inherited great fortunes, how could we ever know the satisfaction that comes from charting our own destinies, creating our own successes, conquering our own obstacles, and climbing the mountains of opportunity that life places before us?

I'm glad I never had everything handed to me. I'm grateful that my parents—who couldn't give me everything my greedy little heart desired—taught me the virtues of honesty, integrity, faith, independence, endurance, and personal drive. What a wonderful legacy for a parent to give to a child!

My past has not hurt me. It has helped me! If you give it some careful thought, you will be able to say the same thing about your past. You will, in spite of whatever hurts and deprivations you've experienced, be able to point to the things that built within you the drive, the determination, and the spirit to "make it."

YOUR GOALS

As you and I begin our businesses and operate them over the years, we have very little difficulty setting business goals. We (hopefully) draft our one-year, two-year, and five-year plans. We set sales targets and growth objectives. We create strategies for business success.

Yet, as natural as goal-setting is in business, many of us think of it as out-of-place in our personal lives—if we think of it at all.

Of course, we all have *general* personal goals. Build a new house, remodel the kitchen, buy a new car, save for the kid's college education, pay off old debts.

But I believe we all need *specific* short-term and long-term personal goals—ones on which our progress can be specifically charted as we work toward them. So we don't become discouraged, our personal goals need to be realistic and attainable.

On any given day, I need to have three dreams . . . three personal goals . . . three planned events that I can anticipate with eagerness. They don't have to be *big* things. They can be as simple as a "date night" with my wife, an invitation to a friend's house for dinner, or a planned drive in the country next weekend. They could include an upcoming vacation trip or tickets to a concert three months from now. The point is, I always try to have *three* things to look forward to. One or two things simply aren't adequate.

The people I know who have given up on their dreams—who don't have anything special to look forward to—have, in essence, given up on living.

Apply your business principles to your personal life. Have one-year, three-year, and five-year plans for your nonbusiness self, as well as for your family.

Write them down. Find—or develop—some system that encourages you to prioritize your goals and allows you to track your progress easily and continuously. I've used two great systems. The first is the *Franklin Day*

Planner by FranklinCovey. It is available in a number of specialized retail stores, on the Internet, or by direct mail. This system is, in essence, a memory jogger that enables you to note action items in the distant future and track back to the notes you took initially, so that details simply don't fall through the cracks.

Your Franklin Day Planner allows you to carry typical "diary" items such as calendars and phone directories, but you can also include client files, exercise logs, credit cards, business card files, expense records, and a zippered pouch for receipts. FranklinCovey also offers city maps, graph paper, spreadsheets, a clock/calculator page divider, and my favorite—perforated, prepunched paper that I can run through my laser printer so that I can make more-or-less permanent records of important information, factual data, and my personal short-term and long-term goals.

If you are more oriented toward computers, I'm sure you've discovered PalmOne (and similar) PDAs. The "sync" feature is fantastic. Write a note on the road; transfer it to your computer. Add a contact on your computer; add it to your PDA. I prefer the PDAs that have built-in miniature "QWERTY" keyboards. My handwriting is illegible, so naturally my "graffiti" is worse.

The book you now hold in your hands was part of my three-year plan. My next book is part of my one-year plan—and it's almost finished. As I sit outdoors looking at the lush forests of Pine, Arizona, or the beautiful Red Rock Country of Sedona, Arizona, working on this book, I am also drafting a set of additional goals. I've finally figured out how important goal-setting really is!

YOUR ETHICS

I'm amazed that my college education contributed any-thing to my success in life. After all, I was somewhat dis-advantaged. The course offerings were so limited. So basic. I was not able, at least in my majors, to register for all of the "enlightened" courses they teach today. In the 1960s, I couldn't register for a course in "business ethics." Imagine that! I never had the help of a text-book—or a college professor—to help me separate right from wrong. Or one shade of gray from other shades of gray, if that's how you prefer to view it.

There is black and there is white. There is wrong and there is right. There's also gray, but there's a lot less of it than most people believe.

It's been demonstrated to me again and again that the biblical edict "As you sow, so shall you reap" is an inviolable law. Think Enron, think WorldCom; and where did Martha Stewart spend a lot of time recently?

The truly successful businessperson in today's society—the one whose success lasts—is *not* the one who lies or cheats to get ahead.

That person follows a simple biblical principle—"Let your Yes be Yes, and let your No be No."

Mean what you say. Keep your word. Hold fast to your promises. Live up to your guarantees. Deliver the service that you sold with the product.

Don't be on the constant lookout for "loopholes." Loopholes were invented by dishonest people to make themselves appear to be honest. Loopholes permit— even encourage—the manipulation of facts for improper purposes.

KEN BLANCHARD AND DR. NORMAN VINCENT PEALE ON ETHICS

You can ask yourself three simple questions to determine if an action or decision you're considering is ethical or not.

THE "ETHICS CHECK" QUESTIONS:

1. Is it legal?

Will I be violating either civil law or company policy?

2. Is it balanced?

Is it fair to all concerned in the short-term as well as in the long-term? Does it promote win-win relationships?

3. How will it make me feel about myself?

Will it make me proud?

Would I feel good if my decision were published in the newspaper?

Would I feel good if my family knew about it?

—From *The Power of Ethical Management* by Ken Blanchard and Norman Vincent Peale
Copyright © 1988 by the Blanchard Family Partnership and Dr. Norman Vincent Peale

A standard that cannot be ignored is that of keeping confidences. From the moment you first violate that rule, you will never be trusted again. One of the things that amazed me for years (though it shouldn't have) is that I had clients who would tell me things well before they told their own employees. They knew that if they said, "Don't repeat this to anyone," I wouldn't even tell my wife.

When you add up the assets of your business, you always include cash on hand, equipment, buildings, fixtures and furniture, vehicles, and inventory. But your biggest asset is missing from that list. You don't include it on your balance sheet because it has no easily determined market value. In fact, it's impossible to attach a dollar amount to it. That asset is your reputation. Guard it. Protect it. Never let it become a liability.

You've heard the old adage "Don't get mad, get even." Over the short term, that philosophy may prove workable. But it certainly doesn't fit with an even older teaching, "Don't repay evil with evil, but repay evil with good."

This is tough advice to follow. It runs contrary to everything most of us have been taught. "Only the strong survive." "You have to be tough to play this game." "Don't let 'em walk all over you."

There is room for kindness in business. There are businesspeople who play the game by the highest standards—and win. It's definitely worth a try.

Ethics should not be subject to the winds of whim. Build your personal life—and your business—on the bedrock of that which is right, and true, and unchanging. You can't go wrong if you don't go wrong.

YOUR SUPPORT SYSTEM

When the difficulties of being in business for yourself drag you down, don't try to make it through your problems on your own. Don't be afraid to utter a cry for help. Find a support group, or a variety of support groups, and welcome them into your life.

Your first line of defense in a nonsense economy and a crazy world should be your *family*. I can arrive home from what I honestly believe has been the worst day of my life, and a warm hug can erase it all. My wife and I can sit down to a beautiful meal that one of us has prepared (to be candid, hers are more beautiful than mine) and, suddenly, slow receivables cease to exist. We can pick up the phone and call other members of our family—none of whom has ever been an independent businessperson—and, somehow, they seem to understand, care, and affirm.

Your *friends* should come right behind your family. My male readers will undoubtedly believe they understand the notion of "male bonding," yet they would never reveal their fears, frustrations, questions, or problems to someone with whom they play poker and watch *Monday Night Football*. It just ain't macho. It ain't cool. Male bonding means you do "guy stuff" together—sports, hunting, or fishing. Nothing more.

My female readers are probably wincing right now. "Honestly!" they're saying. "Men! Who can understand those Neanderthals?" Overall, I believe women have a better notion of what friendship really is and should be. While every human being conceals certain aspects of who they are and what aspirations they have, women are more willing to reveal their thoughts and feelings, fears and dreams. Men would do well to learn how to express their basic needs and feelings with friends who care.

Your third source of support can be *organized small*

groups. These can range from "12-step" recovery groups, to clubs and special interest organizations, to nondenominational Bible studies.

Professional counselors can also be of tremendous support and benefit. Years ago, anyone who saw a psychiatrist or other counselor was viewed as suspect. Today, the stigma associated with counseling has, for the most part, vanished. Counselors can help sort through a variety of personal, marital, family, and professional matters. Career counselors can help with the decision as to whether or not to change direction in life, and business counselors can provide that one gem of truth that can get a troubled business back on track.

Professional and religious retreats have gained great acceptance and are becoming more readily available. In many of these settings, the participants may not have met previously, so they "open up" more willingly as a result. Two of my friends annually attend a three-day retreat for men where the purpose is exactly the opposite. They take a vow of silence for those three days and spend their time meditating, attending vespers, and listening to talks on a variety of life issues. A married couple who are friends of ours tell us that one of the things they do to enhance their marriage is to attend a weekend couples' retreat that's held twice a year.

Churches and synagogues often provide free or low-cost counseling, recovery groups, and other supportive services. I have known many priests, pastors, and rabbis over the years who exhibit a deep caring not only for those in their congregations, but also for those who simply call in times of need. They are able to bring fresh insight to a wide range of questions and problems.

The key to developing an effective support system is that you have to *want* to do it. Seldom will a support person or group come looking for you.

Until you have developed strong ties with support-ive individuals and organizations, you will never know what you've been missing.

THINKING IT THROUGH

What are my keys to maintaining my enthusiasm?

_____

How can I keep a positive attitude? _____

_____

What knowledge do I need to acquire? _____

_____

How will I acquire it?_____

_____

What skills should I learn?_____

_____

How will I learn them? _____

_____

What nonbusiness activities should I pursue? _____

_____

What issues from my past do I need to confront?

_____

What are my top five goals?

_____

_____

_____

_____

_____

Would I want to see my recent decisions/behaviors published in the newspaper? Why? Or why not?

_____

_____

_____

Who should be in my support group? _____

_____

11

Your Employees

As I am writing this, I do not have any employees. I work with independent contractors. The positive side of this is that I can run a profitable business without having a huge payroll, high overhead, or the headaches of HRM—human resource management. (Ask any HR professional about his or her headaches sometime.) On the negative side, I realize that my business will never generate millions of dollars in revenue, nor can I sell franchises. My growth opportunities are limited.

The truth is, if I could operate a successful, growing, multibillion-dollar business without employees, I would. Employees whine, they call in sick, they go on vacation at the most inconvenient times, they take long lunches, they want raises, they demand more benefits, they have PMS (especially the men), they leave without notice, and when they leave, they try to take your best clients with them.

It's impossible to keep them all happy all of the

time. They all have different needs, interests, goals, aspirations, fears, and demands. Rarely do they all get along
with one another. They're jealous and petty. They form
alliances among themselves to try to get the better of
you. They want to work less and get paid more. Make
one false move, and they'll try to form a labor union or
drag you into court.

But almost without exception, employees are a necessary part of doing business. More than that—they're the
lifeblood of your business. Without people, there is no one
to make, sell, or distribute your product. There is no one to
install and maintain your equipment. No one to collect
your receivables or pay your debts. No one to service your
customers or relay your messages.

This is all pitifully obvious. But many of the businesses that are in trouble got there because they overlooked the value and importance of their employees.
Good employees are on the same level as loyal customers and dependable vendors. They are among your
most valuable assets.

The reverse is also true. Incompetent employees—
like fickle clients and undependable vendors—are
among your greatest liabilities.

With a "don't bother me" attitude toward a question, the rude employee can turn your customer into
someone else's customer. Until I had a candid talk with
one of my employees about phone manners, I had several of my longtime customers ask me, "Who is that
angry-sounding person who answered the phone?"
There is no place in a successful business for rudeness.

The unproductive employee can be demoralizing to
the rest of your employees. They will naturally wonder

why someone who doesn't produce as much gets paid as much as (or sometimes more than) the employee who gives it his or her all.

THE EMPLOYEE SCREENING AND SELECTION PROCESS

There are always a lot of people in the job market. Chances are, from the moment you open your doors, you will be flooded with résumés. Chances are they'll all look pretty good, too.

I think of myself as being a fairly bright guy, which makes it difficult to explain why I have made so many dumb hiring decisions. I finally figured out the simple basics of screening and selecting employees. You may consider these to be all too obvious, so feel free to skip this section if you'd like. (And then report back to me in a year—we'll see just how obvious they were!)

Skills

This area is painfully obvious—but often overlooked. Your prospective employees will either possess **all** of the skills you need, **some** of those skills, or **none** of those skills. A big "duh." But you'd be amazed by all the employers who hire people in the **none** column. I have a friend in the medical field (I won't specify which part of it) who hires women only—and hires them based largely on looks. Dumb friend! Bad friend! El Stupido!

I have another friend who always seems to be under-staffed because she can't find the perfect candidate who fits in the **all** category.

Face it. The perfect person rarely walks through the door. So the best practice is to hire the **some** person who has the skills that are best aligned with your present need. Simple example: A candidate who knows how to type on a computer can probably learn Microsoft Word. A candidate who types slowly and can't spell any word with more than two syllables—but who does happen to know Word—probably won't increase in typing speed or spelling aptitude by all that much.

Bottom line: Hire the best **some** you can find.

Training

You may have to offer training in specialized areas, but during the interview process, dig for all the information on the candidate's training that you possibly can. Some training organizations offer certificates that serve as proof of completion.

If you need people who have to be competent in certain software systems and programs, make sure that they are using the same version you are. Software becomes outdated very quickly, so if your applicant is using version 8.3 and you're on version 10.3.5, there will be some catching up involved.

Again, hire the best **some** that you can find.

Experience

Back when I was hiring people to be a part of my creative team, I discovered there are two kinds of experience: **real** experience and **résumé** experience. I learned that it's really important to verify that the applicant can actually do what he or she claims. I developed some "nonstandard" tests that demonstrated what **real** experience the applicant had.

The hiring challenges today are greater than they have ever been. The reason is technology. I prefer the wisdom and experience of older employees, but I value the technological savvy of the younger generation—those people who practically had computers in their cribs. My wife has wonderful wisdom, experience, and sales skills that she has acquired over the years, but I'm having a tough time teaching her how to back up the hard drive on her computer. Our sixteen-year-old daughter has amazing computer skills but has not yet developed all of the other traits an employer would seek.

Sometimes, you can find it all in one person. Hire that person! Usually, though, it's a balancing act. You need to evaluate the skills of the applicants and hire the one whose "operable" attributes most closely match your most urgent needs.

Personality/Temperament

A few years ago, I acquired some invaluable information from my friends Scott Blanchard and Stephanie Rogers that has changed my life. Actually, this information has been around since ancient Greece, but they framed it in a way that made it really useful.

Scott and Stephanie took the major concepts related to the Myers-Briggs Type Indicator (MBTI) and the David Keirsey personality profile (www.keirsey.com) and distilled it all so that even I could understand it.

In a nutshell, they explained that there are four basic

human temperaments. Each of these temperaments can be defined by the "core needs" that are its driving forces. Here they are, along with what Scott and Stephanie suggest are their "mottos."

1. Idealists:
- Meaning and significance.
- Unique identity.

Motto: "All we are saying is give peace a chance."

2. Rationals:
- Self-mastery.
- Knowledge and competence.

Motto: "There's a logical explanation for everything."

3. Guardians:
- Membership and belonging.
- Responsibility and duty.

Motto: "But we've always done it that way."

4. Artisans:
- Freedom to act on impulse.
- Ability to make an impact.

Motto: "Carpe diem! Seize the day!"

While these descriptions are obviously abbreviated—because, after all, this is not a book about temperament—I'm sure you can sense that because people of different temperament types have different core needs, they would bring different skills and perspectives to your company. You can probably also guess that schools and police departments might naturally employ a higher percentage of Guardians, while the employees of computer manufacturers and medical research labs may tend to be Rationals. Ad agencies? Artisans, of course!

Prior to the interview process, it could be very beneficial for you to read some of Dr. Keirsey's material on his Web site or in his books in order to determine which temperament types could add the most value to your company. Then, depending on the laws that relate to employee testing and evaluation (and those laws change all the time), you may want to use some testing materials that help you determine whether or not an applicant is a good match.

Background Check

It is becoming increasingly important to do background checks on prospective employees. My friend, Kevin Klimas, founder of Clarifacts, Inc., a Phoenix-based company that specializes in preemployment background checks, told me that companies place themselves at risk of negligent-hiring lawsuits if they don't conduct such checks.

Kevin said, "Negligent hiring is a legal theory under which employers can be held liable for the unlawful or improper actions of their employees if it can be shown that they failed to make 'reasonable' inquiries into the employee's background and suitability for the position. If the employer knew, or *should have known,* of the risk presented by the employee, the employer can be held liable. Employers found negligent in the hiring process have been subject to substantial financial penalties, including both actual and punitive damages, which are now reaching an average of one million dollars [according to the Workplace Violence Research Institute]."

There are other risks, too. Many business failures are due to employee theft and other forms of dishonesty. This fraud may take the form of padded expenses, vendor kickbacks, theft of equipment, cash skimming, preparing false financial statements, pilfering merchandise, unauthorized purchases, and fraudulent billing practices. Employees at all levels have a significant impact on the success or failure of any business.

When applicants are not properly screened, you can also face potential problems such as workplace violence, sexual harassment, and drug or alcohol abuse.

The basic key to minimizing your risk is not to hire candidates who have committed such acts elsewhere. But you need to have facts on which to base your decision. Here's how to obtain those facts:

County Criminal Record Search

Access to criminal records is available in every county throughout the United States. Most counties provide felony, misdemeanor, and criminal traffic offenses. Information you will want to obtain should include case number, date of offense, filing date, charge(s), type of charge, and outcome.

County Civil Record Search

This search will verify whether the applicant has appeared as a plaintiff or defendant in a civil action. Reports should include type of case, style of case, case number, filing date, disposition date, and settlement amount.

Federal Criminal Record Search

Not all crimes fall under state or local jurisdictions. These searches will reveal violations of federal law such as bank robbery, counterfeiting, kidnapping, interstate drug trafficking, and insider trading.

Employment Verification

Many applicants falsify employment information. Verify present and/or previous employment—specifically, dates of employment (unexplained gaps raise red flags), position held, and ending pay rate (where available). In addition, attempt to obtain reason for separation, eligibility for rehire, job performance rating, and other pertinent information. The amount of information available may be subject to policies of the former employer.

Education Verification

Education history is commonly falsified information on an application or résumé. Verify an applicant's academic history, including dates of attendance, major course of study, degree received and date awarded, and grade point average (if available).

Social Security Trace

This report verifies the name of the cardholder, identifies current and previous addresses (essential for researching criminal history), and any other name(s) associated with the number.

Driving Record History

Motor vehicle reports (MVRs) verify the validity of an applicant's driver's license, including violations, suspensions, and revocations; type of license; and restrictions, if any. Each report spans three to seven years, depending on the issuing state.

Credit History Report

This report provides a profile of the applicant's personal financial management history—indebtedness, payment history, and public record information such as tax liens, judgments, and bankruptcies.

Drug Screening

Drug abusers cost employers through higher rates of accidents, absences, workers' compensation claims, tardiness, use of sickness benefits, and medical benefits usage. Substance-abuse screening tested by a federally approved laboratory is a sound idea.

Professional License/ Certification Verification

Verify the validity of an applicant's professional license/ certification, including the issue date, current status, and disciplinary actions or restrictions, if any.

Reference Interview

Contact professional references to obtain an assessment of the applicant's character, capabilities, and work record.

Design the interview to ask business-related questions to obtain a better picture of the applicant's work history.

When determining what to include in the background check, you'll need to look at the various positions within your organization and request services based on the job classification. For example, requesting a credit history report for a staff accountant position or driving records for a delivery driver position would be both appropriate and highly recommended.

What could happen if you don't perform the appropriate background checks?

In a worst-case scenario, ignoring these checks could lead to the total failure of a business. "There are companies that no longer exist because they hired people who committed acts of violence, harassment, and other forms of misconduct resulting in disastrous civil litigation; or they hired employees who robbed them into nonexistence," Kevin said.

Kevin also laid out some of the legal considerations. "You'd better be informed as to the current guidelines of the Fair Credit Reporting Act (FCRA) as well as the Equal Employment Opportunity Commission (EEOC). The EEOC and other state legislation restrict the use of background information by an employer. Under EEOC guidelines, an employer may not automatically disqualify an applicant with a criminal record. The last thing you need to face is a claim of discrimination. That usually leads to ongoing EEOC scrutiny."

Kevin pointed out that the most important aspect of any preemployment screening program is consistency. Employers with a written policy who are conducting background checks uniformly within job classifications will be able to refute most claims of discrimination.

There are some clear benefits that result from establishing a consistently applied system of background checks.

Minimized Risk

Legal action against employers for negligent hiring is becoming increasingly common. Properly screening employees demonstrates due diligence in the hiring process, thereby giving employers a level of protection against litigation.

Reduced Turnover

The Department of Labor estimates that, on average, it costs a company one-third of a new hire's annual salary to replace an employee. This can include direct costs such as recruitment advertising, time spent reviewing résumés and interviewing applicants, and orientation and training time; indirect costs such as increases in unemployment insurance rates and loss of productivity; and intangible costs such as greater stress and tension, an unstable working environment, and loss of intellectual property. Employment screening assists employers in selecting the right employee, the first time.

Improved Quality of Your Candidate Pool

A formal employment-screening program discourages applicants with something to hide and encourages honesty in the application and interview process. Screening not only discourages undesirable applicants from applying, but also attracts qualified applicants who want to work for an employer who cares about the safety and quality of the workforce.

Savings of Both Time and Money

An enormous amount of time and money is wasted on applicants that do not meet an employer's hiring criteria. Employment screening can filter out unwanted applicants before more time and money are invested.

More Confident Hiring Decisions

There can be a great deal of uncertainty involved in selecting a candidate. Although using instinct in the hiring process is important, basing a decision on hard information is even better. Employment screening is an effective tool for verifying data provided by the applicant and uncovering omitted information.

WHAT TO EXPECT OF EMPLOYEES: THE QUEST FOR EXCELLENCE

Now that you've hired them, how do you get the best from them?

One of my personal philosophies is that while I don't believe in perfection, because, realistically, it can never be attained, I do believe in the *quest* for excellence. I believe in working a little harder, improving the product or service in every way possible, and striving continually to be better at everything I do. "Quality" has long been the buzzword in the business world. Various programs have been developed to ensure that quality happens—from TQM (Total Quality Management) to Six Sigma with all of its Black Belts and Green Belts. But the "quest for excellence" has to be at the foundation of any and all of the more stringent quality programs you implement.

I believe this quest should be formalized in every company's culture and ethic, under whatever phrase or word they choose to use.

The objective of this program should be fourfold. It should:

- Nurture quality work.
- Build commitment to one another (teamwork).
- Assure accountability.
- Reward top performance.

In our increasingly competitive business environment, companies all fight over the pieces of what seems to be a smaller pie. Offshore competition is taking its toll. It is only as management and employees work together in a quest for excellence that they can have the power to successfully fight the ravages of increased competition in a challenging economy.

The Four Keys

1. They will nurture quality work.

Companies that will stay alive and prosper will be run by people who expect quality work from their employees and help them achieve that objective—whether it's through TQM, Six Sigma, or another system. They will recognize that, as competition for every dollar becomes increasingly fierce, they will have to offer a better product at a lower (or more value-oriented) price.

In any business, you have to be aware that there are other companies calling on your accounts and your prospects every day of the business week. They are telling your clients and potential clients that they can do better work (quality) at a lower, or more efficient cost (value) with greater results (profits) than you can. The minute that one of your clients believes their claims, you won't have a client. If your prospect believes it, you won't have a viable prospect.

As a businessperson, you know that quality is crucial. Quality means doing it right. But quality also encompasses value and generates results.

In my old business, advertising, quality often no longer means that the most splendid design will be printed by the most expensive printer. Quality *does* mean that the job is completed within budget, that it fulfills its intended function, and that errors are not made throughout. Errors signal to the client that no one cares . . . that attention to detail is sloppy . . . and that there must be someone out there who can do it better—and do it right.

2. They will build commitment to one another.

Another characteristic that will be common to the successful companies of today and tomorrow will be teamwork. To achieve top quality, everyone on the team must fulfill his or her role.

Great assembly-line workers can't build great cars unless those cars are based on great designs.

The designers must be committed to design great cars. The machinists must be committed to executing great tools, dies, and molds. The assembly-line workers must be dedicated to using those tools and dies in the ways they were designed to be used. And the inspectors who sign off on the completed automobiles must observe the high standards they are intended to follow.

The key is that, for success, everyone must be committed to fulfilling their individual and team roles, rather than trying to redefine those roles to fit their personal interests.

3. They will assure accountability.

There must be some means to measure quality in the broadest sense, and that means is the setting of standards. The standards should apply equally and fairly to all employees, and employees need to have a clear picture of what those standards are. Employees like to know and understand the various criteria on which their performance is being judged. How are they being "graded"? How is score being kept?

It is essential that you establish minimum standards for your own on-the-job performance, as well as that of new people you bring on staff. With the establishment of realistic guidelines, each person will be held accountable for meeting those standards.

4. They will reward top performance.

There is one practice in the world of the NFL that I don't like. And that is, if a team wins the Super Bowl, every player gets the same "winner's share" and the same jewel-encrusted ring, whether he played the entire game or never set foot on the field—even for a second.

While this promotes teamwork, it does nothing for the players who give it everything they've got, even if it means personal pain, possible injury, and the risk of an end to their careers.

I believe that companies should reward top performers—and not automatically give the winner's share and gold ring to every player simply because he or she showed up for the game. From personal experience, I know that some players show up on game day, but they forget their uniforms or are hobbling along on crutches. In my case, I gave them the same rewards as the players who came to the game fully prepared and eager to play. I should have developed a clearly defined system to reward people based on their performance.

Let me quickly add that I am an advocate of equal pay for equal work. A woman who does the same work as a man should receive equal pay—without question, without objection. A woman who outperforms her male counterpart *should* get *more* pay, without question, without objection. When we have succeeded as a nation in equalizing pay and other incentives, we will not have made the average performers into great performers—we will have transformed the great performers into average performers.

If you have fulfilled your ethical and moral responsibility to give everyone an equal right to succeed, without regard to race, creed, color, or sex, you *should* have the right to discriminate on matters of salaries, bonuses, and promotions, based on *measurable* performance. You should be able to do so without fear of litigation, but the days when you can do so are passing quickly.

THE DRIVE FOR PROFITS

In the successful businesses of today, every employee must "buy into" the premise that profits are everyone's concern. And profits are generally based on productivity—on the manufacturing and distribution side, as well as on the sales and management side.

Jobs can exist only if profits exist. Pay increases can be given only when there is an increase in the available amount of money—in a word, profits. But management cannot be held solely responsible for profits. A significant part of the responsibility rests with your employees. In the real world of business, your employees are as responsible for their own paychecks as you, the owner, are. It's time that message became clear. You didn't necessarily go into business to guarantee your employees a job. You went into business and hired employees so that you could guarantee a job for yourself. You can't afford to carry dead weight.

BUILDING MORALE

Advertising—as well as the creativity that produces it—is highly subjective in nature. As one of the primary account executives for my company, I had frequent interaction with our clients. And I can tell you that clients were more prone to criticize than to praise—even when we were doing an outstanding job and their sales were increasing dramatically. Advertising was simply our job, we were getting paid for it, and we were expected to do it well—praise or not.

Because I have received so little positive affirmation for my work over the years, I have not valued praise as much as I should, and I have been slow to praise my employees for their contributions. In fact, when I've hired people in the past, I've said in their final interview, "I don't get much praise, so I don't dish much out, either. Don't take that to mean you're not doing a good job, though."

Well, folks, this is not a philosophy on which great companies are built. It leads only to lackluster performance and job dissatisfaction. It's vital that every employer develop a strategy for building the morale of individuals as well as the company as a whole.

The three most direct tactics for building employee morale are to:

1. **Praise** quality work.
2. **Build** camaraderie and a spirit of teamwork.
3. **Create** an environment in which people know that they will be rewarded for their contributions and will have an opportunity for advancement.

Praise, of course, is easier to lavish on employees who are actually doing a good job. But one crucial truth I've learned from being the father of three children is that *everyone needs praise,* and there is always *something* for which *every person deserves praise.* It may be a stretch some days. You may have to dig a little to find something. But it can be found.

I'm reminded of the story—and I wish I could tell you where I heard it so I could give proper credit—of a schoolteacher who was placed in charge of a group of underachievers and learning disabled students, without that fact being made clear to her at the time. After these kids had spent a year in her class, the school principal came to her and said, "I can't believe the progress you're making with your students. They're performing as well as their counterparts in the mainstream classes."

The teacher, with a look of disbelief on her face, responded, "Why shouldn't they? Just look at their IQs," she said, pointing to the list of students, "126, 142, 138, 123. They're all quite bright! Some are even in the genius category."

The principal examined her list more closely. "Those aren't their IQs," he exclaimed. "Those are their *locker numbers.*"

If you look for praiseworthy traits in your employees, you'll find them. And, as the story illustrates, if you have high expectations, there's a good chance they'll be met.

A word of caution: Employees are capable of detecting false praise. The employee you're praising, along with all those who overhear it, will know whether or not your words are genuine. Don't try to fake it.

Your words of affirmation should follow two paths. Some should be spoken in private, directly to the employee. Some should be in public, to foster recognition and acceptance. Just make sure that one employee isn't singled out for the bulk of your public encouragement.

There are a variety of approaches any company can follow to **build camaraderie and a spirit of teamwork.** Your initial response to some of my tactics may be, "Well, that might work in ad agencies because they're nothing but a bowl of creative flakes in the first place."

You may be right, but try these on for size:

- If you get a piece of good news, no matter how great or small, ring a "good news bell." Hang a bell on the wall in your lobby or conference room. One "gong" is small news, two "gongs" means bigger news, and so on.

  Ring the bell whenever there's a check in the morning mail. Ring the bell when you get a new order from an existing client. Ring the bell off the wall when you get a new client or make a big sale.
- Instead of commemorating Secretary's Day or Secretary's Week, which this aging conservative thinks is horribly sexist, why not observe "Employee Appreciation Week" during the same general time period? Give every employee a potted "mini-garden" designed by a local florist, along with the afternoon off.
- Hold a company golf tournament, complete with trophies for "high gross" and "most putts." Okay, you don't all have to be serious golfers.
- Throughout the life of my company, we observed Martin Luther King, Jr., Day as an official holiday. Because January was always cold and snow-covered in Minnesota, we scheduled a ski outing for the staff. At the end of the day, we raised our mugs of hot apple cider to the memory of a man who gave millions of people a reason to have dreams to call their own.

Of the three tactics for building morale, the most important is to **create an environment in which people know that they will be rewarded for their contributions and will have an opportunity for advancement.**

The most common and accepted way to reward an employee's contributions is through a raise or a promotion. Raises are dependent, of course, on profits. Promotions that involve a new title don't cost anything if the only reward is the title itself—Vice President, Sales, for example. But for a title to be anything other than a trivial gesture, it should be linked to a pay increase. Your employees will quickly see through shallow ploys designed solely to try to make them happy.

There are other rewards that, long term, cost less than a raise but can have almost as much positive impact. Sales contests are one example. The single "plum" of a Caribbean cruise or a trip to Hawaii can increase the productivity of your entire sales department.

My wife, Karla, suggested "time-out" coupons. If a member of the staff had been putting in extra-long hours or had gone above and beyond the call of duty in some way, they were awarded a gift certificate valid at a local restaurant, so that they could take a "time-out." Try it!

It matters little how you recognize employees or what tactics you employ to build morale. It matters more that you *do* it. Employees who are praised, encouraged, promoted, and rewarded are more likely to care, to be productive, and to remain with the company.

KEN BLANCHARD AND SHELDON BOWLES ON CREATING A "GUNG HO" WORKPLACE

Very little that's worthwhile or profitable will happen within your workplace unless your employees are motivated and enthusiastic. In *Gung Ho!*, Sheldon Bowles and I tell the story of Andy Longclaw, a Native American whose grandfather taught him secrets of the forest that can easily be transferred to the workplace. These secrets are based on the special traits of three animals.

SPIRIT OF THE SQUIRREL

Worthwhile Work

1. We must know that we make the world a better place.

2. Everyone must work toward a shared goal.

3. Our values guide all of our plans, decisions and actions.

WAY OF THE BEAVER

In Control of Achieving the Goal

1. We must have a playing field with clearly marked territory.

2. Every person's thoughts, feelings, needs and dreams must be respected, listened to and acted upon.

3. People must be able to do the work, but should be challenged to grow.

GIFT OF THE GOOSE

Cheering Others On

1. Whether active or passive, congratulations must be true. People can detect false praise.

2. There is no real game unless we keep score. Who would care about a basketball game if the scoreboard didn't display progress? Fans cheer progress—every shot that drops through the basket—as well as the ultimate victory.

3. People must be rewarded by both cash and congratulations. Using both forms of reward leads to enthusiasm.

—From *Gung Ho!* by Ken Blanchard and Sheldon Bowles

SETTING EXPECTATIONS

If an employee is ineffective on the job, it is often because he or she has not been properly trained, does not know what his or her employer's expectations are, and isn't redirected when the standards aren't met.

Here's the nutshell version:

- Training.
- Expectations.
- Redirection.

As an employer, you must clearly state your expectations to every employee on a continuous basis. You must make certain they understand the company's goals, procedures, products, and services. Communicating these things only one time won't cut it. It's an ongoing process.

I had always assumed otherwise. "People are bright, receptive, and pay close attention," I said to myself. "They'll catch on right away, and I won't have to repeat anything twice."

Wrong.

If I've learned anything as the result of being in the advertising business, it's that *frequency*—repeating the same message over and over to the same audience—is the key to building brand recognition, being remembered by the consumer, and delivering results in the form of sales. Your employees are the "consumers" of your policies, procedures, goals, standards, and philosophies. They need to be told, told again, reminded, reinforced, and re-reminded. They need to "buy into" everything about the company.

Be direct. Set goals. Teach your people to be good representatives of your company—to care about customers, to help each other, to be a team.

But make sure they're ready to play on the team. Don't expect your employees to deliver miracles if they don't have sufficient experience or you haven't provided adequate training. Can you imagine boarding a 747 jet and then discovering that the captain only knows how to fly 757s and the copilot is proficient only on Airbus 320s? Neither has had one day of training on a 747. On top of that, they have never worked together as a team before.

Good pilots and good team members cost money. Effective training programs cost money. With employees—as with anything else in life—you will never get something for nothing.

When you have succeeded in assembling a team of eager, experienced, trained employees, you can set the highest standards and expect your employees to meet them.

THE JOB DESCRIPTION

No employee should ever be expected to reach for those goals—or even fill an open position—without first knowing what assignments he or she will be asked to fulfill, and what standards will be used to evaluate performance.

This objective is best met through a combination of the employee handbook and a job description. My approach was to provide a detailed handbook that provided basic minimum standards with regard to working hours, company policies, and general expectations. The job description provided information on specific duties and outlined reporting procedures and supervisory responsibilities.

A well-drawn job description should not limit the employee's growth or suppress his or her imagination or eagerness, nor should it describe specific procedures in detail. The latter function is best left to procedural memos, meetings, or job-specific handbooks.

Instead, it should paint a larger picture of the basic areas in which the employee can contribute to the overall success of the company and create a better future for himself or herself.

The first page of each of my job descriptions—past, present, and future—outlines the following:

1. The job title of the employee.
2. The general nature of the position—is it full- or part-time; is it salaried, hourly, or commissioned? Is it union or nonunion; is there a limitation on benefits the company will provide?
3. To whom does the employee report?
4. Who reports to the employee? Who does the employee supervise directly?
5. What is the pay range of the position?

The pages that follow outline the employee's general responsibilities. They do not concentrate on specifics; rather, they encourage both freedom and involvement. For example, the job description I gave to our creative director was broken down into these key categories:

1. **Create**—Participate in regular and unscheduled meetings to develop creative strategies for clients and for specific projects. Focus on combining headlines and copy with illustrations and design to communicate a strong, integrated sales message.
2. **Innovate**—Search out and identify new, fresh, innova-

tive ways to solve advertising/marketing problems, and, when possible, apply them on our clients' behalf.

3. **Estimate**—Work with account people to develop "doable" budgets. Judge the amount of creative time and add costs for outside services to provide a realistic estimate to clients. Communicate and store this information on your computer for quick retrieval. Contribute to profits by making sure that budgets are not exceeded.

4. **Delegate**—Assign tasks to the persons with the best skills and most available time to suitably handle the job. Use staff people first before assigning jobs to freelancers.

5. **Communicate**—State objectives, target budgets, and a clear outline of the job to be done to others in the creative department. Communicate goals, concerns, and problems to the president. Communicate positive and healthy attitudes to other staff members and be a leader among men and women. Don't let bad ideas from others prevent you from pushing for the best solutions. Make sure that communication is multi-level, multichannel, two-way, and "on the table."

6. **Facilitate**—Make it possible for others to better do their jobs, so that duplicated steps and wasted time are eliminated. By using the time of others more effectively, you will use your own time more effectively.

7. **Educate**—Teach others what you know—about computers, type, design, printing, procedures, management, life.

8. **Generate**—Foster excitement, ideas, profits, by encouraging a spirit of cooperation, teamwork,

openness, and enthusiasm toward the agency, its clients, and its creative product.

9. **Cooperate**—Work with your supervisor, with other staff members, and with clients and suppliers so that we can produce advertising and collateral materials that make a difference.

10. **Recreate**—Have fun in your off hours, and take time during the busiest workweek to break for the boat, golf, or an occasional long lunch. After all, "seriousity killed the cat."

While these categories are specific to certain jobs within the context of an advertising agency, they can serve as the foundation for job descriptions in any industry—if one of the underlying goals is to create both independence and interdependence, and both freedom and responsibility, in the workplace.

In every job description, from receptionist to vice president, from media coordinator to copywriter, I stressed that the job was a *team position*. A key concept that I have always tried to communicate is: **"If there's a job to be done, and you're in the best position to do it, it should get done."**

THE NONPERFORMER

When an employee is performing well, it hurts to be forced by business economics into the position of having to let him or her go. It's a little easier (though not much) when you have to dismiss employees because they have failed to perform as expected—or required.

It's vital that you carefully document matters related

to performance so that in the event you dismiss the employee, you have adequate written material to back up your move. One of the reasons why I am an advocate of employee handbooks and written job descriptions is that they can provide the basis for an objective judgment of performance.

There's also no room in business for unrealistic expectations. If you are the owner of a *one-million-dollar* company, you can't hire one new salesperson and expect to be a *ten-million-dollar* company in six months. You need to target a realistic level of growth as your objective.

I have had my share of nonperformers, including an alcoholic who seldom returned from lunch; a horse-loving account executive who claimed to be out on calls when, in fact, many afternoons she was out riding her Tennessee walker; and a person who spent nearly a third of the workday on personal phone calls.

Nonperformers head the list of the people in every company who are not indispensable. They can be replaced by people who truly want to contribute. You owe it to your loyal, caring, hardworking employees to replace them. If you keep them on the payroll with the hope of somehow rehabilitating them, you'll only drag your company down.

THE DISGRUNTLED EMPLOYEE

Throughout the life of my business—especially during the more profitable years, I gave my employees nearly everything you could imagine. Ahead-of-schedule raises; expense accounts; heated indoor parking (a big thing in frigid Minnesota); gift certificates in appreciation of extra effort; medical reimbursement payments for their out-of-pocket health care expenses; tuition reimbursement for college courses they wanted to take; fully paid life, health, and disability insurance; holiday bonuses; "arts" reimbursements (we paid for their concert and theater tickets, which was reported as additional income); golf tournaments and ski outings—if you can name it, we probably did it. (But, sorry, I'd never do that again!)

My philosophy was "Take good care of your employees, and they'll take good care of you." Some will, and some won't. I've discovered through experience that if you offer your employees the moon, they'll be only too happy to take it.

While there are employees who will appreciate your kindnesses and considerations until the day they cross over into eternity, there are others who will turn on you no matter what you do for them. They will bad-mouth you, reveal your trade secrets, and probably go to work for your toughest competitor. I realize this sounds cynical, but it's still a fact.

When an employee's attitude turns sour, you can only hope that you haven't committed some unpardonable sin that could land you in court. Make sure you are never guilty of the following:

1. Don't create a hostile, uncomfortable, or sexist workplace, and don't allow those who work for you to do so.
2. Don't do anything that could be interpreted as discrimination against any person or group of persons.
3. Keep accurate, up-to-date personnel files, and make sure that you have "proof of cause" for every disci-

plinary action you take. (Documentation is everything! Write it down; put the date on it; keep up-to-
date records.)

4. Make sure your employees receive equal pay for
   equal work.
5. Follow the letter of the law with regard to the
   employment practices that apply in your state.
6. Do not put anything in writing that may come back
   to haunt you later. For example, don't write a positive performance review for an employee with whom
   you are having difficulties. In nearly every instance,
   employment files are totally and completely open to
   the employee.
7. Make sure your lawyer has the opportunity to review
   your practices and procedures on a regular basis.
   Laws change, even if your policies don't.

If you violate any of these principles, there's a fair
chance that, in today's litigious atmosphere, you will
face your disgruntled former employees in court.

THE EMPLOYEE WHO WOULD BE BOSS

Every company will eventually employ someone who
thinks he or she should be the boss. If you want him or
her to be, fine. But if you don't, watch out!

These types try to control you. They test you. They
push the limits.

They control meetings by coming late, leaving early,
exhibiting poor attitudes, or acting distracted. Believe it
or not, I had an employee who would actually decide for
himself when a meeting I had called should be over, and

would walk out, saying he had important things to do. This, in spite of the fact that I always tried to keep our meetings as short as possible. The same individual would tell my other employees to contradict my direct instructions, under the premise that his approach was far better.

This kind of employee will test you to see if you really follow your own policies. Often, they think of their contributions as indispensable, and they will nudge the boundaries to see how far you'll let them go.

In poker, two of a kind beats a high card. In business, things are different. Two people on the same level of the "organizational chart" oftentimes believe that, together, they beat the high card—the boss. Don't let that happen!

In order to prevent chaos, your employees have to know that while you will examine all the hands they play, the high card always wins. Yes, you're interested in fresh new ideas. Yes, you appreciate helpful suggestions. But no matter what you've heard to the contrary, successful companies simply can't be run by a committee. Certain aspects can be (for example, new business development committees can be extremely productive), but ultimately, the boss has to make the most crucial decisions.

I'm not advocating that you become a dictator who won't listen to reason or who summarily "executes" employees who express a differing opinion. Once you have made a decision, though, your employees are obligated to stand behind you. When they don't, you have a problem.

To prepare for the inevitable outcome of confrontation—termination of the employee—make sure you have maintained documentation of their questionable actions, hostilities, insubordination, or covert plans. If an employee has fought you for control, generally that strong-willed determination will surface again, under the worst of circumstances.

BUILDING SUCCESSFUL RELATIONSHIPS WITH EMPLOYEES

Your relationship with your employees is partly a formal contract and partly a mutual understanding that should benefit both of you equally. It all distills down to what you owe your employees and what they owe you.

Seven Things You Owe Your Employees

1. A regular, on-time paycheck.
2. A safe working environment.
3. Adequate insurance to protect them from loss from catastrophic illness.
4. Benefits (vacations, holidays, sick leave, retirement plans) in keeping with industry standards.
5. A reward system that is based on performance. (This runs contrary to things such as tenure and unions, and, frankly, it should.)
6. An equal and fair opportunity for advancement, without regard to race, sex, religion, or any other discriminatory factor.
7. Respect for the ideas, suggestions, and aspirations of the employee.

Seven Things Your Employees Owe You

1. An honest day's work for an honest day's pay. (This means keeping personal phone calls to a minimum, actively seeking ways to make meaningful contributions, performing tasks with a high degree of accuracy, reporting for work on time, and not watching the clock for the entire last hour of the day.)
2. Full-time loyalty.
3. Respect for confidential information.
4. Integrity and honesty in all dealings that represent the company.
5. Respect for you, the employer, and for their fellow employees.
6. A positive attitude on the job.
7. Courtesy toward the company's clients, vendors, and competitors.

If each party—employer and employee—can deliver on these very basic lists, you will have laid the foundation upon which, together, you can build a successful company. And as the employer, you will be maximizing one of your most valuable assets.

THINKING IT THROUGH

Am I performing adequate background checks on prospec-

tive employees? _____

If not, what should my plan be? _____

_____

_____

My target date for implementing this plan is: _____

What can I do to embark on "the quest for excellence?"

_____

_____

What are three ways to build camaraderie? _____

_____

_____

_____

Do I have any nonperformers on my team? If so, who

are they and what should be my action plan? _____

_____

12

Your Customers

There are only two kinds of customers in the world: satisfied and dissatisfied. The satisfied customer will generally result in a repeat sale or a continuing relationship; the dissatisfied customer usually will not.

There's a reason my statement is qualified by the words "generally" and "usually."

For example, if you're a real estate agent who sold a certain family their dream house, they may never come back to you with repeat business, even though they were completely satisfied with your service. They love their house and have no reason to buy another one. Conversely, if you're the only supplier of a product or service in a defined market, you may get repeat business from disgruntled customers simply because they have no other convenient choice.

However, customer satisfaction or dissatisfaction has a greater impact than simply on repeat sales. Customers are often your most widespread—and believable—form of advertising. They use the medium called "word of mouth." And there are only two kinds of word of mouth—good and bad.

If you were entirely responsible for your relationships with your customers, you would probably enjoy tremendous and ongoing success. All of your "word of mouth" advertising would be positive. After all, who understands the value of customers more clearly than the owner of the company?

But your employees also enter into the relationships with your customers, and they can have a profound impact on how customer service at your company is perceived. It's vital that you never disparage your customers in the presence of your employees—no matter how irritating or unprofessional those customers may be. Negative attitudes and comments somehow always seem to get back to the customer. Trust me on this one!

You are the one who has the responsibility to teach your employees that you do not pay their salaries, and that you do not pay the bills to keep the company in business. That role falls to your customers. *They* are the reason your employees are employed.

You are the one who must instill in each and every employee the paramount importance of quality customer service. Without top-notch service, your customers will become your competitor's customers.

KEN BLANCHARD AND SHELDON BOWLES ON CREATING "RAVING FANS!"

The last time you pulled into a service station, did you expect someone else to pump your gas for you, or did you do it yourself? Did you expect an attendant to clean your windshield, or were you simply hoping there'd be a squeegee and a bucket of water available? It wouldn't necessarily have to be *clean* water—just water, so that you could clean your windshield yourself.

Creating Raving Fans is all about deciding what you, as a company, want; discovering what your customer wants; and delivering **plus one** percent.

To decide what you want, you have to create a vision of perfection centered on the customer. Perfection, in the case of the service station, could mean pumping the gas for the customer, or cleaning the windshield.

To discover what the customer wants, you have to *ask* and *listen*. The reason you have to ask is that customers often hesitate to tell you about your product or service because they assume no one really wants to know what they think.

A Raving Fan relationship goes far beyond your company's product or service. If you don't listen to your customer's thoughts to learn his needs and desires, you fail to give him what he needs in terms of product or service because you don't know what that need really is. By not listening to him, you're saying his thoughts have no value.

To deliver **plus one** percent means that you not only must have a vision of what you offer and discover what the customer wants, but you must also be consistent—and deliver your product or service properly, time after time, without fail. Once you have that down you can exceed expectations! And that creates Raving Fans!

—Adapted from *Raving Fans* by Ken Blanchard and Sheldon Bowles
Copyright © 1993 by the Blanchard Family Partnership and Ode to Joy Limited

The new emphasis on quality in the world of business today has its roots in customer service—in putting that all-important purchaser of your goods or services first.

Several years ago, I stumbled across a book at my favorite bookstore. It's titled *How to Win Customers and Keep Them for Life,* authored by Michael LeBoeuf, Ph.D. After reading it, I went back to the bookstore, purchased a dozen copies, and essentially forced my employees to read it. They took turns serving as "discussion leaders" on the content of this book during our Monday morning staff meetings. It became mandatory reading for every new employee of the company. I could not recommend it more highly . . . along with the book from which I drew some excerpts above, *Raving Fans,* by my good friends Ken Blanchard and Sheldon Bowles.

As helpful as both of these books are, I hope you

aren't misled into believing that if you follow the authors' principles to the letter, you will never, or even seldom, lose a customer or client. Despite all the solid advice, *the truth is that customer loyalty does not really exist.*

People can and do develop loyalties toward other *people*. Occasionally, they may become truly loyal to a particular *brand*. But they are seldom, if ever, loyal to a *company*. A company is nothing more than a name on a door. It is hardly ever perceived as something that possesses a "personality."

In the chapter on growth, I offered my view of how value is judged, especially in difficult economic times. Quality, I said, takes a backseat to price in the customer's determination of the value of any product or service.

The highest level of customer service in the world often will not win out over the customer's perceived need to "get it cheap."

TIMES OF VULNERABILITY

There are certain times when your company is the most vulnerable—when your relationships with your customers are the most at risk. (By the way, this can also work in reverse. These same times of vulnerability may also provide the best opportunity to win new customers away from your competitors.) Such times are:

1. When the customer's "buyer" changes. This is one that affected us time and time again. The advertising manager or marketing director with whom we had worked leaves, and his or her replacement brings in a team of people with whom he or she is comfortable.

Naturally, we try to build a relationship with the new person, but it doesn't always work.

2. When the customer's owner changes. New owners, of course, bring their former relationships with them, and since they're the boss . . .

3. When the customer's needs change and you are unable to meet the new requirements. Hopefully, you've been watching trends and have been able to respond quickly enough to the changing needs of your customers, but sometimes their needs change suddenly and unexpectedly, and it may not be practical or profitable for you to respond.

4. When a new business offering a similar product or service is able to compete with you directly. For example, if you run a neighborhood grocery store, and a new mega-supermarket opens its doors two blocks away, your customers will likely give them a try.

5. When you make a mistake. Your customers can't afford to lose money or be placed in an awkward position with *their* customers as the result of your errors or omissions.

6. When you fail to deliver as promised. Your customers don't want excuses—they want what they want when they want it.

7. When the economy makes price the most important factor. It bears repeating that in a down economy, if you can't compete on price, you probably can't compete.

Keeping customers—and keeping them satisfied—will be a challenge for nearly every small business. For that reason, businesspeople will be forced to place an increased emphasis on acquiring a steady stream of new prospects and new customers. They will need to evaluate and improve their service, develop a competitive pricing strategy, and adapt their products or services to meet the changing needs and tastes of the customer.

There's only one way to play the game today: *Value your customers; treat them fairly; serve them well.* They *are* your most important business assets.

THINKING IT THROUGH

What customer service issues have been brought to my

attention? _____

_____

_____

How can I go about discovering additional issues that

could translate into loyalty problems? _____

_____

_____

_____

What steps should we take to resolve these issues and

improve service? _____

_____

_____

What can we do to build customer loyalty? _____

_____

_____

_____

Are we aware of any changes in our customers' situations

that could impact our future relationships with them? If so,

what are those changes? _____

_____

_____

_____

13

Your Vendors

In general, all business involves buying something (raw materials or the services of employees), doing something to it (fabricating it, merchandising it, or creating something of value from it), and selling it for more than you paid for it. As the first step of this process, most businesses have to work with vendors or outside suppliers.

Vendors are a vital link in the business chain, yet I've known business owners and managers who treat their vendors as though they represented the lowest form of prehistoric life. They are demanding, demeaning, overbearing, and unforgiving and act as though they could live without the very people who provide the goods and services that keep them in business.

The minute some other vendor walks through these managers' doors with a price that is a few cents lower, they will toss aside whatever relationship they had with their longtime supplier and switch loyalties—if you could call it that.

I've known other business owners and managers who have treated their vendors with the respect accorded to true partners. They are understanding, patient, supportive, and trusting. Of course, they expect good service and fair pricing, but they also reward outstanding performance through loyalty and friendship.

These managers realize that it is vital that their vendors make a profit. Suppliers that are not in a solid financial position cannot provide the levels of service and support, nor the timeliness of delivery, that these astute managers expect. Price pressure can also lead to the lowering of manufacturing standards, and an inferior product from a vendor will ultimately lower the quality of the end product or service.

Naturally, healthy and mutually beneficial relationships between your company and your suppliers must be built on the foundation of trust. You have an obligation to be loyal to those who have served your needs in an effective and timely manner. You owe it to them to make your expectations clear yet reasonable and to allow them to make a fair profit. For their part, your suppliers have an obligation to set fair, competitive prices, to keep you informed as to the status of your order, and to do everything within their power to deliver a product that meets or exceeds your specifications—on time.

The relationship between your company and your vendors—or between your company and your customers as a vendor to them—can be summed up in a few simple "fair trade practices."

SEVEN GUIDELINES FOR VENDORS

1. Realize that a successful business is built on the foundation of many customers who each have a role in that success. Do not try to make all your profit—"a big killing"—from one customer. Treat your small customers as though they are as important as your big customers. They are.
2. Deliver a product or service that meets or exceeds the specifications of your customers.
3. Deliver it on time.
4. Keep your customers informed with regard to any problems that may affect price, quality, or delivery schedules. Nobody likes surprises, except on their birthdays.
5. Pass any unexpected savings you realize along to your customers. It will build loyalty and create goodwill. Ultimately, it will help you fend off your competitors who may have already found the key to the delivery of a better product at a lower price.
6. Let your word be as binding as your written contracts.
7. Appreciate your loyal customers. By this, I don't mean "try to buy them off." But remember what's important to them. If they love golf, drop your business for an afternoon and spend time with them. Help them out with their favorite community service project. *Tell* them you appreciate their business.

SEVEN GUIDELINES FOR CUSTOMERS

1. Set reasonable expectations—make reasonable demands.
2. Do not beat your vendors up on price. Recognize that they must make a fair profit to remain in business.
3. Do not change the rules at halftime. Do not expect more than you bargained for, or change pricing or delivery schedules after the fact.
4. Do not drop a faithful supplier for insignificant or arbitrary reasons. Everyone makes mistakes. The mature customer makes allowances for the occasional mistake.
5. If possible, pay your vendors within their terms, and do not attempt to negotiate new terms of your own. (Do not pay them earlier than their terms require, however, for reasons that are forthcoming in the chapter titled "Your Capital.")
6. Let your word be as binding as your written contracts.
7. Appreciate your vendors. Don't take them for granted. For more than twenty years, we had a vendor who served many of our graphic production needs. Several years ago, to recognize the fact that they had never missed one of our deadlines, we gave them a simple engraved plaque—our "First Annual Lightning Award," on which we added the words, "To the great people who know the meaning of the word 'Rush.'" In the many years since that award was presented, they continued never to miss a deadline for us.

The relationship between you and your vendors should not be adversarial. You're "in this thing together." Without customers, there would be no vendors. And without vendors, virtually no companies would exist. There will never be a time, in any nation or in any economy, when one giant company will meet all the needs of the people. The world will always revolve around buying and selling. There will always be business . . . as usual!

THINKING IT THROUGH

What are we doing to demonstrate to our vendors that we value them? _____

_____

_____

What additional things could we do? _____

_____

_____

_____

14

Your Capital

Hundreds—perhaps thousands—of books have been written about capital. About money. How to acquire it, manage it, control it, invest it, and retire on it.

You could and would learn a great deal from these books. But much of what has been written is specific to a certain economic time or delves into specific investment strategies or assumes that the reader has significant assets to invest.

I believe that what every small business owner needs to do is to remember and apply just a very few basic rules. So I'm going to break the whole discussion down into its simplest form. Even if you believe these points are obvious and basic, it still would not hurt you to burn them into your memory.

THE SEVEN BASIC RULES OF CAPITAL

1. Move it in your door as quickly as possible.
2. Move it out your door as slowly as possible.
3. Pay as little for it as possible.
4. Save as much of it as possible.
5. Watch it as closely as possible.
6. Make sure more of it comes in than has to go out. That difference is called profit.
7. Know when to expect it and how much to expect.

This all sounds so basic, right? But I maintain (and have proven for myself) that if a small businessperson ignores one of these rules, the result is hardship. Ignore two, it's trouble. Ignore three or more, and it's time to write a résumé and contact a headhunter.

In order to understand how significant these basics are, we need to discuss them individually.

MOVE IT IN YOUR DOOR AS QUICKLY AS POSSIBLE

As the result of the good times, I had become inattentive to the need to do regular, timely invoicing of my clients. This had become a deeply ingrained bad habit that was difficult to break when economic times became leaner and meaner.

To correct this problem, I had to retrain our vendors to bill us more quickly, so we could generate our invoices on a tighter schedule.

Then, I had to make sure that our clients were paying us according to terms—2 percent/10 days, net 30.

I knew I had some clients who weren't. In fact, my little company had become the "bank" for a major client with expansive and highly profitable operations in a variety of industries. More often than not, I had to wait 180 days—6 months—to collect the money that was owed to me. I was almost embarrassed to ask clients for money.

To make matters worse, I have never employed a tough, aggressive person to do my "dirty work" for me.

Some of my clients had figured this out. And they used the information to walk all over me. My attitude toward my receivables has cost me literally hundreds of thousands of dollars.

What folly! I finally came to the realization that my receivables were **my money** due to me **for services I had already performed** and **for a product I had already delivered.** I had a perfect right to that cash.

If I didn't have my money, I couldn't use it to pay overhead, or to reduce debt, or to invest, or to save.

No matter whether the economy is in a boom or a recession, it's important to realize that there will always be customers who believe it is their right and privilege to use your money to operate their businesses.

There are a number of simple ideas you can employ to move cash in your door as quickly as possible. Some of them may be applicable to your business.

1. Insist on an up-front deposit as one of your conditions for doing business. Of course, if you operate a retail business and/or accept credit cards, this is a nonissue.
2. If you provide a service that will not be delivered immediately, but for which you will make an ongo-

ing investment of time or materials, develop a plan of "progress billings."

3. Spell out your terms of payment in advance, and make sure they are clear.

4. Follow up on your terms, and immediately go after the past-due money in an aggressive way.

5. If an account turns sour, turn it over for collection or pursue it through the courts without delay.

6. Avoid negotiating your invoices with your customers or clients. Once you head down this path, it's difficult to turn back. Your customers will attempt to negotiate every invoice from that point forward.

As the result of bad experiences, I am now resolved to bill quickly and to get on top of delinquent accounts immediately. The future of Priority Multimedia Group, Inc., depends on my ability to collect for services rendered. And because my current clients would probably have to bear part of the financial burden of bad accounts in the form of increased costs, I owe it to them to be diligent in the matter of receivables collection. I'm pleased to report that my new company has not lost any money due to bad receivables since I did my second start-up in 1995.

MOVE IT OUT YOUR DOOR AS SLOWLY AS POSSIBLE

The longer you can hang on to the cash that comes in your door, the more possible it is to meet urgent demands and take advantage of exciting opportunities that may come your way. The goal should be to have sufficient cash on hand to at least meet the next couple of payrolls, to maintain healthy account balances to enhance your credit report, and to generate some interest income . . . as pitiful as interest rates are nowadays.

In reality, one of the perpetual problems with small business is that no matter how attentive you are to billing and collecting—to moving cash in your door as quickly as possible—there is never enough money to go around (unless you are fortunate enough to be operating a profitable cash-only business.)

The result is that you may have to prioritize your bills—and determine which ones get paid when. While yours may differ, I have my own list of priorities—one that has worked fairly well for me.

1. **Payroll**—Without employees, you have no business. And no matter what great folks they are, miss a paycheck and they're "outta here" quick.
2. **The government**—The withholding taxes you collect from your employees is not your money. Don't *ever* treat it as though it is. The government—both federal and state—wants its money, and it wants it *now*. The penalties and interest charges are too steep for you to consider using tax money as a viable form of short-term financing.
3. **Insurance**—This is your protection against disaster. If you don't pay your insurance company, they won't pay you when your building burns down, or an employee contracts a serious illness, or your delivery van gets rear-ended.
4. **The phone company**—It takes just a few seconds for these folks to pull your plug.

5. **Other essential utilities**—Electricity, water. The stuff that makes the world go around!

6. **Your most crucial vendors**—The suppliers you need the most deserve to be *at least* this close to the top of the list.

7. **Credit cards, leases, loan payments**—You can usually get a grace period on these items. After all, they'll just collect more interest from you as a result, and interest charges are how they make their money. I really believe that they would actually prefer that you never pay off the principal, so they can go on collecting interest.

   Please understand that I don't *want* to be late on any payments, and I do pay the required late fees when I am. And remember, a good credit rating is vital to the future of your business, so do everything you can to protect it.

8. **Rent or mortgage payments**—It generally takes a long time for your mortgage holder to foreclose on a loan or for your landlord to turn you out on the street for default on a lease. For one thing, banks and institutional investors aren't interested in getting their property back. And landlords would rather get some kind of payment from you than have empty space on their hands. As long as you convince them that you're doing everything you can to continue to pay your obligations, they'll usually work with you. In difficult economic times, some landlords have willingly renegotiated leases midterm, to the tremendous advantage of the tenant.

9. **Noncrucial suppliers**—These are the vendors you don't really need to stay in business. It hurts to say

this, because I've been viewed from time to time as one of those vendors. But we *are* talking priorities here—so during those times when it's impossible to pay everyone on demand, these poor folks come in last.

10. **Club dues**—Club membership is about the most nonessential thing you do with your money. And, for the most part, people aren't exactly lining up to join private clubs, so the club's management will usually work with you.

11. **Lawyers and accountants**—Hey, *they* make *you* wait! Just remember all those times you've called their offices and heard, "I'm sorry, he's in conference and can't take any calls," or, "I'm sorry, she's taking a deposition and will be tied up all day." (And I actually *like* my attorney and my CPA. It's simply that when it comes down to a question of whether I keep my phone service or pay my lawyer first, I have no choice but to write the check to the phone company.)

Of course, the goal in prioritizing your payments must always be to keep your suppliers happy and preserve your credit rating.

One key I've discovered that enables me to keep my suppliers reasonably content with my payment schedules is to use as few of them as practical.

There was a time in our business when we used up to seven or eight photographers in a typical one-month period, to shoot product photos, models, ad layouts, brochure photos, and so on. The problem was, thirty days later, they all wanted their money. And because some of the projects on which they had worked had not yet been billed, and others had been invoiced to slow-paying clients, I did not have adequate cash to meet their demands. Those we were less likely to use again right away had to wait for their money.

I eventually used just two or three photographers in a month's span. And I used the same two or three on a continuing basis. I knew that I could pay at least part of the outstanding debt before I asked them to do another job. They were basically happy, and I was living under a lot less pressure.

There is, however, an inherent and obvious risk in having too few established relationships with suppliers. If you rely on one key vendor in every category, and haven't established backup relationships with others, you run the risk of being "cut off," which, in the worst case, could effectively put you out of business.

It's crucial that you understand that I am not, under any circumstances, suggesting that you ignore your bills, drag out payments that you *could* make, and create hardship for others, or "stick" the people to whom you owe money. I'm simply saying, hang on to your money as long as you can, and, during times when you're cash poor, have a plan for assigning priorities to your payables.

PAY AS LITTLE FOR IT AS POSSIBLE

One of the all-time dumb things I've ever done is to finance some of my computers, video equipment, and office furnishings on credit cards. I have traditionally enjoyed a good credit rating and have signed a number of equipment-lease deals at very favorable rates, but for some reason, I took the easy way out and rang up massive charges on credit cards. So instead of paying 6 percent or 9 percent or even 11 percent, I was paying 13.9 percent, 16.8 percent, 19.7 percent, or even 21.3 percent on bank credit cards. These are the same banks, by the way, that are paying 1 to 2 percent on savings accounts—at least at the time this is being written.

In the future, I'm going to take advantage of some of the lease options that make provisions for upgrades and offer fund balances.

The lesson that I've learned is to research financing options so that I pay as little as possible for the money I borrow. It may take some extra effort to find the best rates or financing options, but over the long term, it's worth it.

I've had some positive experiences with loans that offer floating interest rates tied to the prime rate or some other factor. In the best plans (at least the best for predicting cash needs), the monthly payments always stay the same, but the term, or number of payments required, changes. My last airplane was financed for a seven-year term under such a plan, and immediately after I purchased it, interest rates began to slip. I ultimately paid off my loan in six years and four months.

SAVE AS MUCH OF IT AS POSSIBLE

There was a time when making money in the advertising business was about as easy as growing weeds. In the late 1970s and early 1980s, despite double-digit inflation, double-digit interest rates, and nearly double-digit unemployment, the cash would just roll in.

I am completely embarrassed to tell you what I did

with it. And I deserve to be. But we're going to learn something here.

In addition to buying four boats (not all at the same time), two airplanes (also not concurrently), a company Mercedes, a corporate sports car, an office-full of hand-crafted walnut desks and conference tables, and a stereo that could fill the Houston Astrodome with rich, bassy lows and crisp, brassy highs, I *entertained.*

Princess Di—may she rest in peace—would have loved the way I entertained. I wore a tux. I knew how to order dinner in really poor French. I also knew lots of people with their hands out—the concierge, the mâitre d'hôtel, the captains, the waiters, and even the guy in the restroom who handed me a towel.

We were fortunate to have clients in both New York and Los Angeles—two great cities in which to entertain.

To properly amuse our New York clients, my creative director and I would make advance reservations for the hottest play on Broadway, check into The Plaza, and book pretheater dinner reservations at Windows on the World, with its stunning view from the very top of one of the twin towers of the World Trade Center. (How I miss those towers. It is heartbreaking to go to New York and not see them.) After dinner, we'd take a limo to the play. Following the curtain calls, it was a carriage ride through Central Park.

Of course, the properly trained business traveler always has to bring back gifts for the kids from FAO Schwarz and a trinket or two from Tiffany & Co. or Alfred Dunhill of London for the spouse.

The L.A. client didn't require the same level of atten-tion. But entertaining still involved an outstanding dinner at the Sportsmen's Lodge in Studio City or the Inn of the Seventh Ray in Topanga Canyon, or at one of the great ocean-view restaurants in Malibu.

You can only imagine how terrific I thought it was to finally get a client in San Francisco, the city of aftershocks, pretty bridges, and plentiful restaurants!

Things weren't too bad back in the Twin Cities, either. There were private clubs to join, new restaurants to try, and long business lunches to enjoy, featuring—you guessed it!—sushi!

We threw lavish Christmas/Hanukkah parties in our office for our clients and suppliers, complete with live entertainment. The next day, it would be the staff's turn. Overnight hotel rooms for everyone, limo to dinner, live music or perhaps a magician to entertain, and gifts and bonuses for all.

Meanwhile, the savings accounts, certificates of deposit, and other investments stayed about even. That's because I wasn't saving—I was spending.

But did I learn anything through all of this? It would not appear so. I noticed that we were doing so well near the end of 1991 that I decided I should share our good fortune with one and all.

Our holiday office party for 200 or so of our closest friends featured two Renaissance-period musical acts, two live Santas, plenty of food and drink, and me in my brand-new tux. To draw this crowd, we mailed 500 videotapes of a special homespun musical number we called "The Christmas Wrap," which featured our staff "rapping" on camera to the beat of an original musical track.

The next night, it was the overnight in individual suites in a local hotel, the limo, and dinner for the staff in a beautiful Victorian mansion that some claim is haunted. Some people simply don't learn. I appear to be among them.

In defense of our holiday festivities, I have to add that two fine charities did benefit. We gathered hundreds of toys for inner-city kids, as well as new clothing for both children and adults. And, instead of giving our clients a fruitcake or a weekly planner or other present, we made a donation in their names to Habitat for Humanity, an organization that provides low-interest loans on quality housing to families who might not otherwise have a home of their own. (Check into it: www.habitat.org. You could get involved!)

I have a newfound interest in saving, but that has prompted an interesting question: "When I do manage to accumulate some cash, where should I put it?"

I've lost enough in the stock market to know that I don't want to put all of it there.

My real issue with investing in other companies—especially small to medium ones—is that I have no say in how they're run, where **they** invest my money, or how they will respond to changing technologies and changing markets. The world is moving fast, and I'm doing all I can to *keep up* with the changes in my industry, let alone *anticipate* those changes. I plan to take the conservative approach.

As a result of that thinking, we now hold investments (limited though they are) in Pacific Rim mutual funds, European funds, conservative U.S. growth funds, certificates of deposit, a variety of IRAs, a good 401(k), regular savings accounts (which are a joke these days, but at least they're highly liquid), and whole life insurance.

Many of my financially astute associates ridicule whole life insurance, pointing to the fact that term insurance provides essential protection when it is most needed (the early earning years) at a fraction of the cost of whole life. But, frankly, I don't buy insurance for protection alone. It is not my goal to make my children wealthy when I die. Let them start their own businesses and make it on their own. The best gift my parents gave me was a sense of urgency about "doing it for myself," and the feelings of pride in accomplishment that resulted.

My whole life policies are with one of the best-rated, most financially sound companies in the country. If they go under, there probably won't be an economy to worry about.

The major advantages I've found in whole life insurance are: the premium is predictable because it stays the same as I get older, the money I put in is returning 12 percent or better in dividends and paid-up insurance, and, when I need quick cash, I have always been able to borrow it at 8 percent, even when interest rates were at their all-time high. On top of all that, I can pay back my loans on my schedule. And when I retire, I can choose to take out my money in the form of an annuity, with a guarantee that payments to my survivors will continue for a minimum of ten years if I die within that period. Does our great national retirement plan, Social Security, offer that? No, but it should, considering what I pay into it!

You have probably developed, or will develop, an investment strategy that puts mine to shame. I hope so! But, above all, I hope you set aside a significant portion of your earnings in some form of "savings" program. There will likely be lean times ahead, and you will be in a better position to survive them if you plan for them during the good times.

WATCH IT AS CLOSELY AS POSSIBLE

Throughout this book, I've bared my soul and pointed out the big mistakes I've made through the years, in the hope that you won't make the same ones.

Here's one of my biggest mistakes.

I haven't, until recently, watched my receivables. Something this simple just shouldn't be overlooked.

I haven't asked for cash up front from clients whose credit is doubtful. I haven't asked for credit applications, I haven't checked their credit status, and I haven't moved quickly enough to collect when things turned sour.

In the old days, I very seldom sent out monthly statements to follow up the original invoices. Now I realize how important that is!

I now watch my receivables. And I do more than watch. Now the emphasis is on collecting.

But there are other aspects to watching your capital. They are: watching your expenses and watching your payables. The first of these will be covered in the point that follows, but the latter deserves attention here.

I once had an employee who didn't understand that ad agencies are supposed to bill clients for the gross amount for an ad and pay the media the net amount. The difference is called the "agency commission." It amounted to 15 percent of the gross. That's how we made a considerable portion of our money.

This individual had a unique approach to the situation: Bill the client for the net amount, and pay the media the gross amount. It wasn't until a magazine publisher phoned us to ask why we were being so generous that we discovered the problem.

The point is, don't assume anything. Don't take it for granted that your outgoing invoices are correct. Spot-check to make certain that suppliers are being paid no more than they deserve. Make sure that the amount they bill you is the same as their estimate, or the same as the number that appears on your purchase order.

In short, make sure that a competent person on your staff is checking, cross-checking, verifying, and reporting any discrepancies to you. And take the time to recheck for yourself from time to time.

MAKE SURE MORE OF IT COMES IN THAN HAS TO GO OUT

One of the ways to make sure that more money comes in than has to go out is to watch your expenses carefully. Loosely translated, that means watch your overhead.

The notion of "fixed overhead" is, in my experience, a myth. There was never anything fixed about my overhead. Parts of it may have been fixed, but I'm not sure which parts they were. Health insurance premiums increased. The percentage on the employer's share of FICA went up nearly every year. Employees expected raises. The cost of basic phone service increased. Letterheads, business cards, and forms cost more every time we reprinted them. That doesn't sound like "fixed overhead" to me.

What I *have* learned in more than three decades in business is that while my overhead is never fixed, it *can* be watched and controlled.

In most businesses, the two biggest expenses are inventory and payroll. Depending on the business, one may outstrip the other dramatically. A book could be written on inventory control, and, fortunately for you, several have been.

Although my businesses of yesterday and today are based on people, ideas, and technology rather than inventory, I believe I have some observations worth noting.

The key to inventory is to meet the end demand, whether that demand is for quantity, timely delivery, or diversity. Where many companies go wrong is that they don't balance those three factors. They get wrapped up with the "just in time" strategy to the point where one slip does them in. Or they adjust inventory based on today's sales and are unable to meet tomorrow's demand.

One of the worst cases of inventory management I've ever seen occurred in a small gift shop in an upscale specialty shopping mall in an affluent Twin Cities suburb. This shop positioned itself as the source of the perfect gift for the person who had everything. Their shelves were stocked with the unique, novel, hard-to-find, high-tech gadgets that excite people like me.

I was so enthusiastic about the store that I pitched them to become a client of my ad agency. I had visions of their concept becoming a chain of nationwide franchises. And I'd be in on the ground floor. (In fact, someone actually did it soon thereafter. They called their company The Sharper Image.) Unfortunately, I think, for both of us, they refused my offer. They believed their upscale location was enough to carry them.

As I continued to visit this store, I noticed that their offerings were becoming less unique, less novel, less high-tech—in fact, ordinary. They weren't searching out new, exciting products, and they weren't stocking enough of what they did have. The shelves were becoming bare.

Here's the climax of this story. One holiday season, my staff gave me a gift certificate for this store. I went there to cash it in. And, to my surprise, my favorite store—the one that used to be jammed with goodies I craved—didn't have *one* thing that I wanted.

I cashed in my gift certificate on something I didn't really want, because I guessed that they'd be out of business within a few months. And, sure enough, they were. In their misguided attempt to make sure that more cash came in than went out, they had depleted their inventory of the very things they needed to sell to remain in business.

The opposite approach also poses significant problems. A former client, a boat dealer, felt certain that the way to sell more boats was to make sure that the showroom floor and outdoor lot were jammed to capacity with new boats. This seemed to work when interest rates were low. But then, they suddenly ballooned, and he was faced with the high cost of financing his "floor plan." He obtained a second mortgage on his house to see him through. It didn't. His business succumbed to the heavy load of excessive interest costs. More was going out than could possibly come in.

To determine your cash needs, try to take into account the many changes that could occur—in interest rates, taxes, operating expenses, and the increased costs of raw materials or inventory. Have a strategy to deal with those changes if and when they occur, so that you're not caught short. Have cash in the bank or be in a position to raise selected prices or reduce certain costs quickly. Make sure your relationship with your bank is healthy and secure. The worst time to go scouting for a new bank is when you need to.

KNOW WHEN TO EXPECT IT AND HOW MUCH TO EXPECT

With a few short-term exceptions, my business always looked good on paper. I always had substantial assets, significant receivables, and a healthy backlog of orders. At the very same time, I looked in the checking account and found that it was running on empty.

When that happened, I looked at receivables and tried to predict how sound they were and project when I could expect them to turn to cash. And just when we thought we knew the payment habits of a certain client, that client threw us a curve. Thirty days suddenly became ninety. As the inevitable result, our payables slowed down and our vendors got a little nervous.

Today, in my current business, I do a regular cash flow analysis and projection. I can't believe that The Gottry Communications Group survived as long as it did without this information.

The bottom line—to use an overworked term—is that no matter how great your product or service is, no matter how timely your delivery is, no matter how professional your employees are, if you're not following the seven basic rules of capital, you're opening the door to almost certain disaster.

THINKING IT THROUGH

What policies could I establish (especially with new clients/customers to move cash in my door more rapidly?

_____

_____

What can I change in order to move cash out my door as slowly as possible? _____

_____

Where should I place cash/how should I use cash when it is available? _____

_____

What steps can I take to reduce the interest I pay?

_____

Where can I find money to stash away? What can I consolidate? What purchases can I delay or cancel? What should I consider selling to raise reserve capital?

_____

_____

What procedures/policies should I follow if I notice negative changes in cash flow and collections? _____

_____

How often should I examine my pro forma to determine if there are ways to increase profits?_____

Which clients pay in 10 days? 15 days? 30 days? 45 days? 60 days? _____

_____

Based on that knowledge, how much money can I expect to receive in 10 days? 15 days? 30 days? 45 days? 60 days? _____

_____

What specific steps can I take with each specific client to speed up receivables? _____

_____

_____

15

Your Relationship with Your Community

No matter what size your business is—or someday will be—there are tremendous rewards that result from caring about others.

Under federal tax law, corporations can give away up to 10 percent of their taxable profits. (They can actually give away as much as they want. They just can't take the excess as a tax deduction.)

Ten percent of profits doesn't sound like much, but if every corporation were to follow this guideline, this nation would have much less poverty, substandard housing, and far fewer diseases and hungry children than it does now.

What, then, can we do to impact our communities? To give back to the people who have helped us succeed in our business endeavors?

The avenues for service are almost endless and readily available. You don't have to do something on a grand scale. Begin with something small. Discover how great doing it makes you feel, and you'll be eager to do more.

What are some of the things I have done over the years?

Because my team and I created print advertising and collateral material, we often donated our creative work to charitable organizations whose purposes we supported. We created brochures for a Twin Cities program that helps, counsels, and comforts children who are victims of sexual abuse. We produced direct mail pieces for an organization that places orphans from a variety of Third World nations with loving families.

To help others benefit from our experience in radio, television, and video production, we created commercials and programs for the March of Dimes, the Minnesota AIDS Project, and the Children's Program of Northern Ireland, an organization that transported young kids from their strife-torn environment and placed them in American homes for the summer months. In 2003, we created and produced a video for UMOM New Day Centers—homeless shelters in Phoenix. We didn't get paid for it because our services were donated, but we did have the satisfaction of winning two national awards for our work—and helping a worthy organization raise money from the private sector.

Over the years, I've volunteered to ring bells for the Salvation Army, I've spent an annual day cleaning up a city park, and I've sold roses to raise money to support the local food shelves, provide a source of fresh water for impoverished villages in the Dominican Republic, and purchase coats, mittens, and scarves for disadvantaged schoolchildren.

If none of these ideas appeals to you, here are some other things you could consider:

You could sign up for the Adopt-a-Highway Program, and you and your staff could keep a one- or two-mile stretch of highway free of litter. (In most cases, the name of your company appears on a sign along the stretch of road you maintain—an added public relations benefit.)

You could plan visits to—and holiday programs for—the people confined to the long-term care facilities in your area.

You might want to consider making provisions for time off work for those who want to volunteer to work with Boys Clubs/Girls Clubs or lead a Girl Scout or Boy Scout troop.

Many communities have programs to deliver meals to the elderly or immobile people who are confined to their homes. They need drivers. You and your employees could do that!

There may be a program that needs volunteers to cook and serve meals to the poor and homeless. Here in Phoenix, I know of many churches and other groups that sign up to serve one meal each week at the UMOM New Day Centers. As a side benefit, they develop an esprit de corps among themselves that would be the envy of any company!

Every small business owner should have a sufficiently developed "environmental conscience" to do the small things we all can do. Take the painless step of providing recycling containers for aluminum cans, glass bottles, and paper. Cancel multiple subscriptions to publications, and route one or two copies throughout the office instead. Produce "rough" copies of your laser-printed documents on the back sides of previously printed paper. Use recycled paper and packaging products whenever possible. And resist the "overpackaging" of the products you manufacture.

If you are a successful businessperson, you have a responsibility to give something back to your local community—and to our global community. You also have the opportunity to provide leadership to your employees, so that they can experience the rewards and self-esteem that result from service to others.

Don't base your decisions on what you believe might be the eventual benefits to your company. Ask, rather, how your involvement will benefit your community and make it a better place for you and your employees to live. I guarantee you will never regret it!

THINKING IT THROUGH

What products or services that we offer could benefit worthwhile charities? _____

_____

What specific examples of community involvement could I set for my team? _____

_____

How could I gain the involvement of customers/clients in

local causes? _____

_____

_____

Are there any statewide, nationwide, or international

causes we should consider? _____

_____

_____

Should I consider giving employees time off to volunteer

for community activities? _____ If so, what

kinds of activities should be encouraged? _____

_____

_____

What types of activities should not be allowed? _____

_____

_____

PART THREE

Conquering
Your Natural
Enemies

16

Busy-ness

I'd pay big bucks, if I had them, for days with more hours in them. The twenty-four each of us gets simply aren't long enough to do everything that needs to be done. The demands of my business—coupled with my writing commitments—could easily consume all twenty-four hours.

But while I love my business, I don't want to spend every minute of every day enslaved by it. I strive to balance my time so that my wife and I can build our relationship . . . so that my teenage daughter and her adult brother and sister can share their daily victories and defeats with a caring, involved father . . . so that I can read, reflect, and learn during my few private moments . . . so that I can enjoy the larger circle of family and friends . . . and so that I can serve my community through my involvement in helping meet the needs of others.

I'm a committed believer in play, too. There's no

harm in taking a break in a busy week to shoot nine—or even eighteen—holes of golf. There's no evil that results from spending an extra day at the cabin over the Fourth of July weekend. Your business won't be irreparably damaged if you work out at a health club three days a week, or take a Friday afternoon off to go boating or hiking with your family. In fact, your company may be better off as the result of the "mind cleansing" qualities of play.

What all of this means in terms of my business is that I have to be as productive as possible during business hours. And, if I am to achieve the goals I have set for my company, I have to ensure that my employees are as productive as possible, too.

This means taking control of "The Great Time Wasters."

- The commute.
- The telephone.
- The morning mail.
- E-mail.
- Meetings.
- Systems and procedures.
- Paperwork, reports, and memos.

THE COMMUTE

If you live in an area where traffic congestion turns your commute into a major time commitment (L.A., Dallas, or even Phoenix, for example), or if trips to other parts of your city are a routine part of your business day, you need to maximize your use of that otherwise minimally productive time.

In addition to the obvious answers, such as attaching your headset and placing and returning calls on your cell phone, or catching up with the world through news radio, I've found a couple of other productive activities.

I like to turn my drive time into learning time through CDs or audiocassettes. Many of the CDs I listen to are related to business issues. But I also listen to the so-called "self-help" programs, including those motivational gems from the likes of Zig Ziglar and Dr. Denis Waitley. And a recent "find" for me is a series of CDs by Robert T. Kiyosaki about investing in rental property. I've listened, I've followed his advice, and it's worked!

I also carry a small tape recorder or digital voice recorder in the center console or on the passenger seat, so that if I have an idea worth remembering, I can get it down in audio form. This alternative is a lot quicker and safer than trying to fumble with paper and pen to jot something down.

I've found, too, that I can cope with traffic better by listening to calming music—classical or so-called "smooth jazz."

Although it's difficult to pull off if you're in business for yourself, through carpooling you can gain valuable ideas and insights from other people. You can increase your knowledge and understanding of world events, and, occasionally, you can pick up a valuable business lead. If carpooling is not a feasible option for you, at least suggest it to your employees—so that your company can do its part to reduce wasteful gasoline consumption.

THE TELEPHONE

As much as I love my cell phone because it makes my drive time more productive, I hate routine phone calls while I'm working on my computer. Nothing interrupts a great thought more effectively than a phone call, and nothing irritates me more than a caller who doesn't understand when the call should end. Add to that the problem of "telephone tennis," and you have the essence of my frustration with phones.

I have a friend in business who takes every call that comes in for him without having any calls screened whatsoever. That would drive me crazy. Just the calls from the stock and commodity brokers who want to add me to their client lists, or the long-distance providers who want me to switch to their service, would chew up the bulk of my day.

I rely on caller ID and voice mail to screen my calls. If I don't recognize a number, I'll wait to see if the caller leaves a message. I can skip through useless voice mails quickly, so that saves a lot of time. If you have a receptionist who answers your phones, prepare—and ask your receptionist to study—a list of the important people with whom you have significant relationships—clients, suppliers, prospects, and friends. If a caller isn't on that list, the call should be handled by someone else and referred to you only after all the details are known—name, position, company, phone number, and purpose of the call.

If I'm in the middle of a project—writing a book or editing a video, for example—but I know that I have some errands to run and I'm going to be in my car for an extended block of time, I bring all my messages with me and return the calls on my cell phone. When I leave the meeting or appointment I drove to, I pick up new messages and return those calls on my trip back to the office. (Again, use a headset, please!)

Another effective habit to develop is to return all calls during specific "phone blocks." Set aside 10:30 to 11:00 in the morning, for example, to return all early-morning calls, and 3:30 to 4:00 in the afternoon to return all late-morning and afternoon calls. Incoming calls after 4:00 P.M. get returned the next morning. If you do business in other time zones, you'll need to adjust your phone times.

Of course, if your business relies on incoming calls for sales, these techniques will probably not apply.

THE MORNING MAIL

Every book or article I've ever read on office efficiency offers the same advice: "Handle each piece of paper only once. Answer it in writing, respond to it by phone, delegate it to someone else, file it, or throw it away. Whatever you do, do it immediately to reduce clutter and frustration."

Great advice. But I can no more follow it than I can flap my arms and expect to fly. My tendency is to sift through the pile of daily mail and look for the important stuff. *That* I respond to immediately. The less urgent items get placed in priority piles.

Part of my problem with the daily mail is that, because one of the things I've always done is to create direct mail packages for many of my clients, I like to see what techniques other direct mailers are using.

Another problem is that, thanks to *Macworld* magazine, The Sharper Image, and others for whom I have "opted-in," I have made it onto nearly *everyone's* mailing list. You would not believe the catalogs I get in the mail. Because these fine companies have gone to the trouble and expense to send me their literature, I feel morally obligated to read it all.

You want to drive your spouse crazy? Put a three-foot stack of magazines and catalogs next to your bed, and keep the bedside light on for at least an hour after he or she tries to go to sleep.

It gives me great pride to be able to report, however, that I am in recovery. I now throw away (read that: recycle) at least three-fourths of this bulk before I read it.

I've also developed a series of prepackaged responses for a wide range of other mail, from résumés to requests for charitable contributions and free writing and design work.

And I now handle every piece of paper only *twice*. That's progress, believe it or not. I'm confident that I'm on the road to recovery!

E-MAIL

While my "Britney Spears," "free" and "Viagra" spam filters have been quite effective, I still get a lot of junk . . . with "real" e-mail sprinkled in from time to time. The best way I've come up with to deal with all of this is to deal with it—on the same day. Dump it in the trash as quickly as I can. Then answer the real e-mails right away, even if I have to offer a brief response accompanied by an apology. I copy the e-mail to myself as a prompt—especially if it requires an additional response from me.

I have eliminated a lot of the hassle of responding to e-mails by creating multiple "signatures." Your e-mail program likely offers you a convenient way to do this. I assign clear and concise names to all of my signatures so that I know which one to include in a particular reply. And, by the way, signatures don't have to appear at the bottom of your e-mail. You can drag them, or cut and paste them, to anywhere you want. Saves you lots of time.

My basic signature includes my contact information along with a sales message that usually promotes my latest book. Other signatures range from "Thank you for taking the time to write to me. It's always great to hear from my readers, and I'm so pleased that my book helped you." Oops! I probably should not have revealed this little secret to you! Truthfully, though, I actually do respond personally to every complimentary e-mail that I receive. So far!

MEETINGS

Want to waste a lot of time? Have a lot of meetings!

Meetings can be one of the greatest threats to productivity faced by any business. My belief has long been that you can either hold meetings or you can do real work.

But there are some meetings that are inevitable—and necessary. Among the valid purposes they can have are:

- To communicate information efficiently to everyone on your staff and get their feedback.
- To obtain timely reports from employees.
- To conduct interviews with job applicants.
- To conduct job performance reviews.

- To analyze procedures and develop strategies.
- To solve a specific problem.

There are ways to conduct more productive meetings and reduce the amount of wasted time.

First, set and adhere to a strict starting time. Don't let people hold up the meeting by wandering in whenever they feel like it. One of my more strong-willed former employees used to want to exhibit control and make a statement about how important he was by making his grand entrance several minutes after the rest of us were seated. After all, he must have reasoned, he was crucial to any discussion we might have, and, indeed, I was delaying the start of any discussions until he arrived and settled in. Eventually, I calculated how much productive time he was destroying, so I restated the need to begin meetings on time and began to do so. In subsequent meetings, we were well into our agenda by the time he arrived. He didn't like it, but he didn't change, either. For that reason and many others, during my period of economy-driven "right-sizing," I concluded that his maverick behavior was something I did not need.

Second, set and adhere to a strict stopping time. When a meeting lasts beyond its useful life, it becomes less and less productive, and more of a social event. Make sure that when you have handled all old and new business, you end the meeting.

Third, limit the attendance at all meetings to only those people who need *to attend.* The larger the meeting group becomes, the more unwieldy it becomes. Hopefully, your company doesn't employ insecure babies whose feelings get hurt if they're not included in a particular

meeting. This is more of a problem in smaller companies than in medium to larger ones. At one time, I felt I
had to include everyone in every large-scale meeting to
avoid hurt feelings. While I have always been sensitive to
the need to make everyone feel that they are part of the
team, I recognized the need to limit the size of meetings
and explained that productivity (profits) are more
important than meetings. If an employee could be
doing his or her job instead of attending a meeting,
that's what that employee should be doing.

Fourth, establish a set agenda in advance. Have a well-
defined purpose for the meeting and know what topics
you want to cover as well as how much time you want to
allow for each topic. In the advertising business—and
possibly in your business—there is one notable exception. The free-wheeling, unstructured brainstorming
session. Sometimes it's better to let wandering minds
wander, especially when the goal is a creative solution.

*Finally, keep an accurate record of who attended, what was
discussed, who contributed to the discussions, and what was
decided.* This exercise has three functions: It will help you
weed out unnecessary attendees, it will help you eliminate unnecessary or unproductive meetings, and it will
help you follow through on decisions and individual or
group assignments, so that you don't have to schedule
the same meeting again to discuss the same topics.

SYSTEMS AND PROCEDURES

Some companies can be so bogged down in systems and
procedures that they become immobilized. They let
their operations manual dictate their every move, with

the argument that to ignore procedures is to invite chaos.

As the owner of a business, you have the choice. You can do the work of busy-ness or do the business of work. You can run your business, or you can let your systems run it for you.

Every company in these high-tech times seems to have a computer addict among the ranks. I made the mistake of letting our resident computer-head set up some new, efficient office systems based on the latest time-saving software.

The first problem I encountered was that, while he was hired as a creative director and was responsible for generating a certain amount of billable time (profits) each week, he immediately began to devote much of his time and attention to his real love—the Mac on his desk. The result: reduced income for the company.

The second problem I encountered was that some of the "efficient office systems based on the latest time-saving software" were a complete waste of time, energy, and money.

One program, Office E-mail (a predecessor of today's e-mail), was supposed to make the relaying of phone messages and other interoffice communications more speedy and efficient. Every time my computer beeped at me, I knew I had a message. I would have to switch from what I was doing to Office E-mail, retrieve my message, and, after I had read it, respond by e-mail. Then, I would have to electronically "throw it away"—a two-step process during which my computer asked me, "Are you really sure you want to throw this away?"

All this, in a company of only ten people in an office

that was less than one-hundred feet end-to-end, and thirty feet crossways. After months of frustration, I finally made an executive decision. "If you have a question for me, write it down, come see me in my office, or call me on my phone extension. If there's a phone message for me, jot it down on one of those pink 'While You Were Out' slips." The minute I took myself off Office E-mail, everyone else asked if they could do the same, because they disliked it as much as I did. The guy who set it up in the first place kept the program on his computer, but since there was no one else to talk to on the system, he eventually gave up.

E-mail today has taken on an entirely new role. But, please, if you're twenty feet away from someone you need to talk to, go talk to him or her! It's far more personable! And it actually often takes less time!

Don't let systems take over your business. It will be difficult to regain control. Sometimes simple manual systems are actually better than computerized systems. Other times, computer reports are far superior. Determine where you need people, where you need computers, and where you need to apply common sense. Don't let giant software companies tell you how to do what you need to do.

PAPERWORK, REPORTS, AND MEMOS

Do you have Memo Writers on your staff? These are the people who feel the need to leave a paper or e-mail trail covering every thought and deed. I don't know if they're frustrated would-be journalists, if they're trying to prove how much work they accomplish, or if they simply want backup in the unlikely event you ever end up in a courtroom face-off.

Some time ago, one of our clients told the story of an employee who made certain that his brilliantly conceived memos would be read by the boss. He would type up the memo, photocopy it twice, keep one copy for his files, and then send the boss the original plus one copy. Both copies would have the key points highlighted by a yellow marker, and a yellow Post-it note would be attached, with the directive "Please see the attached memo" written on it. He would then do a follow-up e-mail asking, "Did you receive my memo regarding such-and-such?" I swear this is true. I have seen these critters. They are incredible.

If you must write memos or e-mails, keep them brief and to the point. There's no need for flowery language or detailed explanations. Instead, train the people who read your memos to ask you questions if there's something they don't understand. (Okay, maybe go into more detail than responding with the letter "C.")

You will be able to gain mastery over the time wasters if you always remember this key point: The purpose of business is to create and sell a product or provide a meaningful service—at a profit. If the activities you and your staff pursue on a daily basis do not contribute to that goal, they are nothing more than time wasters. They are busy-ness.

THINKING IT THROUGH

How can I gain the most benefit from my commute?

_____

_____

How can I take control of telephone calls? _____

_____

_____

How can I conquer the stacks of mail? _____

_____

_____

How can I master the flow of e-mail? _____

_____

_____

How can I make meetings more productive? _____

_____

_____

How can I streamline (or even eliminate) systems and procedures? _____

_____

_____

How can I reduce the amount of paperwork, reports, and memos with which I have to deal? _____

_____

_____

17

Busybodies

There's a good possibility that there are murderers on your staff. Cold-blooded, calculating killers. Their immediate victim is time. Their ultimate victim may be your company.

I wish I had all the time to kill that those on my staff did. But it was—and is today—my company. I have always skipped lunch to try to make it work. I have always begun my day early and ended it late.

Do you have two (or more) employees who think it's their job to gossip? Is the coffee machine their most important business tool? Is lunch with one another the most essential activity of the business day? Does your office telephone hold the key to success for their entire social life? Do they step outside to make calls on their cell phones? Do they delight in telling fellow employees that you're "the Enemy," but "if you stick with me, I'll show you the ropes and we'll take control of that boss of ours"?

I discovered the hard way that one rotten attitude can spoil the whole barrel. I knew that the problem had been festering for some time. My mistake was that I didn't confront it head-on—immediately.

It's easy to let things slide, especially the things that involve confrontation and conflict. No one wants to get into an argument. No employer wants to "ruin" someone's life by laying him or her off in difficult—or even good—economic times.

Fortunately for me, the three people on my staff who had "busybody-itis" left of their own accord. They were replaced by people who really cared about the company and wanted to see it succeed.

But while the busybodies were still a part of my life, they succeeded in aggravating me beyond description. The reason was that there was simply no way to deal with them that didn't involve their getting angry, creating a bigger stir, and compounding the problem.

For example, if someone I needed to see was on a personal phone call, I used to mouth the words, "Come see me when you're finished," and then walk away—and wait for him or her to finish and get back to me. It occurred to me that this was wasting my time, and that the message wasn't getting through.

I realized that people might have an occasional need to make a personal call during working hours, but they should have had enough respect for me and the company to keep those calls to a minimum and to keep them brief, or to make them during breaks. The problem was that those repeated calls would last twenty minutes to a half hour each. Finally I concluded that if they couldn't control their calling habits, I would try to control them.

My initial solution was to stop by first, mouth the words that I wanted to talk to them, and leave for one minute. Then I would return and stand at the offending person's desk until he or she decided to hang up. A few of them considered this action on my part to be an invasion of their privacy, but I viewed their phone calls to be an abuse of my valuable time—and a form of direct stealing from the company.

Then I hit on the ultimate solution. These people didn't have enough to do. Either I had to find more meaningful work to occupy their workdays or I needed to thin out the staff. No boss likes to lay off employees, but when profits are being squeezed, an "early retirement" or two could easily be the best option.

The truth is, most people like to be busy. Good employees don't like to sit around and do nothing. If they have something significant to do and they enjoy their jobs, the days fly by!

THINKING IT THROUGH

What can I do to make sure that my team produces everything I need them to produce? _____

_____

What can I do to ensure that all of my employees are fully engaged? _____

_____

Which employees need more attention in that area right now? _____

_____

What can I do to keep people busy doing productive work? _____

_____

_____

Which employee(s) is (are) not contributing right now?

_____

_____

How can I help him/her/them make greater contributions? _____

_____

_____

What can I do to build teams based on accountability?

_____

_____

18

Sloppiness

If "loose lips sink ships"—as the old military saying goes—it is equally true that "sloppy work sinks businesses."

When you first saw the word "sloppiness" as the heading of this chapter, you probably thought its content would focus on employees and the sloppy work habits that seem to prevail on the job today. Yes, we'll be getting to that matter in a few pages. But the best place to begin is with the boss—the entrepreneur who started the company.

THE SLOPPY EMPLOYER

The most effective small business owners and managers have successfully overcome what may be their natural tendencies to be a bit "sloppy." There are several simple keys that help conquer this problem:

1. Be committed to follow-through, both for yourself and your employees. Draft a schedule of the recurring tasks you need to complete and check them off as you complete them.
2. Make sure that employees submit reports on time so that you know what's going on in your business. You need to know, for example, whether or not your salespeople are actually selling.
3. Focus on the important tasks. Prioritize, so that you don't get caught up in small details. Learn how to "triage."
4. Verify that someone is maintaining your database—of customers, prospects, vendors, distributors, government agencies, and so on. Sloppy record-keeping can destroy your company.
5. Stay on top of collections of credit accounts.
6. Don't wait until the last minute. Inevitably, something will come up that will cause delay. Anticipate the unexpected.

As a small businessperson, you have *so much* to do. Some things will simply have to wait. The key is to know what things can wait and what things need your immediate attention.

KEN BLANCHARD AND STEVE GOTTRY ON "TRIAGING"

The concept of triage as it applies to your business life is based on wartime medical practices. When the battles rage all around, wounded soldiers are rushed to the medical unit, where a triage nurse is assigned to assess the severity of their injuries and the likelihood of their survival.

Those soldiers with minimal non-life-threatening wounds are sent to the back of the treatment line, as are those severely injured soldiers who have little chance for survival. Top priority is then given to those whose injuries can be effectively treated and whose lives can be saved.

Throughout your business career, you will face countless instances in which you must triage effectively in order to be the most productive.

Each of your tasks will likely fall into one of three very straightforward columns: **Yes, maybe,** and **no.**

The **yes** tasks are:

- Those things you **have** to do and **want** to do.
- Those things you **have** to do but **don't want** to do.

The **maybe** tasks are:

- Those things you **want** to do but **don't have** to do.

The **no** tasks are:

- Those things you **don't want** to do and **don't have** to do.

I am constantly amazed by how many **no** tasks people place in the **yes** or **maybe** columns, and how many **maybe** items find their way into the **yes** column. Golf would be my best personal example. It takes tremendous resolve on my part to keep from moving a game of golf from my **maybe** column to my **yes** column!

But I can promise you that if you can learn to triage successfully in every business situation, your odds of staying in business will increase dramatically!

—Adapted from *The On-Time, On-Target Manager* by Ken Blanchard and Steve Gottry
Copyright © 2004 by the Blanchard Family Partnership and Priority Multimedia Group, Inc.

There are four things that need your immediate attention—four areas than cannot be the victims of your own sloppiness and lack of triaging skills:

1. The needs of your employees, or interpersonal communications matters. Train them, encourage them, manage them, support them, empower them, and then let them do their jobs!
2. The needs of your customers or clients. You need to contribute to *their* success! You need to make sure that they are your raving fans!
3. The need for cash. You need a continuous flow of it on a regular basis in order stay in business!
4. The need to cover your behind—legally, morally, financially. *Do* the details!

I addressed the first point in the chapter "Your Employees," the second in the chapter titled "Your Customers," and the third in "Your Capital."

The fourth point also deserves some discussion, because I have learned the hard way that sloppiness in this area will ultimately hurt your business.

There is a tendency on the part of many business owners to procrastinate on some matters and skip over the details on others. The excuses usually sound valid. After all, the reason for being in business is not to perform nonessential "busy work." The basic needs of any business are to perform the tasks that directly affect productivity and produce income. There are, however, administrative tasks that cannot be overlooked. This is my short list of "must-do's." Consider it for your business.

- Make sure your insurance is up-to-date, that all potential perils are covered, and that everyone who should be enrolled in various health, disability, and life insurance programs really is.
- If you require signed contracts from your employees (such as noncompete/nondisclosure or general employment contracts), make sure they are signed before their start dates, and that they are uniformly required of all employees.
- If you operate a service business, your contracts with your clients should also be in order, and if a matter comes up that may get resolved only in court or in arbitration, you should take action quickly.
- All forms and reports required by the government should be filed accurately and without delay. You should perform periodic checks to make sure you

comply with all current regulations. Don't take it for granted that every employee or every department is automatically in compliance.

· Your sales tools should be up-to-date and readily available. You should never run out of forms, check blanks, letterheads, business cards, and other routine materials.

· Your inventory control system should be accurate and should provide sufficient lead time for reordering/restocking.

If you are sloppy in any of these areas, there's a good chance your errors and omissions will be staring you in the face down the road. Ultimately, no business can afford sloppy management.

THE SLOPPY EMPLOYEE

One of the most difficult issues I faced during the restructuring of Gottry Communications and my subsequent second start-up was that my new employees had to correct the mistakes, oversights, and poor performance of their predecessors. When my new team discovered these problems, they realized that no one who had gone before them had even so much as followed the basics of their job descriptions or adhered to the most elementary procedures. The sad truth is that all of this was mostly my fault. I'm the one who let things slide into disarray. I was out at the airport, gassing up my airplane.

There's absolutely no challenge associated with finding sloppy workers who don't produce. The challenge is in finding, hiring, and retaining the competent, detail-oriented employees you want and need, because every other company out there wants and needs them, too.

Sloppy workers can lose customers for the company, and it can cost you huge sums of money to correct their mistakes. Their poor-quality work could even result in life-threatening situations.

In our business we created and produced a significant number of printed pieces for our clients, including brochures, catalogs, annual reports, and direct mail packages. It wasn't all that uncommon for the larger of these projects to cost $25,000, $50,000, or $100,000 or more, when all of the costs of writing, design, photography, and printing were totaled. A major error in one of these projects (for example, placing the pages in the wrong order) could lead to the client's rejection of the entire piece. We'd have to eat the cost of printing—often the major cost in the project. (In the case of this book, imagine what would have happened if the book bindery had placed Chapters 4, 5, and 6 ahead of Chapters 1, 2, and 3. Every copy would have had to be scrapped.)

To prevent errors and omissions, we established an elaborate system of checks, cross-checks, and sign-offs, which we called our "set in stone" procedures. This system was quite effective, but invariably, when someone on the staff took a shortcut (usually because it was a "simple job" that didn't require all those cross-checks), a mistake slipped through and we had to throw away the job. When an ad said "Prudential *Reality* Group" instead of "Prudential *Realty* Group," we had no choice but to rerun a corrected version of the ad at our expense. Fortunately, the client had a sense of humor, and we didn't lose the account as a result.

Sloppy work can even become a life-and-death matter, as I nearly discovered. My airplane was in the shop for a mandatory annual inspection and was returned to service with a clean bill of health. I was about to take it out for a flight when I decided that I'd better remove the cowling that covered the engine just to make sure that all the bolts, clamps, hoses, and wires appeared to be there—and in the right places. I discovered that the mechanic had left a screwdriver sitting on top of the engine. Had I not found it, it could have easily slipped and slid into the path of the belt that drives the alternator. In flight, this could have precipitated a mechanical chain-reaction that may have ended in disaster. (Mechanics who work on airplanes, like the pilots who fly them, are certified by the FAA, a department of the federal government. It *does* make me wonder, sometimes.)

It's a simple fact of life that everyone makes mistakes. As the boss, it's your responsibility to make sure that systems are in place to both minimize mistakes and diminish the negative effects of the mistakes that do occur. It's also your responsibility to pay attention to your business—to make sure that you "mind the store" and follow through on the hundreds of little details that are a daily part of small business. Don't let poor work habits trigger the domino effect. There may be no way to stop the chain reaction once the first domino falls.

THINKING IT THROUGH

What sloppy habits do I need to deal with personally?

_____

_____

What tasks do I personally need to triage? _____

_____

_____

Who among my employees has sloppy habits? _____

_____

_____

What are those habits? _____

_____

What can I do to help those employees triage?_____

_____

What "set in stone" procedures do I need to establish to

minimize errors and increase profits? _____

_____

_____

19

Debt

I am convinced that the leading cause of insomnia, hypertension, and irritability among the ranks of small business owners is excessive debt. The kind of debt that causes you to toss and turn half the night as you repeatedly ask yourself, *How am I going to find the money to cover all of this?*

That's not to say that debt isn't inevitable or necessary. No business that I know of can operate completely free of debt. Equipment has to be financed. Buildings require mortgages. And having an adequate inventory to meet demand usually requires financing.

But there are ways to control debt, so that it doesn't control you. I've implemented some of these controls in my business almost from the start. Others I've discovered more recently, as the result of the ravages of the up-and-down economy and the need to finance my current business venture.

First, don't buy things you don't really need, until

such time as you don't really need the money you'll have to spend to get them. Invest in things that will make you money. Over the years, anytime I had some "extra" money, I spent it on things that added no real value to my company. In other words, these acquisitions didn't increase my power to generate sales or income. Earlier, I mentioned my travel-and-entertainment habits, but that's just the so-called tip of the iceberg. I spent money on artwork, decorative antiques, mirrored walls, upgraded carpet and window treatments, and big-time stereo systems for every employee's office—among other things. Instead, I should have been investing in meaningful production tools, better software, buildings, land, and cash reserves.

Second—and this almost sounds contradictory—don't buy cheap things over and over. Buy quality the first time. This is something I've usually done right. I had a walnut desk of a simple modern design custommade for me in 1973, and it is still the desk in my office today. I bought a top-quality leather executive chair in 1977, and I finally had to discard it in 1999, when the leather on one of the arms finally cracked through. In contrast, I've done considerable bargain hunting and have purchased low-grade leather conference-room chairs that haven't lasted two years. You usually *do* get what you pay for (hardly ever more than you pay for, but often less), and the cheap stuff has always proven to be just that—cheap.

Third, to make sure you don't get tired of the quality things you buy, avoid fads and trends. Buy solid traditional designs or clean, simple modern designs. Make sure the materials used are enduring natural products rather than the trendy man-made substances that might look totally out of place in a year or two. If you walked into my office today, you would probably admire my desk, without having any idea that it is a "modern" design that's more than 30 years old. (Oh, that's right, you would; you read about it here.) The point is that I'm still pleased with many of the purchases I made 15 or 20 or 30 years ago—and I would probably still have been pleased with most of the things I had to sell under duress. In fact, here's an exercise for you. Rent the DVD of the 1962 James Bond film, *Dr. No,* and take a close look at the bedrooms into which the mad scientist's henchmen escort Sean Connery and Ursula Andress. Those still-stylish sets are the work of skilled set designer Ken Adam, and they are a tribute to the nature of enduring design.

Fourth, reread the chapter on capital, and memorize what I said about financing with high-interest credit cards. I'm convinced that bank cards were invented by the devil himself.

Fifth, don't go into debt on fancy cars. All cars have three things in common, whether they are a Rolls-Royce, Mercedes-Benz, Jaguar, Buick, Chrysler, Hummer, Chevrolet, Honda, BMW, or Ford. They break down, they depreciate, and eventually, they become old, ratty, and nearly worthless. Okay, I know. You need the flashy car to enhance your image. That may be true, but let's be reasonable here. Do you really gain more "image" by driving a $55,000 or an $85,000 car than you would by motoring around in a $25,000 or $35,000 car? If it's that important to you, then buy a clean, well-maintained, pre-owned example of the make you want. Most people won't know the difference. Or care. (True, there are "collector" cars that actually appreciate—I know someone who bought a Ferrari for $20,000, put some "sweat equity" into it, and sold it for $400,000—but you have to know what you're doing.)

Sixth, sell equipment, furnishings, and other assets that you don't need as soon as it occurs to you that you don't need them. The longer you wait, the less these items will be worth. I had the good fortune of selling four computers that I didn't need about three months before the manufacturer offered a major price reduction on a very similar replacement model. Had I waited, the prices on my used equipment would have dropped dramatically and instantly. I did wait too long on another piece of outdated equipment, and I ran numerous classified ads to sell it—with no response. I eventually paid someone to haul it away.

Seventh, use any new cash you generate (via the sale of equipment or other means) to reduce or eliminate the long-term debts on which you pay the highest interest rates. I realize that interest is a business deduction, but you have to earn the money to pay the interest to take the deduction. Interest costs you—no matter what.

Eighth, refinance your long-term debt and consolidate as much of it as you can at lower interest rates. You will have to run the numbers to make sure the bottom line works, but don't overlook this option. During the recent period of declining home mortgage interest rates, businesspeople were standing in line with the rest of America, refinancing their homes. Because I have every intention of staying in my present home for several more years, I jumped at the chance to lower my interest rate by 2⅛ percent. After wrapping the minimal closing costs into the new loan, I will come out "even" in less than a year, and gain after that. It was simply the smart thing to do. Yet, many of the same businesspeople who jumped at the chance to refinance their homes continue to make payments on equipment and business loans at yesterday's interest rates. (Yes, I realize that interest rates change, and as you read this book, they could be headed in either direction. Just make sure you watch them—and do your best to do the right thing at the right time.)

The result of following these simple suggestions is that you will reduce your debt load, conserve future capital, sleep better at night, and be less crabby toward your employees, friends, and those with whom you have close, lasting relationships.

THINKING IT THROUGH

Where am I paying too much interest? _____

_____

_____

What have the trends in interest rates been over the past

six months? _____

_____

_____

On what accounts should I try to renegotiate interest rates?

_____

_____

What debts should I reduce as quickly as I can?

_____

_____

What debts can I eliminate right now? _____

_____

_____

What impact will debt reduction/elimination have on
my bottom line? _____

_____

_____

Should I investigate new sources of financing? _____

What should I look into? _____

_____

_____

20

The Government

It may be a bit of an exaggeration on my part to include the government on the "enemies" list. After all, the government provides good and valuable services without which we could not be in business. Streets and highways are about the simplest example there is.

On the other hand, the government expects your cooperation in several areas, and if you do not comply with its regulations, you could, indeed, discover a new enemy.

Here are a few quick suggestions that will help you prevent any unfortunate confrontations:

- Pay taxes on time, and file all forms and returns by the due date—unless you can afford to pay penalties and interest. Any accountant will tell you that once you've "flunked" a tax audit, no matter how small the error or omission, it is likely that you will be a perpetual target for audit. This can get to be quite expensive in terms of professional services and lost time.

- Don't blur the distinction between what is a legitimate business expense and those things that should be categorized as personal expenses. Personal use of a company automobile is one obvious area. Personal use of company credit cards is another. I don't so much as use a postage stamp from the postage meter to mail a personal letter or bill without paying back my own company.
- Carefully scrutinize your "travel and entertainment" expenditures. The IRS does not want people to write off their vacations. I believe the safest way to play the game is to write off expenses only when the trip is 100 percent for business and does not have any personal component whatsoever. That means that even though it worked out well for my board of directors to hold a meeting in southern California while my family and I were there on a vacation trip, I did not claim any business expenses or deductions for the trip. My view, however, may be more conservative than that of your accountant.
- Know, understand, and follow the government's directives related to discrimination, equal opportunity, sexual harassment, and other matters.
- Make sure your workplace is safe and up to code.
- Check your licenses and permits to be certain that they are all current.
- Post required government posters in a conspicuous place. (Posters such as minimum wage and occupational safety and health are in this category.)
- Treat government employees who may pay you a visit with courtesy and respect. For the most part, you'll

find that they are people with lives similar to yours—they may have families, cheer for the same sports teams, shop at the same grocery stores, and do their absolute best on the job.

These are ways to avoid conflict . . . but even the government offers some room for improvement. What are the best ways to accomplish this?

The first one is, you can help *elect businessmen* and *businesswomen* to positions in local, state, and federal government. If you are able to identify a probusiness candidate, do more than vote for that person. Volunteer to work on the campaign. Drum up support from other businesspeople. Write supportive letters to the editor. Put a campaign sign on your lawn. Make a contribution to the campaign fund. We need more people in public office at every level who understand our concerns and needs.

Second, you can *join an organization that helps your voice be heard* on Capitol Hill. There is strength in numbers—a single voice may be ignored by our lawmakers, but many voices speaking in unison cannot be dismissed so easily. I would suggest that you consider joining your local chamber of commerce as well as an organization such as the National Federation of Independent Business (NFIB). NFIB was established primarily for the purpose of lobbying on behalf of the concerns and interests of small business. For a modest annual membership fee, you are able to participate in regular membership surveys, the results of which define the organization's legislative priorities. You also receive a "report card" on the voting record of all senators and congressmen on issues crucial to small business, as well as a nifty little magazine called *MyBusiness*. (I've listed the address and phone number for NFIB's membership office in the Appendix.)

We have only one federal government, like it or not. We need it to be a government that is our friend, not our adversary. We need to follow the guidelines set forth by government bodies. And we need to work harder to elect people who have been in business and understand that small business is the foundation of our economy. It's the only way our voice will be heard and our treatment will be equitable.

THINKING IT THROUGH

What systems/procedures are in place to make sure I comply with all requirements for filing government reports and forms on time? _____

_____

Do I and my employees clearly separate personal expenses/charges from business expenses/charges? _____

Are my licenses and permits current? _____

Am I missing any necessary documents? _____

Are there any safety modifications I have not yet made?

_____

Am I willing to commit some of my time and money to research the positions on business of the various candidates for U.S. Senate, U.S. House, state legislature, and city government? _____ What am I willing to do to get the best probusiness candidates elected?

_____

_____

21

Addiction

Alcohol. Cocaine. Pills of various shapes, sizes, and content. These are the things that come to mind when the word "addiction" is mentioned.

Chemical addictions are serious, true, and impact your company's ability to produce your product or provide service to your customers. But there are other less visible—and equally insidious—addictions that can wipe your slate clean. Addiction in any form is the enemy of business.

The most common addiction is *workaholism*. And the most common defense for workaholism is, "My company won't survive if I don't give it all I've got." Addictions, though, are often triggered by an avoidance mechanism. Excessive hours at work can often be used to avoid an unpleasant home life or other non-work-related responsibilities. The office, store, or shop becomes a "comfort zone" in which one can focus on a single set of problems, rather than face the larger sphere of problems associated with this complex experience called life.

Workaholism can often result from the *fear of delegating*. There are four components that underlie this fear:

- "No one else can do the job as well as I can do it."
- "If I assign the task to someone else, I'll probably have to do it all over anyway."
- "If someone does it better than I can do it, unless I'm at the 'employer' level rather than the 'manager' level, I could eventually be out of a job."
- "So I guess I'll just *do it all myself, procrastinate* on the really *important things,* prove to anyone who cares that I really am a workaholic, and ruin my life beyond all recognition."

Yes, delegating is a fearful process. People *do* fail. In delegating, the real trick is to find employees whose failure rate is so low that a profit can be made in spite of those failures. Obviously, if the cumulative cost of an employee's mistakes exceeds the potential revenue that could be generated by the work tasks they perform, that employee is more of a liability than an asset and should be replaced.

I believe that no one initially intends to be a workaholic. The pressures of business sneak up on the owner, and slowly and imperceptibly, he or she goes into the office earlier and earlier—and leaves later and later.

This level of "devotion" to work is not good for the family, for relationships, for marriage—and if you never "turn it all off," you are never able to refresh your mind.

Workaholism is even more likely to become a problem in a recession, when it becomes increasingly difficult to keep your head above water. You come to believe that the only way to improve your financial position is to put in those extra hours in the office, store, factory, or shop.

Technology addiction has recently become a problem for companies that utilize computers and other electronic marvels. Usually it strikes the owner of the company, but in my case, I told you that it attacked one of my employees.

One of the problems directly associated with technology addiction is that when a company puts a new technology in place, there is a learning curve associated with it. You lose productivity because your employees are in training. Ultimately, the results could be positive, but try to evaluate in advance whether the proposed technology will ever compensate for the lost time and eventually pay for itself. We made some software changes a few months ago that still have not had a positive impact on productivity. In fact, even though the training cycle has been completed, the new system is more time-consuming and generates more needless paper than the old system.

As owners, we often find ourselves paying our employees to learn new information that will likely change before they have assimilated it all. In our businesses, countless hours are lost to the learning demands of ever-changing technology.

Toy addiction seems to be reserved for business owners of the male gender. This is the one that got me. I am a marketer's dream—an early adopter. I want to "be the first on my block" to get the new this-or-that.

I was one of the first people I knew to own an electronic calculator, way back in the early 1970s. It cost me $425. Now I can buy one that's smaller, performs more functions, doesn't require a huge, heavy AC adapter, has easier-to-read numbers, and costs a mere $3.99.

I paid $4,000 for my first Motorola portable cellular phone. Of course, I could use it the very first day they started cellular service in the Twin Cities. Now tiny phones that take pictures, permit text messaging, receive e-mails, and allow Web browsing are dirt cheap—if not free, assuming you sign the right contract.

When I bought my first compact disc player, it cost $400, and there were only a handful of titles available on CD—priced at $20 or more each. Today, you can buy a machine that plays DVDs, CDs, mp3s, and who knows what else for less than $100—in some cases, much less. And I recently paid a buck a piece for brand-new, factory-sealed DVDs. (Okay, so one of them was an old John Wayne movie, one was a Shirley Temple classic, and the others were such gems as episodes of *The Beverly Hillbillies,* so it could be argued that I got what I paid for.)

Toys can be cars, boats, airplanes, computers, or innumerable kinds of gadgets. If their acquisition gets in the way of running an effective, productive, and profitable business, it's time to take another look at them.

Perfectionism is an addiction that drives far too many owners of small businesses. In a previous chapter, I pointed out that while I don't believe in perfection, I believe in the *quest.* I believe each of us should always strive to do a better job. The difficulty arises when the boss forgets that "perfection will never become reality."

Valuable employees can be driven from the company as the result of unrealistic expectations.

As an employer—as a human being—you have to accept the fact that people make mistakes. You will never find the perfect employee. Good management involves reducing the frequency of your workers' mistakes and controlling the negative impact of those mistakes on profitability. At our company, we operate under a simple philosophy: "The more pairs of eyes that scrutinize a job, the better that job is likely to become, and the fewer the errors that are likely to be overlooked."

The *longing for acceptance and recognition* is an addiction with the hidden power to destroy a small business. Its most common symptom is the inability to say "No." As a result, the boss accepts every offer to head up charitable drives, serves as the chairman of every civic committee, prepares speeches for every worthwhile audience, and performs at least one "good deed" every day.

Usually, the motives can be rationalized. "A responsible businessperson has an obligation to give back to the community" or "It's great PR for the business." Good points. I believe in PR, and, as you know, I believe in giving back to the community. But I don't believe you should get so involved that your business goes down the tubes and your family doesn't remember what you look like. Don't let a healthy longing for acceptance and recognition become an addiction that controls you.

The list of addictions that could afflict the small businessperson is a long one. I know of those who are sexually addicted, who are compulsive gamblers, and who are even addicted to daily religious rituals.

It really doesn't matter whether the addiction is chemical, social, sexual, religious, or material, any compulsive behavior is likely to destroy you, as a businessperson, or your company—most likely both. If you, or someone who knows you intimately and cares about you, becomes aware of a potential problem, your first step should be to seek professional help. Quickly, courageously, and without embarrassment or hesitation. Don't let pride do you in. You're worth too much. Your family, your friends, your employees, and your customers all value you.

THINKING IT THROUGH

Am I aware of any addictions that I need to control? If so, what are they? _____

_____

What steps should I take to overcome my addiction(s)?

_____

_____

Am I aware of any employees who are struggling with addictions? If so, who are they? _____

_____

_____

What plans/programs should be explored to help them?

_____

_____

In what ways am I a perfectionist? _____

_____

Am I imposing unreasonable demands on my employees?

If so, what are they? _____

_____

_____

22

Fear

If being in business for oneself meant easy and abundant money, total freedom and independence, no pressure, pleasant vacations, plentiful diversions, restful nights and worry-free days—in other words, a problem-free life—*everyone* would be doing it.

But it's never happened in the past, it ain't happening now, and it ain't going to happen in the future.

Anyone who has ever been in business knows that it's never "steady as she goes." There is turbulence, uncertainty, and pressure. There are demands that, at times, seem overwhelming. Ultimately, the life of every small businessperson is impacted by the most dreaded of all emotions—fear. And that list of fears borders on the infinite.

Will my customers return again?

Will my clients renew their contracts?

Will I be able to make the next payroll?

How will I pay my bills?

What will happen if my key employees leave the company?

Is my family doing okay in the midst of all my business concerns?

What will be the result of this or that particular decision?

What will I do for a living if my business fails?

And ultimately: Will I be able to retire in comfort and security?

In a robust, growing economy, all of these fears can be sublimated with a certain degree of success. The fear of whether or not there will be enough money to cover the next payroll crops up from time to time, but, for the most part, when business is good, fear is reduced.

A recession, particularly a long and grueling one, provides a sharp contrast. Fear keeps the average business owner awake at night. I know, because, over the years, I have spent a lot of long hours in the fear closet.

I'm not an expert on the psychological implications of, or control of, fear. There are other books that explore the subject in depth. You can find them online or at your closest bookstore.

But I have learned four things about fear that have helped me better understand and deal with it.

The first is that *fear is common to all of us*. We all have our own favorite fears. The big, tough former head coach of the Oakland Raiders, John Madden, I am told, is terrified of flying. He travels from city to city to fulfill his sports telecast assignments by motor coach—a luxurious palace on wheels. I, on the other hand, loved flying my own plane, but I'm afraid of climbing tall ladders. Some business owners I know are afraid of public speaking; others are afraid of water. What is one person's rational fear may seem completely irrational to another.

The fear that is shared by virtually everyone I know, though, is the fear of failure. None of us wants to be a flop. We want to be the brightest and the best in our chosen business ventures. Understanding that this fear is not uncommon is the first necessary step in dealing with it.

The second thing I've come to understand about fear is that *it is "just" an emotion*. It's not an irrefutable law of science or nature. It's not set in stone. That's why our fears change over time. We're not always afraid of the same things, because our fears change with both age and circumstance.

The third point about fear is that *it's controllable*. The key to controlling it is to understand it. **Why** does this or that particular fear exist?

For example, if John Madden understood flying—how airplanes work, why flying is truly the safest form of travel—he might conquer his fear of flying. Knowledge is power. (On the other hand, I am convinced that ladders will never be safe!)

If, as the result of the process of acquiring knowledge about a fear, we are able to change the circumstances that surround it, we can control or eliminate it. If we are unable to change those circumstances, the fear will be an ongoing "reality" for us.

Here's an example: I have the fear that I will not be able to make my next payroll. My fear is based on the knowledge that I do not have enough money in my payroll account. Based on that knowledge, I realize that I must change my circumstances, first, for the short term, and ultimately, over the long term. Short-term changes could include borrowing from the bank, collecting a receivable, selling an asset, or cashing in a certificate of deposit. Long-term changes could include reducing overhead, raising prices or profit margins, increasing the speed of the billing cycle, cutting back on the size of the staff, or gaining wage concessions.

If I am unable to change any of the circumstances that led to the original problem, my fear of not meeting the next payroll will be an ongoing "reality" for me.

Finally, fear has a roommate—a close and constant companion called "tension." Unfortunately, unchecked tension can lead to all sorts of health problems, including headaches, high blood pressure, heart attack, and stroke.

To deal effectively with tension, I believe it's important to have diversions that are totally unrelated to work. They could include hobbies, music, or exercise—anything that takes your mind off the problems at hand.

I'd like to be able to report that I am "fear free," but that is simply not the case. What I can report is that I refuse to allow my fears to control my life. That's because many of my fears have become reality—and that fact did not irrevocably ruin my life. The reason is that I never experienced "the fear of starting over!" I was ready to stand up, dust off my clothes, and go at it again. Small business has too great an appeal to me.

If your worst fears ever come to pass—if you lose a major client or can't make payroll or two of your employees start a competing company and take half of your business with them—those situations do *not* have the power to destroy you. Unless you let them.

Overcome fear by facing it, then moving on!

THINKING IT THROUGH

What are my greatest fears right now? _____

_____

_____

What is my plan for dealing with them? _____

_____

_____

Am I willing to discuss my fears with someone else?

_____

_____

With whom can I discuss them?_____

_____

_____

23

There's Always Tomorrow!

I hate to be the one to tell you this, but someone has to.

There's a good chance your new or current business could fail. In fact, varying research indicates that 30 to 40 percent of general business start-ups fail in the first year, 60 to 80 percent fail by the end of the fifth year, and 85 to 90 percent fail by the end of ten years.

I was surprised to learn that, despite my long-held belief to the contrary, restaurant start-ups actually fare slightly better than general businesses. Research shows that 26 to 27 percent of new restaurants fail in the first year, 50 to 60 percent fail by the end of the third year, and 70 percent fail by the end of ten years. A little better, but still somewhat intimidating.

I need to qualify those numbers for you, however. The determination of failure rates for small businesses is impacted by differing definitions of "failure." Failure is used to describe anything from bankruptcy, to closure for the sole reason that the owner wasn't making as much profit as he or she wanted. Closure of a business does not necessarily translate into failure, but in most of the statistics quoted, small business closures were included in the "failure" percentage. Most statistics I found did not offer any indication as to what kind of failures were included, but that doesn't really matter, because even if the margin of error is 25 percent, the numbers are still bleak.

So why do people risk everything to go into business?

I've scattered several reasons throughout this book. Your reason to start a new venture may be that you got laid off and want to try something new. Perhaps you simply want to be your own boss. Maybe you've "done it all" and you seek the challenge. Possibly you recognize that if you're successful, you will make more money than you could by working for someone else.

I took business failure rates and the other challenges of small business ownership into consideration when I opened my own ad agency.

On that very first day, the battles began. I fought recessions, inflation, downsizing, employee disloyalty, and a host of other challenges. I defied the statistics and made it to five years. I even celebrated the twentieth anniversary of my business. Then, just a few years later, my ad agency became a statistic.

That left me with only one option. I decided to start a new business.

I knew it would have to be a different kind of business designed to fill new and emerging needs. I knew I'd have to run it in new ways. I knew I'd have to control overhead more tightly than I ever had before. But I knew that my only option was to pick up what few pieces were left and start a new venture.

I believe that once an individual has had a taste of the independence, freedom, and sense of accomplishment that a small business offers, that individual will never be satisfied working for someone else.

My hope is that this book will help your business succeed, and that the fact that I began anew will inspire you to pursue your dreams no matter what comes your way.

Throughout the preceding pages, I've focused primarily on the business aspects of my story, because that's the information that will best help you face your present and future business challenges. But there are still some missing pieces of my personal story—things that may inspire you to maintain hope and demonstrate the depth of your character and the scope of your leadership skills.

Yes, I told you about the car accident, the broken bones, the lightning strike, the attack of the giant ants, and my dad's losing battle with cancer. Huge downers. Every one of them.

But I have not yet told you that when I woke up every morning during those dark years, I was greeted by the warm smiles and tight hugs of my wife and daughter. I haven't told you about the glory of the changing leaves in the fall, or the beautiful sunrises and stunning sunsets that seemed to be painted in the sky just for me.

I haven't told you about the never-failing support and encouragement I received from my entire family, or the remarkable realization that my friends were going to stand by me—no matter what. I honestly thought that when the goodies were gone, my friends would be gone, too. I soon discovered that they didn't care about the "toys" with which I entertained them, the parties at which they were my guests, or the rather lavish lifestyle I shared with them. They cared about me! What a wonderful awakening that was!

The introduction to this book was probably all you needed to convince yourself that I was being driven by materialism. I'm certainly not going to tell you that there's something wrong with driving a nice car, owning a boat or airplane, furnishing your house with fine furniture, or carrying a Tumi computer bag. I *am* telling you that I've had all those things, and they'll never replace family, friends, or peace of mind. I'm telling you that my priorities have changed.

Will I always want to own and operate a successful growing business? Yes!

Do I still have dreams to chase? Yes!

Will I continue to look with some envy at companies such as 3M and Microsoft, which were once small businesses and are now profitable industry giants? Of course!

Am I willing to pursue success at the expense of my marriage and family? Never!

Is the accumulation of money the reason for my existence? Absolutely not!

It's finally occurred to me that when one does have money, it should be used to enrich the lives of others to the greatest extent possible. As I go about the business of growing my business, it is clear to me that I have a share of the responsibility for the poor, the hungry, the homeless, the elderly, and the ill. While I've always had a heart for the less fortunate, I haven't always done my full share. I'm the only one who can change that.

Am I going to be driven by fear? Not a chance! You'd be amazed by how well I sleep these days!

Am I going to let anger toward the people who have let me down and broken my trust build up and destroy my peace of mind? No! People will always be people. I know they'll disappoint me from time to time. In facing the situation of my former employees who violated their contract and took away some of my clients, one of the things I realized was that I had to practice what I preach. I could either be angry, and allow that anger to eat me alive, or I could forgive them for wronging me. I chose the latter and wrote them a letter and told them they did not have to adhere to the terms of a court-ordered settlement and make payments to me for the business they were doing with my former clients. I never received a reply to my letter, but I know I did the right thing. My anger has been erased—completely.

Ultimately, I had to ask myself this question: "Am I going to do my best under the circumstances?" **No!** I'm not going to let circumstances control my life. I'm going to do *better* than they allow. I'm going to live a positive, hopeful life, in spite of the circumstances, because I believe I have a positive hopeful future!

Some of my friends and business associates have noticed that the glum, depressed person who lost his money, sold his Mercedes, said good-bye to his airplane, let go of his toys, closed his office, and moved to sunny Arizona to start over is having one "kick" of a time at it. Yup, I admit it. I'm having fun! I'm wearing a bigger smile than I ever have before. My wife no longer asks, "Are we rich yet?" She asks, "Are we having fun yet?" I answer, "Yes!" And she agrees.

I have confidence in our future together.

But how about your future? What can you expect?

As you come to the end of this book, I want you to know that you can be certain of some things in life—in addition to "death and taxes."

You can be certain that operating a small business will always be a great adventure—because you will always confront the unexpected. That's exciting, and it's one of the many things that make being an entrepreneur so appealing to me.

You can also be certain that the economy will always have its peaks and valleys, and that the changing economic environment will affect every business to some extent. As a businessperson, you will always have to adapt to change, and perhaps rethink and redirect your dream.

You can count on technology to change, too. Just as the computer revolution impacted my advertising business by enabling some of my clients to do their work in-house, there are other—now unimaginable—technological changes ahead. Be alert to the changes that could affect your industry and your business, and consider your possible responses carefully. Seek the advice of others, as well.

You can also be assured that you and I, if we are true entrepreneurs, will never be satisfied reporting to someone else. We will find a way to be in business for ourselves. We will create our own golden opportunities. We will remain positive . . . hopeful . . . energetic. We will anticipate every tomorrow with eagerness.

And we will use every bit of common sense we possess to achieve business success and positively impact the lives of our employees, our suppliers, and our customers!

APPENDIX

FOR INFORMATION ON MEMBERSHIP IN THE NATIONAL FEDERATION OF INDEPENDENT BUSINESS, WRITE TO

National Federation of Independent Business
53 Century Boulevard, Suite 250
Nashville, TN 37214
Phone: (615) 872-5800, (800) NFIB-NOW
Fax: (615) 872-5899
www.nfib.com

PARTIAL LISTING OF BUSINESS CONSULTING ORGANIZATIONS AND INDUSTRY ASSOCIATIONS
(Please note that many of these organizations have local chapters that would welcome your inquiry and membership.)

American Association of Healthcare Consultants
5938 North Drake Avenue, Chicago, IL 60659
Phone: (888) 350-2242, (773) 866-2770
Fax: (773) 463-3552
www.aahc.net

American Council of Engineering Companies
1015 15th Street, Suite 802, Washington, DC 20005
Phone: (202) 347-7474   Fax: (202) 898-0068
www.acec.org

American Society for Training and Development
1640 King Street, Box 1443, Alexandria, VA 22313–2043
Phone: (800) 628-2783, (703) 683-8100
Fax: (703) 683-1523
www.astd.org

Association of Consulting Chemists and Chemical Engineers
P.O. Box 297, Sparta, NJ 07871
Phone: (973) 729-6671   Fax: (973) 729-7088
www.chemconsult.org

Association of Executive Search Consultants
12 East 41st Street, 17th Floor, New York, NY 10017
Phone: (212) 398-9556   Fax: (212) 398-9560
www.aesc.org

Association of Internal Management Consultants
86 Clarendon Avenue, West Rutland, VT 05777
Phone: (802) 438-2882   Fax: (802) 438-9859
www.aimc.org

Association of Management Consulting Firms
380 Lexington Avenue, Suite 1700, New York, NY 10168
Phone: (212) 551-7887   Fax: (212) 551-7934
www.amcf.org

Association of Professional Materials
Handling Consultants
8720 Red Oak Boulevard, Suite 201, Charlotte, NC 28217
Phone: (704) 676-1184   Fax: (704) 676-1190
www.mhia.org/apmhc

Financial Executives International
200 Campus Drive, Suite 200, Florham Park, NJ 07932
Phone: (973) 765-1000   Fax: (973) 765-1018
www.fei.org

Franchise Consultants, International
Franchise Association
1350 New York Avenue, Suite 900, Washington, DC 20005
Phone: (202) 628-8000   Fax: (202) 628-0812
www.franchise.org

Independent Computer Consultants Association
11131 South Towne Square, Suite F, St. Louis, MO 63123
Phone: (800) 774-4222, (314) 892-1675
www.icca.org

Institute of Management Consultants
2025 M Street Northwest, Suite 800, Washington, DC
20036–3309
Phone: (800) 221-2557, (202) 367-1134
Fax: (202) 367-2134
www.imcusa.org

International Network of Merger and Acquisition Partners

525 Southwest Fifth Street, Des Moines, IA 50309
Phone: (515) 282-8192   Fax: (515) 282-9117
www.imap.com

National Association of Export Companies

P.O. Box 3949, Grand Central Station, New York, NY 10163–3949
Phone: (877) 291-4901   Fax: (646) 349-9628
www.nexco.org

National Association of Personal Financial Advisors

3250 North Arlington Heights Road, Suite 109, Arlington Heights, IL 60004
Phone: (800) 366-2732, (874) 483-5400
Fax: (874) 483-5415
www.napfa.org

Professional and Technical Consultants Association

(Membership concentrated in Northern California)
543 Vista Mar Avenue, Pacifica, CA 94044
Phone: (800) 747-2822, (650) 557-9911
Fax: (650) 359-3089
www.patca.org

Public Relations Society of America

33 Maiden Lane, 11th Floor, New York, NY 10038–5150
Phone: (212) 460-1400   Fax: (212) 995-0757
www.prsa.org

Society for Human Resource Management
1800 Duke Street, Alexandria, VA 22314
Phone: (800) 283-SHRM, (703) 548-3440
Fax: (703) 535-6490
www.shrm.org

Index

acceptance, longing for, 297
accountability, 188, 190
accountants, 142, 231, 287
   advice from, 60, 62, 118, 121
   bankruptcy and, 142
   payment of, 231
accounting software, 59
acquisitions, 105
Adam, Ken, 283
addiction, 293-96. *See also* substance
   abuse
Adobe Photoshop, 57
Adopt-a-Highway Program, 247
advertising, 96-102, 105, 128
   budget, 101-2
   media-based, 74, 76-83
   public relations vs., 96
   public service, 246
   purpose of, 97-99, 101
   "word of mouth," 212
   yellow pages, 83-84
advertising agencies, 77, 82
   commissions, 238
   getting most from, 99-101
   reasons for using, 99
advice
   bankruptcy filing, 142-43
   downsizing, 132-33
   sale of business, 118
   second start-up, 150
   sources of, 59-63
   See also information sources

affirmations, 158
agenda, meeting, 261
airline industry, 67
alcohol abuse, 182, 293
Allied-Signal, 105
"all-in-one" customer, 103
American Airlines, 67
America West Airlines, 67
Amway, 86
analysis, boss's role in, 46
anger, 311
anti-Semitism, 159
Apple Computer, 24, 25
Architectural Digest, 82
Artisans (temperament type), 180, 181
assets
   acquisition and, 105
   bankruptcy and, 142
   corporation and, 38
   limited liability company and, 37
   liquidation and, 118, 145
   long-term debt and, 131
   partnership division of, 35
   revocable trust and, 121
   S corporation and, 39
   sole proprietorship and, 34
assets, building on, 153-249
   capital and, 11, 225-44
   community involvement and,
      245-49
   customers and, 211-18
   employees and, 175-210

(assets, building on, cont.)
  owners and, 155–74
  support system as, 170–73, 309–10
  vendors and, 219–23
attitude, 156–62, 209
attorneys. *See* lawyers
audiocassettes, 255
avoidance, 293–94
Avon, 86

background check, employee,
    181–87
  consistency in, 185–86
bankruptcy, 118, 139–44
  corporate, 37
  legal advice and, 142–43
  worksheet, 143–44
banks, 31, 32, 242
barriers, market entry, 14
Bayfields, Inc., 120
Beatles, The, 158
Bible, 17, 28, 161
bigotry, 159–60
billboard advertising, 74, 83
bill-paying priorities, 229–31
BlackBerry PDA, 56–57
Blanchard, Ken
  on customer service, 213–14
  on employee motivation, 197–98
  on ethics, 169
  on servant leadership, 47
  on triaging, 273–74
  on vision and mission, 27
Blanchard, Scott, 179–80
Bloomington (Minn.) Chamber of
    Commerce, xxii
bonus programs, 75
book clubs, 90
books
  as information source, 54, 152
  uplifting, 158–59
Boom, Corrie ten, 158
boss (owner), 155–74
  attitudes of, 156–62

control and, 206–8
courage of, 164
customer relations and, 97
divestiture of company by, 117–23
downsizing steps by, 129–38
employee obligations of, 208–9
enthusiasm of, 155–56
ethics of, 47, 168–70, 191–92
fears of, 301–5, 311
goals of, 165–67
knowledge of, 162–63
past experiences of, 164–65
personal income uncertainty of,
    20–21, 164
planning-stage role of, 45–46, 47,
    48
second-start-up and, 145–52,
    308–9
skills of, 163–64
sloppiness of, 271–76
support systems for, 170–73,
    309–10
worksheet questions, 173–74
Bowles, Sheldon, 197–98, 213–14
Boys Clubs/Girls Clubs, 247
Boy Scouts, 247
brainstorming sessions, 261
branding, as competitive edge, 24–25
brand loyalty, 14, 93, 215
Brookstone, 90
bureaucracy, 69–70
business counselors, 172
business ethics. *See* ethics
business expense. *See* expenses
business partners. *See* partnership
business plan, 18–19, 44
business structure, 44
  downsizing restructuring and,
    129–38
  selection of, 18, 33–39
  simplicity of, 69–70
BusinessWeek (magazine), 55
busybodies, 267–70
busy-ness, 253–66

worksheet questions, 265-66

"buy/sell" agreement, 119

cable television, 74, 77-79, 86, 92

caller ID, 256

camaraderie, building of, 193, 195

capital, 225-44
    basic rules of, 226
    bill-paying priorities, 229-31
    expense monitoring, 238, 239-42
    incorporation needs, 11
    investing of, 236-38
    lavish spending of, 234-36
    new business needs, 18, 28-33
    new sources of, 108-9
    second start-up and, 150
    worksheet questions, 243-44
    See also cash flow; loans

career counselors, 172

carpooling, 255

cars, 283-84, 288
    driving record, 184, 185

cash
    acquisitions and, 105
    debt reduction and, 284
    liquidation and, 118, 145
    needs determination, 241-42
    start-up sources of, 31-32
    See also capital

cash flow, 32, 33, 227-29, 274
    downsizing and, 135
    priorities and, 229-31
    regular analysis/projection of, 242
    too-rapid growth and, 102, 104
    See also receivables

catalog outlets, 74, 86, 90, 258

CDs (compact discs), 255, 296

cell phones, 256, 257, 296

chambers of commerce, 61, 289

change, 46, 312
    evolution stage and, 112-13, 115
    growth stage and, 70-71

Chapter 11 vs. Chapter 7 bankruptcy,
    142

charities, 236, 246

Charmin, 24

Chick-fil-A, 24, 25

Children's Program of Northern
    Ireland, 246

churches, 172

civil record searches, 182

Clarifacts, Inc., 181

clients. *See* customers/clients

club dues, 231

clubs, direct mail, 89-90

cold calls, 73

collections, 228, 238, 272

commercials. *See* television
    advertising

common sense, 18

communication, 202

community relations, 245-49
    workshop questions, 248-49

commuting time, 254-55

compact discs, 255, 296

compensation
    paycheck regularity and, 208
    pay raises as, 196
    payroll and, 143, 229, 240
    performance-based, 188, 191-96,
        206, 208
    as salesperson's incentive, 73
    uncertainty of owner's, 20-21, 164

competition, 66-68
    barriers to entry and, 14
    boss's adaptation to, 46
    marketing and, 72-97
    market share and, 67-68
    from off-shoring, 1-2, 67, 71
    positioning and, 24-25
    price and, 67, 109, 216
    value and, 66-67
    winning new customers and,
        215-16

competitive edge, 24-25, 99
    up-to-date technology as, 71-72

computers
    competitive edge and, 71-72

(computers. cont.)
    employee skills in, 179
    PDAs and, 167
    productivity and, 134, 147, 262–63
    See also Internet; software
conceptualization, boss's role in, 45,
    46
confidentiality, 169–70, 209
consolidation, debt, 284–85
consultants, 60–61
"content creation," 146–47
contests and promotions, 74, 93–94
    for employees, 75, 196
Continental Airlines, 67
continuity programs, direct mail, 89,
    90
contracts
    client, 275
    employment, 43, 275
control, 206–8, 263
cooperation, 203
corporate giving, 245
corporate veil, 37–38
corporation, 18, 33, 37–38
    advantage of, 38
    incorporation capital and, 11
    layers of management and, 69–70
    legal insulation of, 34, 37–38
    name availability for, 24
    S type, 33, 38–39
    tax law and, 245
cost per thousand viewers, 77
costs
    advertising, 78, 79, 101–2
    control of, 66–68
    of employee screening/
        replacement, 186–87
    See also investment needs and
        financing; overhead
counselors, 60, 172
county record searches, 182
coupons, 75, 80, 82, 93, 98
courage, 164
courtesy, 176, 209

creativity, 85, 89, 100, 135, 201
credibility, 97
credit. *See* debt; loans
credit cards, 230, 232–33, 283, 288
credit history. *See* credit rating
creditors. *See* debt; loans
credit rating, 38, 184, 185, 230, 231
criminal record searches, 182, 183, 185
cross-training, 40
Custom Craftsman Printing, 140
customer loyalty, 14, 71, 93, 105, 140,
    221
    vulnerability in, 215–17
customers/clients, 74, 76, 211–18
    addressing needs of, 274
    competition for, 66
    contracts with, 275
    effective salesperson and, 73
    employee treatment of, 176, 209,
        212
    filling needs of, 274
    loss of, 128–29, 131, 215–16
    mission statement and, 25
    non-payment by, 139–40, 160–61
    overdependence on single, 103, 128
    payment by, 226–27
    pro formas and, 33
    quality and, 189
    replacement of, 133
    rules of, 97
    too-rapid growth and, 103, 104
    trust of, 170
    of vendors, 221–22
    worksheet questions, 217–18
customer service, 103, 212–15
    outsourcing of, 2, 67
    staffing and, 39

Daniels, Peter J., 158
database maintenance, 272
David (biblical king), 161
debt, 281–86
    acquisition and, 105
    bankruptcy and, 142–43

cash flow and, 102
corporations and, 37–38
downsizing and, 130–32, 135, 141
honoring, 140–41
liquidation and, 145
partnerships and, 36
paying off of, 140, 145–46, 284
recovery plans and, 135
refinancing/consolidation of, 284–85
renegotiation of, 130–32, 140, 146
sole proprietorships and, 34
unnecessary, 282–83
worksheet questions, 285–86
See also bankruptcy; loans
decision making, 150, 164
deficit spending, 2
delegating of work, 202, 294
delinquent accounts, 228
delivery, 109, 216
deposits, up-front, 227
differentiation, product/service, 72
digital photographs, 12, 59
direct mail, 74, 86, 87–90, 257
creative examples of, 89
direct marketing, 74, 86–92
discount coupons, 75, 80, 82, 93
discrimination, 192, 205, 208
government directives on, 185, 288
disgruntled employee, 204–6
dishonesty, 160, 182
distinguishing benefit, 24–25
diversification, 109
divestiture, 117–23
second start-up after, 145–52
types of, 118–22
worksheet questions, 122–23
"Do Not Call" lists, 91
downsizing, 127–38
bankruptcy vs., 140–41
business dry spell and, 128–29
recovery plan, 133–36
self-honesty and, 136
steps in, 129–33

worksheet questions, 137–38
See also second start-up
dreaming stage, 5–16, 56
FANAFI principle and, 12–14
guidance during, 10–11
for second start-up, 148
worksheet questions, 15–16
driving record, 184, 185
Dr. No (film), 283
drug abuse, 182, 184
DVDs, 57–58, 147, 296
Dylan, Bob, 158

"early bird" specials, 75
economic conditions, 2, 70, 71, 127, 216
fear and, 302
education, 47, 162, 183, 202
EEOC, 185
800 numbers, 91
election campaigns, 289
e-mail
direct marketing by, 86
productivity and, 258–59, 262, 263, 264
pros and cons of, 55, 56–57
e-marketing, 74
Employee Appreciation Week, 195
employee benefits, 135–36, 147, 204–5, 208
employee contracts, 43, 275
employee handbook, 41–43, 200, 204
employees, 19, 39–43, 175–210
addressing needs of, 274
background checks on, 181–87
bankruptcy claims and, 142–43
busybodies among, 267–69
carpooling and, 255
company standards and, 135, 181–82, 190, 200
competition for, 65
contests and promotions for, 75, 196
cost control and, 66, 69

(employees, cont.)

customer relations and, 76, 97, 176, 212

delegating work to, 294

disgruntled, 204-6

downsizing and, 129-30, 134, 135-36

eagerness and youth of, 69

equitable treatment of, 160, 190, 191-92, 206

firing of, 43, 135, 203-4, 207-8

in focus committee, 113-14

growth stage and, 69, 71

implementation stage and, 51-53

independent contractors vs., 134, 147-48, 175

job descriptions for, 200-203, 204

laying off of, 129-30, 149

limits testing by, 206-8

mission statement and, 25-26

morale building and, 192-98

nonperformance by, 203-4

obligations of, 209

obligations to, 208

owner interaction with, 155-56, 208-9

owner's heirs and, 120

payment of. *See* compensation; payroll

performance excellence and, 187-92

planning stage and, 39-43

policies for, 41-43, 200, 206

productivity of, 209, 254-64

profit orientation of, 192

record-keeping on, 205-6, 208

as resources, 51-53, 113-14

rudeness of, 176

salespeople, 73-74, 93

screening/selection of, 177-87

second start-up and, 149, 150, 276

selling business to, 119

servant leadership of, 45-46, 47

setting expectations for, 198-200

sloppiness and, 160, 276-78

standards and, 135, 190, 198-200

state laws and, 42-43, 206

stock ownership plan for, 108-9, 121

temperaments of, 179-81

training of, 40, 57-58, 71, 178, 199, 200

turnover reduction and, 186

unproductive, 176-77

values and, 160

worksheet questions, 210

See also team building

Employee Stock Ownership Plan, 108-9, 121

employment contract, 43, 275

Enron, 168

entertainment, business. *See* travel and entertainment

enthusiasm, 155-56, 203

entrepreneur. *See* boss; small businesses

"environmental conscience," 247-48

Equal Employment Opportunity Commission, 185

equal opportunity, 191-92, 206, 208

government directives, 288

equal pay for equal work, 191-92, 206

equipment

downsizing and, 135, 141

leasing deals, 232-33

quality of, 282-83

selling of surplus, 284

equity, liquidation and, 118

equity financing, 31

ESOP (Employee Stock Ownership Plan), 108-9, 212

estate tax, 120

estimate, 202

ethics

employee, 181-82, 209

owner, 47, 168-70, 191-92

evolution stage, 111-16

worksheet questions, 116

excellence, quest for, 187-92

expectations, setting, 198-200, 204

expenses
    business vs. personal, 288
    debt and, 281–86
    downsizing cuts in, 130, 134
    employee fraud and, 182
    monitoring of, 150, 238, 239–42
    travel and entertainment, 130,
       234–36, 288
    See also overhead
experience
    of employees, 178–79
    of owner, 164–65
    second start-ups and, 149–50, 276

facilitation, 202
failure
    beginning again after, 146, 148–52
    delegating of work and, 294
    fear of, 303
    small business rates of, 307–8
Fair Credit Reporting Act, 185
fairness, 42
faith, religious, 161
family
    divestiture and, 120–21
    as investors in start-up, 31
    as support system, 171, 309
FANAFI principle, 12–14, 19–20, 111,
    112
    as key to business success, 12–14,
      115
Fast Company (magazine), 55
fax marketing, 86, 92
FCRA (Fair Credit Reporting Act), 185
fear, 294, 301–5, 311
    worksheet questions, 305
Final Cut Pro, 57
finances. *See* capital; cash; cash flow;
    debt; overhead
find a need and fill it. *See* FANAFI
    principle
firing
    company standards and, 135
    documentation and, 207–8

    of nonperforming employee,
      203–4
    "wrongful discharge" suit and, 43,
      208
"fixed overhead" myth, 239
focus committees, 113–14
Forbes (magazine), 55
Ford Motor Company, 46
forecasting, 32–33
foreclosure, 230
forgiveness, 160–61, 311
Fortune (magazine), 55
Fox News, 24, 25
franchise, 7, 8, 106
FranklinCovey, 167
Franklin Day Planner, 166–67
fraud, employee, 182
freelancers. *See* independent
    contractors
frequency, 199
friends, 171, 309–10
future, clear vision of, 47

"gifting" of business, 120
Gift of the Goose, 198
Girl Scouts, 247
global economy, 1–3, 162
goals, 165–67, 199
gossip, 267
Gottry, Karla, xxiv–xxv, xxvii, xxix, 9,
    36, 73, 74, 121, 127, 147, 149,
    179, 196, 311
Gottry Communications Group, Inc.,
    The, 23, 145, 147, 148, 242
government, 275–76, 287–91. *See also*
    taxes
Graham, Billy, 158, 161
gross rating points, 77
growth stage, 65–110
    advertising and, 97–102
    competition and, 65–66
    cost control and, 66–68
    eager employees and, 69
    growth strategies and, 104–9

(growth stage, cont.)
    hazards in, 102–4, 109
    marketing and, 74, 76–97
    product differentiation and, 72
    worksheet questions, 110
grudges. *See* forgiveness
Guardians (temperament type), 180,
    181
Gung Ho! (Blanchard and Bowles), 197
"gung ho" workplace, 197–98

Habitat for Humanity, 236
HarperSanFrancisco, xxii
Hart Schaffner & Marx, 17
hatred, negative effects of, 159–60
health insurance, 208
heirs. *See* inheritance
Herbalife, 86
hidden costs, 28–29
holidays, 195
"home shopping" channels, 86, 92
honesty, 209
Honeywell, 105
horizontal markets, 107–8
hostile work environment, 205
How to Be Happy Though Rich (Daniels),
    158
*How to Win Customers and Keep Them for
    Life* (LeBoeuf), 214
HRM (human resource management),
    175
Humphrey, Hubert, 158

Idealists (temperament type), 180
Idea of the Month Club, 52
ideas, 52–53, 202, 208
iGo, 90
image, costs vs., 68, 283–84
implementation, boss's role in, 45
implementation stage, 49–64
    filling in missing pieces and, 50–51
    internal resources and, 51–53
    outside resources and, 53–63
    preopening tasks of, 49–50

inbound telemarketing, 91
Inc. (magazine), 55
incentives, 74, 75, 93
income. *See* compensation
income tax. *See* taxes
incorporation. *See* corporation
independent contractors (freelancers),
    134, 147–48
    advantages of using, 147, 175
India, 2–3
information sources, 51–63, 113–14,
    162–63, 255
    for evolution stage, 113–14
inheritance
    of parent's company, 120
    wealth from, 7, 8, 165
innovation, 72, 201–2
Innovations for Success Program, 52
insurance
    as employee benefit, 208
    owner, 229, 275
    See also life insurance
insurance agents, 62
integrity, 73, 209
intellectual property, 7, 8, 13, 31
interest rates, 233, 241, 284–85
internal resources, 51–53
International Advertising Festival of
    New York, xxii
Internet
    as information source, 55–57
    as marketing tool, 12, 74, 84–86
    See also Web site
inventions, 7, 8
inventory control, 29–30, 240–41, 276
investment counseling seminars, 60
investment needs and financing, 18,
    28–33
    business structure and, 34, 38, 39
    cash flow and, 32, 33, 102
    evolution stage and, 114
    growth capital and, 108–9
    hidden costs and, 28–29
    outside costs and, 30–31

pro forma and, 32–33
  sources of financing and, 31–33,
    108–9
investments, 7, 8, 60, 150
  strategies for, 236–38
investors, 31, 38, 62
invoicing
  employee fraud and, 182
  monitoring of, 238–39
  payment terms and, 33, 222,
    226–28
  timely, 134–35, 226
IRS, 147–48, 288

job descriptions, 200–203, 204
  employee redefining of, 52–53
"just in time" inventory, 240

keeping confidences, 169–70
Keirsey, David, 179, 181
Kentucky Fried Chicken, 143
kindness, 170
King, Martin Luther, Jr., 195
Kirby vacuum cleaner, 86
Kiyosaki, Robert T., 36, 255
Klimas, Kevin, 181, 185
knowledge, 162–63. *See also*
    information sources
Kodak, 12
Kroc, Ray, 8

Labor Department, 186
Lands' End, 90
late fees, 230
law. *See* legal issues
lawyers, 60, 206
  as advisers, 62
  bankruptcy and, 142–43
  divestiture and, 121–22
  payment of, 231
layoffs, 129–30, 149
laziness, 160
leadership, 45–46
  five steps to, 47

learning
  from experience, 149–50, 276
  from internal resources, 51–53
  knowledge and, 162–63
  of skills, 163–64
leases, 230
LeBoeuf, Michael, 214
legal issues
  business structure and, 18, 33, 34,
    37–38
  employee policies and, 42–43,
    185–86, 206
  See also bankruptcy
L'Engle, Madeleine, xxii
Levi Strauss, 1
licenses, 184, 288
Liemandt, Jack, 17
life insurance, 31, 236–37
limited liability company (LLC), 18,
    33
  description of, 36–37
  legal insulation of, 34
  name availability for, 24
liquidation, 118, 141, 145
L.L. Bean, 90
LLC. *See* limited liability company
loans
  business structure and, 34
  Employee Stock Ownership Plan
    and, 108
  interest rates, 233, 241, 284–85
  payments on, 230
  renegotiation of, 130–31
  for start-up financing, 31–32
  See also bankruptcy; debt
lobbying, 289
location
  of business start-up, 18, 21–22
  of new branches, 105–6
  of office space, 68
  of second start-up, 148
Longclaw, Andy, 197
long-term debt, 102, 131, 284
loopholes, 168

lottery, 7
loyalty
   brand, 14, 93, 215
   customer, 14, 71, 93, 105, 140, 215, 221
   employee, 136, 204, 209
   vendor, 219, 220

Macy's parade, 94
Madden, John, 302, 303
magazines
   as advertising tool, 74, 81–82
   contests and promotions, 94
   as information source, 54–55, 113, 162, 163, 290
mail, 257–58. *See also* direct mail; e-mail
mailing lists, 87, 88, 89
management layers, 69–70
manufacturing, 1–2, 22, 67, 71
March of Dimes, 246
marketing, 72–97, 128
   contests and promotions, 75, 93–94
   customer relations, 76, 97
   direct marketing, 74, 86–92
   incentives and premiums, 75, 93
   Internet, 74, 84–86
   media advertising, 74, 76–84
   point-of-purchase materials, 75, 94–95
   public relations, 75–76, 95–97
   See also advertising
markets
   finding new, 114
   horizontal and vertical, 107–8
market share, 67
Martin Luther King, Jr. Day, 195
Mary Kay, 86
materialism, xxii–xxv, 310
Maytag, 24
MBTI (Myers-Briggs Type Indicator), 179
McDonald's, 7, 8
meal delivery, 13

media advertising, 74, 76–84
   public relations placements vs., 96–97
meetings, 259–61
memo writers, 263–64
Mercedes-Benz, 24
mergers, 104–5
Microsoft, 310
Microsoft Word, 57, 59
middle management, 70
Miller, Mark, 47
Minnesota AIDS Project, 246
minority groups, 159–60
mission statements, 25–27
mistakes
   learning from, 150
   negative effects from, 216, 276–78
morale building, 192–98
mortgage payments, 230
motivation
   boss's role in, 45, 47
   rewards as, 188, 191–96
motor vehicle reports (MVRs), 184
"must-do" list, 275–76
MyBusiness (magazine), 290
Myers-Briggs Type Indicator, 179

name of business, 18, 22–24, 104–5
National Federation of Independent Business, 289–90
National Geographic (magazine), 82
natural enemies, 251–305
   addictive behaviors, 293–99
   busybodies, 267–70
   busy-ness, 253–66
   debt, 281–86
   fear, 301–5
   government, 287–91
   sloppiness, 271–79
natural resources, 2
negligent hiring, 181, 186
neighborhood. *See* location
networking, 61–62
new capital, 31–33, 108–9

newspapers
  advertising in, 74, 80–81
  as information source, 163
  public relations placements in, 75,
    76
NewTek, Inc., xxii
Newton, Isaac, 66
NFIB (National Federation of
    Independent Business), 289–90
Nielsen ratings, 77
nonperforming employee, 203–4
Northwest Airlines, 67

Office E-mail, 262–63
office space
  downsizing and, 130, 131–32, 141
  image and, 68
  rent/mortgage payments and, 230
off-shoring, 1–2, 67, 71
Oldsmobile, 100
online sales, 12, 84–86
opportunity, employees and, 193, 196
organization, boss's role in, 45
organized small groups, 171–72
outbound telemarketing, 90–91
outdoor advertising, 74, 83
outside costs, 30–31
outside resources, 53–63, 162
  advisers, 62–63
  consultants, 60–61
  Internet, 55–57
  organized small organizations,
    171–72
  peers, 61–62
  publications, 54–55
  seminars, 59–60
  software, 58–59
  trade associations, 60
  videos/DVDs, 57–58
  worksheet questions, 64
  See also information sources;
    support system
outside services, 65–66
outsourcing, 2, 67, 71

overhead, xxvi
  control of, 66, 68
  downsizing cuts in, 128–30, 131,
    134, 135
  expense monitoring and, 238,
    239–42
  too-rapid growth and, 103, 104
overstaffing, 39
owner. *See* boss

PalmOne PDA, 167
paperwork, 263–64
partnership, 18, 33, 119
  problems of, 34–36
past-due invoices, 228
patents, 13, 31
pay. *See* compensation
payables. *See* invoicing
payment terms, 33, 222, 226–28
payroll, 143, 229, 240
PDAs, 167
Peale, Norman Vincent, 156, 158, 169
peers, support/advice from, 61–62
perfectionism, 296–97
performance
  objective basis for judging, 204
  reward system based on, 188,
    191–92, 193, 196, 208
permits, 184, 288
"Personal Book of Affirmation," 158
personal goals, 166–67
personal guarantees, 38
personality
  of effective salesperson, 73
  of employee, 179–81
personal lines of credit, 31
personnel. *See* employees
Peter, Laurence J., 69
Peter Principle (Peter), 69
phone calls
  manners and, 176
  personal, 204, 209, 268–69
  productivity and, 204, 209,
    256–57, 268

phone company, payment of, 229
photography, 12, 59
planning, personal, 167–68
planning stage, 17–48, 49
    boss's role in, 45–46, 47
    business plan development and,
        18–19, 44
    business structure selection and,
        18, 33–39
    employee needs and, 39–41
    employee policies and, 41–43
    essential questions about, 18–19,
        48
    first plan draft and, 44
    investment needs and, 28–31, 39
    location of business and, 18, 19–21
    naming of business and, 22–24
    positioning and, 24–27
    timing of start-up and, 21–22
    worksheet questions, 48
play, importance of, 253–54
point-of-purchase materials, 74, 75,
    94–95
politicians, 289–90
Pope, Alexander, 162
P-O-P materials, 74, 75, 94–95
positioning, 18, 24–27
positive attitude, 156–62, 209
posters, government-required, 288
praise, importance of, 193–95
premiums, 74, 75, 93
preopening phase, 49–50
preservation/evolution stage, 111–16
press conferences, 75
price, 98, 216
    advertising agency and, 100
    competition and, 67, 109, 216
    evolution stage and, 114
    value and, 66–67, 215
    vendors and, 220, 222
price wars, 67
Priority Multimedia Group, Inc.,
    146–47, 228
problems, acknowledging, 129

procrastination, 275–76
product benefit, 98
productivity, 209, 254–64, 275, 295
    commuting time, 254–55
    technology and, 134, 147, 262–63
products or services
    advertising of, 97–102
    differentiation of, 72
    expansion of, 106–7, 114
    FANAFT principle and, 12–14,
        19–20, 111, 112, 115
    marketing of, 72–97
    new competition to, 216
    payment for, 227–28
    positioning of, 24–25
    viability of, 109
professional counselors, 172
professional license/certification
    verification, 184
professional retreats, 172
profit margin, 67
profits, 19
    as advertising's purpose, 102
    budget estimation and, 202
    bureaucratic draining of, 70
    corporate tax law and, 245
    employee orientation toward, 192
    wise investment of, 150
profit-sharing plan, 108
pro formas, 32–33, 40, 89
progress billings, 228
promotions. *See* contests and
    promotions
promotions, employee, 196
Proverbs, 17, 161
Prudential Realty Group, xxii, 277
Psalms, 161
public offering, 119–20
public relations, 74, 75–76, 95–97, 99
    benefits from, 96–97

quality, 98
    customer service, 212–15
    nurturing of, 188–90, 193

purchasing of, 282–83
value and, 66, 215
QuarkXPress, 57

racism, 159, 160
radio advertising, 74, 79–80
raises. *See* compensation
Rationals (temperament type), 180, 181
Raving Fan relationship, 213–14, 274
Raving Fans (Blanchard and Bowles), 214
reading, informational, 54–55, 113, 162, 163, 290
reality, 14
real vs. résumé experience, 178–79
receivables
downsizing and, 135
as financing, 32
monitoring of, 150, 238–39
terms of, 226–28
See also cash flow
recognition
of employee top performance, 188, 191–96
longing for, 297
record clubs, 90
record keeping
database maintenance and, 272
employee documentation, 205–6, 208
of meetings, 261
recovery plan, 133–36
recreation, 203, 253–54
redirection, 199
reference interview, 184–85
refinancing debt, 284–85
reinvention, 47
relationships, valuation of, 47
religion, 161, 172–73
renegotiating debt, 130–31, 140
rent payment, 230
reports, 263–64, 272
reputation, as asset, 170

research, 11, 30
on advertising audiences, 77, 79
Internet use for, 56
See also information sources
respect, 209
results, valuation of, 47
résumé vs. real experience, 178–79
retail
new locations and, 105–6
point of purchase, 95
retreats, 172
revocable trusts, 121
rewards. *See* compensation
"right to work" states, 43
risk, 103, 150, 182–83
Rogers, Stephanie, 179–80
Rotary Club, 61
rudeness, 176

safety, workplace, 288
salary. *See* compensation
sale of business. *See* selling/divestiture stage
sales, 276
as advertising's purpose, 101–2
business forecasting and, 32
direct, 86–87
downsizing and, 128, 135
online, 12, 84–86
recovery plan's focus on, 134
tools for, 276
See also marketing
salespeople
incentives and premiums for, 93, 196
key qualities of, 73–74
Salvation Army, 246
Sanders, Harlan, 143
savings, 233, 235, 236
Schuller, Robert, xxii, 156, 158
S corporation, 18, 33, 38–39
advantage of, 39
search engines, 84–85, 86
second-mortgage loans, 31

second start-up, 145–52, 308–9
  definition of, 148
  learning from experience and, 149–50, 276
  worksheet questions, 151–52
self-help programs, 255
self-honesty, 136
  selling/divesting stage, 117–23
  second start-up and, 145–52
  taxes and, 117–18, 121
  worksheet questions, 122–23
seminars, 59–60
servant leadership, 45–46
  five steps in (SERVE), 47
service organizations, 61, 246
services. *See* products or services
sexism, 205
sexual harassment, 59–60, 182, 288
shareholders. *See* stockholders
Sharper Image, 90, 240, 258
  Sound Soother, 159
show business, 7, 8
signatures, e-mail, 259
Simon, Neil, 7
Six Sigma, 188, 189
skills
  of employees, 177–78
  of owner, 163–64
slipups, day-to-day, 136
slogans, 24–25
sloppiness, 271–79
  of boss, 271–76
  of employee, 160, 276–78
  worksheet questions, 279
small businesses, 1–3
  building on assets of, 153–249
  challenge of, 308–12
  downsizing of, 127–38
  dreaming stage, 5–16, 45
  evolution stage, 111–16
  failure rates, 307–8
  growth stage, 65–110
  implementation stage, 49–64
  natural enemies of, 251–305

  planning stage, 17–48, 49
  second start-up, 145–52, 308–9
  selling/divesting stage, 117–23
small groups, 171–72
smiling, 155, 156
Social Security trace, 183
software, 295
  bundling of, 93
  as competitive edge, 71–72
  downsizing and, 134
  outsourcing and, 67
  productivity and, 262
  as resource, 58–59
  training on, 57–58, 178
sole proprietorship, 18, 24, 33
  drawbacks of, 34
Solomon (biblical king), 17, 161
spam/spam filters, 56, 258
special sales events, 75
Spiegel, 90
Spirit of the Squirrel, 197
Sporty's Pilot Shop, 90
Standard Publishing, xxii
Standard Rate and Data Service (SRDS), 82
standards, employee performance, 135, 190, 198–200
start-ups
  planning first, 17–48, 49
  second, 145–52
  See also small businesses
state laws, 42–43, 206
Stewart, Martha, 168
stockbrokers, 62
stockholders, 38, 39, 62
  employees as, 108–9
  public offering and, 119–20
Stoner, Jesse, 27
stupidity, 160
substance abuse, 182, 184, 293
success, visualization of, 158
suggestion boxes, 52
suppliers. *See* vendors
support system, 61–63

downsizing and, 132–33
    as owner asset, 170–73, 309–10
synagogues, 172
systems and procedures, 261–63

take-out services, 13
tape recorder, 162–63, 255
target markets, 107–8
tariffs, 2
tax audit, 287
taxes, 33, 241, 287
    bankruptcy and, 142
    corporate giving and, 245
    estate, 120
    "gifting" of business and, 120
    independent contractors and,
        147–48
    payment on time of, 287
    sale/divestiture of business and,
        117–18, 121
    S corporation and, 39
    sole proprietorship and, 34
    withholding, 229
team building, 150, 188, 189–90, 193,
    195, 199–200, 202–3
technical service, outsourcing of, 2,
    67, 71
technology
    addiction to, 295, 296
    changes in, 13, 312
    for cost control, 66
    employee skills in, 179
    evolution stage and, 113, 114
    growth stage and, 66, 70, 71–72
    impact of, 70
    productivity and, 134, 147, 262–63
    work output and, 147
telemarketing
    direct marketing and, 74, 86,
        90–91
    outsourcing of, 2
telephone. See phone calls
television advertising, 74, 77–79
    advantages/pitfalls of, 78–79

temperament, 179–81
tension, 304
term insurance, 237
terms of payment, 33, 222, 226–28
theft, employee, 182
Thomas, Clarence, 59, 60
3M, 310
"time-out" coupons, 196
time wasters, 254–64
timing, of start-up, 18, 19–21
tolerance, 160
top performance, 188, 191–92, 193,
    196
Total Quality Management (TQM),
    188, 189
"toys," xxii–xxv, 150, 234, 310, 311
    addiction to, 295–96
    downsizing and, 132, 136
trade associations, 60
trade journals, 113
trademarks, 13
trade policy, 2
traffic building, 93–94
traffic counts
    business location and, 21–22
    sales forecasting and, 32
training, 40, 178, 199, 200
    in technology, 71
    of telemarketers, 91
    video/DVD for, 57–58
transit advertising, 74, 83
travel and entertainment
    downsizing cuts in, 130
    lavish spending on, 234–36
    tax deductions and, 288
triaging, 272, 273–74
trust, 150, 169–70, 220, 311
trust fund, revocable, 121
turnover, employee, 186

UMOM New Day Centers, 246, 247
understaffing, 39
Undis, LeRoy, 140
unemployment, 2, 70, 71

Unique Selling Proposition, 24, 25
United Airlines, 67
United Properties, xxii
University of Minnesota, 10
up-front deposits, 227
up-to-date information, 18
up-to-date technology, 71–72
USP. *See* Unique Selling Proposition
utility bills, payment of, 230

value
    basis of, 66–67, 215
    perception of, 98
values
    boss's embodiment of, 47, 168–70
    of employees, 160
    See also ethics
vendors, 219–23
    debt renegotiation with, 131
    downsizing and, 131, 135
    employee courtesy toward, 209
    guidelines for, 221
    guidelines for customers of,
        222–23
    invoicing and, 226
    loyalty and, 219, 220
    paying off of debt to, 140, 146
    payment of, 226–27, 230–32
    too-rapid growth and, 103, 104
    worksheet questions, 223
venture capitalists, 31
verification, employee applicant
        claims, 183, 184
vertical markets, 107–8
video clubs, 90
videos/DVDs, 147, 296
    as information source, 57–58
vision
    of company, 27
    servant leadership and, 47

Visual Communications Services, Inc.,
        22–23
visualization, 157–58
voice mail, 256

Waitley, Denis, xxii, 255
Walljasper, Eric, 149
Wal-Mart, 76, 106
Walton, Sam, 106
Warner Bros. Distribution, xxii
Way of the Beaver, 197–98
wealth, 165
    eight ways of gaining, 7–9
Web site, 74, 84–86, 147
    elements of successful, 84–85
    as marketing tool, 85–86
whole life insurance, 236–37
Wired (magazine), 55
wisdom experience, 179
withholding taxes, 229
word, as binding, 222
"word of mouth" advertising, 212
workaholism, 293–95
workplace environment, 205, 208
workplace violence, 182, 185
Workplace Violence Research
        Institute, 181
WorldCom, 168
World Wide Pictures, 139
"wrongful discharge" suits, 43, 208

yellow pages advertising, 74, 83–84
Young, Richard, 120

Ziglar, Zig, xxii, 158, 255

ABOUT THE AUTHOR

Steve Gottry was the founder and president of The Gottry Communications Group, Inc., a full-service advertising agency and video production firm based in Minneapolis, Minnesota. He formed the company in 1970, and served a variety of organizations across the nation. Among his clients were HarperSanFrancisco, Career Press, Zondervan Publishing House, Prudential Commercial Services—changed since then—Warner Bros., World Wide Pictures, United Properties, Alpha Video, NewTek, Inc., Pemtom Homes, and Standard Publishing. His firm was the winner of a number of national awards, including three Silver Microphones for radio and an award for direct mail from the International Advertising Festival of New York.

In May of 1991, his agency was named "Small Company of the Year" by the Bloomington Chamber of Commerce. Steve was recognized as the "Small Business Advocate of the Year" by the chamber in 1995.

Steve is the coauthor (with Ken Blanchard) of *The On-Time, On-Target Manager* (HarperCollins, New York, January 2004) and the coauthor (with Linda Jensvold Bauer) of *A Kick in the Career,* (from Priority Multimedia Group, Inc., Mesa, AZ, October 2004). He has coauthored a novel and has also written a book to help would-be screenwriters develop stories. He has written the screenplays for four produced television and video/DVD projects and also writes, produces, and directs commercial and industrial videos.

He and his wife, Karla, moved their family to Arizona in 1996 to leave the colder climate of Minnesota in order to enjoy 320 days of warm sunshine every year! He teamed up with Ken Blanchard in October 1998 to collaborate on a number of publishing projects and has since developed writing relationships with several other best-selling authors.

Steve was recently named Writer-in-Residence at Grand Canyon University in Phoenix, where he teaches a class titled "Writing as a Career." He is a member of Toastmasters International and an officer with the Dobson Ranch Club. A man of many interests, he is an instrument-rated pilot, an avid semi-pro photographer, and a devoted Arizona Diamondbacks fan. He loves the outdoors and prefers to write at a remote campsite, near the ocean, in beautiful Sedona, or simply "out by the pool."

The author welcomes your comments. *He is also available for speaking engagements on the subject matter of* Common Sense Business, The On-Time, On-Target Manager, *and* A Kick in the Career.

If you wish to contact him, write to:

Steven R. Gottry
P.O. Box 41540
Mesa, AZ 85274–1540
or: gottry@mac.com
Web site: www.commonsensebusiness.biz